DATE DUE

DEMCO 38-296

GYÖRGY LIGETI

György Ligeti, 1982. *Photo courtesy of Schott-Archiv/Andersen*

GYÖRGY LIGETI
A Bio-Bibliography

Robert W. Richart

Bio-Bibliographies in Music, Number 30
Donald L. Hixon, Series Adviser

GREENWOOD PRESS
New York • Westport, Connecticut • London

Library of Congress Cataloging-in-Publication Data

Richart, Robert W.
    György Ligeti, a bio-bibliography / Robert W. Richart.
      p. cm. — (Bio-bibliographies in music, ISSN 0742-6968 ; no. 30)
    Includes bibliographical references and index.
    ISBN 0-313-25174-6 (alk. paper)
    1. Ligeti, György, 1923- —Bibliography. 2. Ligeti, György,
    1923- —Discography. I. Title. II. Series.
    ML134.L57R5   1990
    016.78'092—dc20   90-14022

British Library Cataloguing in Publication Data is available.

Library of Congress Catalog Card Number: 90-14022
ISBN: 0-313-25174-6
ISSN: 0742-6968

First published in 1990

Greenwood Press, 88 Post Road West, Westport, CT 06881
An imprint of Greenwood Publishing Group, Inc.

Printed in the United States of America

The paper used in this book complies with the
Permanent Paper Standard issued by the National
Information Standards Organization (Z39.48-1984).

10 9 8 7 6 5 4 3 2 1

For Anna

Contents

Introduction

György Ligeti is surely one of the most significant composers alive today. For some, Ligeti (or at least his music) may be known because Stanley Kubrick used his music (without permission or remuneration) in the film *2001: A Space Odyssey*. An indication of his influence can be found in *Bakers Biographical Dictionary of Musicians* (7th ed., edited by Nicolas Slonimsky, 1984). Ligeti is one of approximately ten percent[1] of the entries who is initially identified with an adjective. The adjective is "innovative" and it fits well. I feel it also important that Ligeti has been able to combine beauty and emotional meaning with innovation. My first conscious contact with his music was at a performance of the *Ten Pieces for Wind Quintet*. I was immediately attracted by this music, and found myself (to borrow a phrase from Zippy the Pinhead) "having fun." The ability of his music to evoke such direct reactions is as important as its ability to reward analysis.

The pronunciation of his name is a matter of some confusion: as in all Hungarian names the stress is on the first syllable, rather than the often heard Li-*get*-i. The composer himself comments, "But it doesn't matter. Say it as you please."[2]

The lively wit and eager intellectual exploration of this man are infectious. Several of the translators who helped me on this project later remarked that they were fascinated and moved by Ligeti's writings and the literature surrounding him.

My goal in this bibliography has been to describe rather than to evaluate the material. Naturally, quite a bit of judgment is required in determining what items are to be listed, but most of the time I have limited my annotations to summary as opposed to criticism. The book is divided into four sections: 1. Biography. 2. Worklist (numbered W1, W2 etc.). 3. Bibliography (numbered B1, B2 etc.). 4. Discography (numbered D1, D2 etc.).

---

[1]Weschler, Lawrence. "Profiles: Boy Wonder II." *The New Yorker*, Nov. 24, 1986, p. 60.

[2]Soria, Dorle J. "György Ligeti: Distinguished and Unpredictable." *Musical America*, 107, no. 12 (Sept. 1987): 27. *See*: B57.

Although the first section is very grandly termed a biography, I want to emphasize that it is obviously only a brief survey intended to acquaint the reader, if necessary, with the basic and widely available facts of Ligeti's life. Users of this book who are already familiar with these facts have no need to read it. The subtitle "a bio-bibliography" refers not to equal biographical and bibliographical treatment of my subject, but to bibliographical treatment of the life and works of this composer.

The bibliography is divided into two parts: writings by Ligeti and writings about Ligeti. The largest section in the latter part consists of concert and record reviews. Reviews have been given special emphasis here as in other books in this series. In most cases, a quotation from the review is presented (and translated if necessary) in order to summarize the reviewers opinion. Cross references link all items dealing with each individual musical work. For example, the worklist item for *Atmosphères* gives references for each mention of this work in the discography and bibliography. An appendix lists in chronological order all of the concerts (apart from opera performances) devoted entirely to works by Ligeti. Since this bio-bibliography emphasizes performances in particular, I felt that these important performances should be given some prominence.

Writings listed in the bibliography date from the 1940s onward. The bulk of material was written after Ligeti's 1956 flight to the West. My cutoff point is the end of 1987. A handful of items have come into my possession since then and I have included them here, but I have not actively sought out material published since 1988. When an item is available in various translations, I have cited the original language and have noted other available manifestations. For the sake of consistency I cite titles of musical works in English if the title is generic (for example Double Concerto rather than Doppelkonzert). Otherwise, titles are given in the original language. The emphasis of this bibliography is on published materials. For a more complete list of manuscripts, sketches and unpublished writings, see Nordwall, *György Ligeti: Eine Monographie* (*See:* B119). Publishers have occasionally issued writings by Ligeti under titles other than those assigned by the author. In these cases Nordwall lists the original, authentic title and makes note of any spurious ones. Since my emphasis is on published material, I have listed the published title in all cases and make note of Ligeti's original title. I hope this practice proves useful and complementary to Nordwall's list. Ove Nordwall's archives of Ligeti manuscripts, which is located in Stockholm, should be noted here as the most important source of information on Ligeti.

Samuel Johnson wrote in the preface to his dictionary, "It is the fate of those who toil at the lower employments of life, to be rather driven by the fear of evil, than attracted by the prospect of good; to be exposed to censure, without hope of praise; to be disgraced by miscarriage, or punished for neglect, where success would have been without reward.... Every other author may aspire to praise; the lexicographer can only hope to escape reproach, and even this negative recompense has been granted to very few."[3] This state of affairs exists for bibliographers as well. I apologize in advance for errors that I am sure I have made, and I ask users of this bibliography to report these "miscarriages."

---

[3]*A Johnson Reader*, edited by E.L. McAdam, Jr. & George Milne. New York: Pantheon Books, 1964. p. 118.

I would like to thank Mr. Ligeti's personal secretary, Dr. Louise Duchesneau for providing much valuable information. My warmest thanks also to Mr. Ove Nordwall who gave generously both information and moral support. In addition, he taught me how to address letters to Europe correctly!

This project was supported in part by funds from the Walter Gerboth Award of the Music Library Association. Don Hixon has provided valuable advice and input, and was a tremendous help in tying up loose ends toward the end of the project. Michael Gray was very generous in provided good advice and information on the discography. I want to thank David Griffin and Gwen Culp of WLN for making word processing and printing equipment available. I also want to thank Donna Schumann of WLN for giving generously of her expertise in personal computers and also in typography. The following people have also helped in sending information and translating:

Linda Barnhart, University of California, San Diego
Michelle Biget, Universite de Haute-Normandie
Jacques Boulay, editor, *Sonances: Revue musicale Québécoise*
David Bowman, Los Angeles Philharmonic Association
Elaine Breach, Washington State University
Christopher Claypoole, Detroit Symphony
Jane Piper Clendinning, Yale University
Susan Clermont, Library of Congress Music Division
Ludwik Erhardt, editor, *Ruch Muzyczny*
Helene Fereira, The Evergreen State College
Stephen M. Fry, University of California, Los Angeles
Mary Louis Greer, University of Louisville School of Music
Angelika Hoffmann, Schott
Eric Hughes, *World Encyclopedia of Recorded Music*
Michel Jolivet, Seattle
Vincent Jolivet, Seattle
Andy Josa, Eugene
Juliet Lambert, New York Philharmonic
Lutz Lesle, Hamburg
Kathleen McMorrow, University of Toronto
Marc Mandel, Boston Symphony Orchestra
Andrea Raab, Schott
James Ralston, Seattle
Dena Ryz, Seattle
Fred Sallis, Berlin
Erkki Salmenhaara, University of Helsinki
Klaus Schumann, *Süddeutsche Zeitung*
Anna Seaberg, King County Library, Seattle
Laila Vejzovic, Washington State University
Denise Wagner, The Pittsburgh Symphony Orchestra
Ulf Wiman, University of Washington, Swedish Dept.
Friederike Zimmermann, Hug Musikverlage

I would also like to thank the following organizations for sending material and information:

The Almeida Theatre Company, London
Caprice Records

Muszika
Nederlandse Sint-Gregoriusvereiniging
Neue Musikzeitung
Nutida Musik
B. Schotts Söhne
The South Bank Centre
Staatstheater Stuttgart
Der Tagesspiegel (Berlin)
Città di Torino, Assessorato per la Cultura
Die Welt
Wergo Schallplatten
Die Zeit

I want to thank Steve Willis for not constantly asking me, "Are you finished with that Ligeti book yet?" To Anna, my dear friend and wife: Thank you for your endless patience and support. Finally, I would like to thank my mother and father for teaching me to finish what I start.

GYÖRGY LIGETI

1

Biography

György Ligeti's mother and father were Jewish Hungarians who settled in Dicsöszentmárton in Transylvania during World War I. They stayed when the area became part of Romania, and on May 28, 1923 the town (now called Tîrnăveni) became György's birthplace. György's mother, Ilona Ligeti, née Somogyi, was an ophthalmologist. His father, Sándor Ligeti, was an economist and banker who also wrote books on economics from a radical socialist point of view. György's father had been born with the German surname Auer, but changed it to the Hungarian equivalent Ligeti.[4]

When György was six years old the family moved to Kolozsvár (now known as Cluj, in German known as Klausenburg), the cultural center of Transylvania. Here he heard operas and concerts, listened to the family's battered old gramophone, and developed an interest in music. When György was 14 his brother Gábor (five years younger than György and gifted with perfect pitch) began taking violin lessons. György persuaded his parents to allow him to study piano so that he and Gábor could play sonatas together.[5] At the same time he began composing. He wrote many pieces at this early stage without any knowledge of harmony or orchestration. In 1941 a Hungarian-Jewish publishing firm called "Ararat" organized a song-writing competition. Ligeti entered a song called "Kineret" with a text by Palestinian poet Rachel Blovstein, translated from Hebrew into Hungarian by Hubert Adler. This song won a prize and was published.

Ligeti's father had planned to send György to the University of Cluj to study physics, but by this time anti-Jewish laws had been passed making it very difficult for Jews to enter the university. Since it was not possible to study science, György's father allowed him to enter the Cluj Conservatory to study composition. Ligeti studied with Ferenc Farkas in Cluj and also with Pál Kadosa in Budapest until January 1944, when he was drafted into the Forced Labor Service. For Jews, this meant treatment as prisoners of war. Ligeti's unit transported heavy explosives to the front. However dangerous and cruel this life must have been, the service saved Ligeti from the fate of

---

[4]The violinist Leopold Auer was György's great uncle.

[5]"Musikalische Erinnerungen aus Kindheit und Jugend." In *Festschrift für einen Vertreger: Ludwig Strecker, zum 90. Geburtstag*, edited by Carl Dahlhaus, 54-60. Mainz: Schott, 1973. *See*: B102.

many Jews who were deported in the spring and summer of 1944. György's mother, father, and brother were sent to Auschwitz, and only his mother returned. In October of that year, Ligeti deserted during a battle at the front. The remainder of his unit was later imprisoned in the concentration camp Mauthausen. He made his way on foot back to Cluj and stayed there until the war was over. During much of this time he was ill with pleurisy, a recurrent illness he had acquired during forced labor. When the war ended Ligeti went to Budapest to continue his compositional training. He studied with Sándor Veress, Pál Járdányi, and again briefly with Farkas. After graduation in 1949 he obtained a grant to study Hungarian and Rumanian folk music in Transylvania. Ligeti spent the year following in the footsteps of Bartók and Kodály, collecting folk songs in villages.

In 1950 an appointment as Lecturer of Harmony, Counterpoint, and Formal Analysis at the Ferenc Liszt Academy of Music brought some financial security. While teaching there he wrote two texts on classical harmony. This was a difficult time for experimental composers. Hungary was completely isolated from the west so that the music of Schoenberg was unknown and Stravinsky and Bartók were heard only to a limited extent. Music that was too advanced could not be performed, so Ligeti's public work was limited to Hungarian folksong arrangements. At the same time he had a strong urge to write more complex works in private:

> I was 27 years old and living in Budapest, completely isolated from
> all the ideas, trends, and techniques of composition which
> developed in Europe after the war .... In 1951 I started to
> experiment with simple structures of rhythm and sound in order to
> build up a new music from nothing. My method was Cartesian to
> the extent that I considered all the music that I already knew and
> loved as not binding on me - even as invalid. I asked myself:
> What can I do with a single note? What can I do with its octave?
> What with one interval? What with two intervals? What with
> definite rhythmic relationships which could form the foundation of a
> whole based on rhythm and interval? In this way several small
> pieces were composed, chiefly for the piano. From these
> questions and the attempt to solve them, certain characteristics
> appeared which were not wholly unconnected with serial ideas.
> This seems to me remarkable since I arrived at them from a
> completely different starting point and via a completely different
> path.[6]

In 1955 many cultural restrictions began to be lifted and musicians were able to hear and study new music. For a brief moment it appeared that Hungary was on its way to a quick and complete liberalization. Then came the uprising in the fall of 1956, which was brutally crushed by the Soviets. During this period, Ligeti is said to have left an underground shelter during a battle, in order to listen to a radio broadcast of Stockhausen's *Gesang der Jünglinge*.

Ligeti and his wife, Véra, left Hungary in December of 1956. He arrived eventually in Cologne where he met Karlheinz Stockhausen and began studying the new music of the west. It was reported that he arrived in

---

[6]György Ligeti, quoted in program notes by Ove Nordwall for phonograph record: *Duo Pohjola* (BIS 18). *See*: D48.

Cologne in a state of exhaustion and immediately lost consciousness. "He was taken first to hospital and then to Stockhausen's house, where he slept for 24 hours and refused all food. On waking he broke into a four-hour-long conversation about new music and electronic music, then he went back to sleep for another day and another night."[7] Ligeti, however stated in a letter to Ove Nordwall that this account was "unneccessarily dramatized."[8] It was during this time he analyzed Boulez's *Structure Ia* for *Die Reihe*. He also worked at the electronic music studio in Cologne, and composed three electronic works. He settled in Vienna, and today he resides part time in Vienna and part time in Hamburg.

He quickly established a reputation as a profound and engaging theorist. Studies on musical form, "space" in music, and electronic music, as well as analyses of works by Webern and Boulez were published in rapid succession in 1960 and 1961. He continued to publish theoretical works through the 1960s and 1970s.

Ligeti's first introduction to world prominence as a composer came in 1960 at the Festival of the International Society for Contemporary Music (ISCM) in Cologne. Here his orchestral composition *Apparitions* was first performed. This event was a critical and popular success. *Apparitions* won first prize in the ISCM competition in 1964. His next work, *Atmosphères* was introduced at the 1961 Donaueschingen Music Festival. This second orchestral work brought the motionless background of *Apparitions* to the fore. To produce this static music in which subtle changes are still perceptible, Ligeti developed a technique he calls "micropolyphony." This technique makes use of canonic procedures, but with so many voices and with the entrances so close together that it is impossible to perceive the imitative nature of the music. A contrasting style developed in *Artikulation* (1958), *Aventures* (1962) and *Nouvelles Aventures* (1965). This style is characterized by (openly) contrapuntal texture and disjunct, fragmentary melodic material. *Aventures* and *Nouvelles Aventures* are concert pieces for three solo vocalists with instrumental accompaniment. The text consists of phonetically notated syllables without meaning. These pieces were staged using a variety of interpretations. In 1966 Ligeti wrote his own "libretto" with stage action but no plot.

In the early 1960s Ligeti composed several ironic or satirical pieces in which his sense of humor can be seen as well as some of his views on musical aesthetics. These include *Fragment* (1961), *Die Zukunft der Musik* (1961), *Trois Bagatelles* (1961), and *Poème symphonique* (1962).

The sixties were an incredibly productive period. Ligeti's next large work was the *Requiem* (1965). This work displays the composer's previously developed styles within a choral setting. The *Requiem* was awarded first prize by the ISCM in 1966, and the Beethoven Prize of the City of Bonn in 1967. *Lux aeterna* (1966) and *Lontano* (1967) again make use of micropolyphony, but now certain intervals are given prominence adding an element of harmony. *Lontano* was awarded first prize in the UNESCO competition in 1969. In the *String Quartet No. 2* (1968) Ligeti began experimenting with micro-intervals and continued in *Ramifications* (1969), the

---

[7]Wörner, Karl H. *Stockhausen: Life and Work.* University of California Press, 1973. p. 237.

[8]Nordwall, Ove. *György Ligeti: eine Monographie.* Mainz Schott, 1971. p. 61. *See:* B119.

Double Concerto (1972) and *Clocks and Clouds* (1973). These years also saw the creation of the *Concerto for Violoncello* (1966), *Ten Pieces for Wind Quintet* (1968), the *Chamber Concerto* (1970), and *San Francisco Polyphony* (1973-74). *Continuum* (1968) is noteworthy in that it forebodes Ligeti's use in the 1980s of multiple layers of rhythmical and metrical patterns. The titles of the first organ study *Harmonies* (1967) and the orchestra piece *Melodien* (1971) are an indication that by this time Ligeti had moved away from music perceived as large chromatic clusters. The second organ study *Coulée* (1969) is essentially an organ version of *Continuum*.

Ligeti makes use of many images and metaphors both within his music and in describing his music. This is not to say that these works are programmatic, but ideas and images recur (*See*: B198). One such image that is found frequently is that of a precise mechanism gone awry. This style can be seen in *Poème symphonique, Continuum*, the third movement of the *String Quartet No. 2*, the third movement of the *Chamber Concerto*, and piece no. 8 from *Ten Pieces for Wind Quintet*.

Ligeti went to see the film "2001: A Space Odyssey" on a tip from a friend. He was amazed to find that over 30 minutes of his music had been used without consent or even his knowledge. The context of the film and the juxtaposition with music of Johann and Richard Strauss showed Ligeti's music in an uncharacteristic light. In a 1973 interview Ligeti commented, "They took the music from my recordings. I knew nothing about it. When I heard about the film I wrote MGM and producer Stanley Kubrick. They wrote back: 'you should be happy. With this movie you have become famous in America.' I wrote back: 'I am not happy. You took my music and you did not pay me.' But I didn't want to sue. I am not so commercial. Lawyers met. In the end I got $3,500."[9]

Monument-Selbstportrait-Bewegung for two pianos (1976) displays a further step in the composer's search for new means of expression. This work makes use of complex superimposed meters, and shows the influence of American minimalism. The second movement is a tribute to composers Steve Reich and Terry Riley.

In 1967 Göran Gentele approached Ligeti about writing an opera for the Royal Swedish Opera. His first idea was another *Aventures et Nouvelles Aventures* type of anti-opera with no real meaning or plot. His working title at this time was "Kylwiria," an imaginary land he had created in childhood. After making a few preliminary sketches, Ligeti concluded that he needed a real plot in order to fill an entire evening. In 1969 he planned a comic opera based on the Oedipus legend. This work was to have an understandable plot, but still no meaningful text. When Gentele died in 1972, he abandoned this plan and chose a libretto based on *La Balade du Grand Macabre* by the Belgian playwright Michel de Ghelderode. Ligeti worked with Michael Meschke to condense and "Jarryfy" the libretto (i.e. render it even more absurd, in the style of Alfred Jarry).[10] *Le Grand Macabre* was performed by the Royal Swedish Opera in Stockholm in 1978. With characteristic irony, he

---

[9]Soria, Dorle J. "Artist Life." *High Fidelity/Musical America* 23 (Dec. 1973), p. MA6.

[10]This background on *Le Grand Macabre* is taken from "Zur Entstehung der Oper *Le Grand Macabre*." *Melos/Neue Zeitschrift für Musik* 4 (1978): 91-93. *See*: B44.

called this work an "anti-anti-opera." It has been performed many times in many languages and always evokes strong reactions, one way or the other.

Illness prevented the completion of any new works between 1979 and 1982. This was a turning point in Ligeti's career which signalled the beginning of a new phase of creative activity. In 1982 he completed his *Horn Trio*, a work with strong ties to musical tradition. The eighties have seen the creation of two sets of choral pieces, a piano concerto, a first set of piano etudes for which Ligeti won the Grawemeyer Award in 1986, and five *Nonsense Madrigals* commissioned by the King's Singers. He is presently working on a new opera based on Shakespeare's *The Tempest* with a libretto by Geoffrey Skelton. Influence on his work of the 1980s came from the music of Conlon Nancarrow, fractal geometry and Central African polyphony.

Part of Ligeti's importance as a composer lies in the fact that he has explored new paths for music, having rejected in the late 50s the most favored techniques of post-Webernian serialism on one hand, and aleatory on the other. Never content to settle into a compositional routine, Ligeti has continued to develop new techniques and reexamine his aesthetic position. He expressed this attitude in a 1978 interview: "To sum up the stylistic changes my music has gone through, first of all I should say that whenever I feel that certain melodic or rhythmic models or formal structures have gone stale, I switch my interest to some other area, but my basic approach remains unchanged. What did actually happen? Having gone through *Apparitions*, *Atmosphères*, the *Kyrie* of the Requiem, I felt that total chromaticism, the world of filled cluster had ceased to have any more interest for me. If I went on composing that type of music it would simply be an imitation of my earlier work, I would just be chewing the cud.... I tend to want to do something new, if possible. I am not after novelty for its own sake, I do not want to assume absurd postures, but if something has already been it is ready, complete, gone and done with."[11]

Another aspect of Ligeti's career has been his work as teacher and lecturer. He has earned a reputation as an enthusiastic and absorbing speaker. In the sixties he lectured at the Darmstadt Music Courses and at the Stockholm Music Academy. He has taught composition courses in Madrid, Bilthoven (The Netherlands), Essen, Jyväskylä (Finland), Berlin, Tanglewood, Siena, and Aix-en-Provence. He was Visiting Lecturer and Composer-in-Residence at Stanford University in 1972. He was Professor of Composition at the Hamburg Musikhochschule from 1973 to 1988.

As of this writing Ligeti is reportedly working on a violin concerto and *Piano Etudes* no. 10-12.

---

[11]*György Ligeti in conversation with Peter Varnai, Josef Häusler, Claude Samuel and himself.* London: Eulenburg Books, 1983. p. 31-32. Translated from the Hungarian by Gábor J. Schabert. *See:* B61.

2

Works and Performances

I. Selected Works to 1956

For a complete list of works to 1956, see Nordwall, Ove. *György Ligeti: Eine Monographie* (*See*: B119). A revision by Fred Sallis of the pre-1956 worklist is forthcoming as of this writing.

W1. *Polyphonic Etude* (1943; unpublished)
      For piano four hands. Ove Nordwall has a copy of the ms. *See*: App. II, p. 173.

      Première

  W1a.   1985 (Oct. 27): Stockholm; Stockholm Konserthuset; Eva Nordwall and Kerstin Larsson, piano.

W2. *Idegen földön* (1945-46; Schott; 3:15)
      "Far From Home." For 3-part women's choir a cappella. Words by Bálint Balassa and folksongs. 1. Siralmas nékem (Lament). 2. Egy fekete holló (A black bird). 3. Vissza ne nézz (Don't look back). 4. Fujdogál a nyári szél (Summer breeze). German translation by Hilger Schallen; English by Desmond Clayton.

      Première

  W2a.   1971 (April 17): Stockholm; Radio Chamber Choir; Eric Ericson, conductor.

W3. *Magány* (1946; Schott; 2:30)
      "Solitude." For 5-part mixed a cappella chorus. Words by Sándor Weöres. German translation by Hilger Schallen; English by Desmond Clayton. *See*: App. II, p. 171.

Première

W3a.   1948 (May 21): Budapest; Bartók kollégium kórusa; Lászlo
Udvardy, conductor.

Other selected performance

W3b.   1983 (May 18): Stuttgart (South German Radio); Schola Cantorum
Stuttgart; Clytus Gottwald, conductor.

W4.   *Három Weöres-dal* (1946-47; unpublished)
Three songs for soprano with piano. The third song was lost, but
Fred Sallis reconstructed it from sketches. Words by Sándor
Weöres. 1. Kalmar jött nagy madarakkal (The peddler came with a
big bird). 2. Táncol a Hold (The noon dances) (ms. belongs to O.
Nordwall). 3. Gyümölcsfürt (Grapes).

Première

W4a.   1948 (May 25): Budapest; Edit Géncs, soprano; György Ligeti,
piano.

W5.   *Two Capriccios for Piano* (1947; unpublished)
Ms. belongs to O. Nordwall. *See*: App. II, p. 173.

Première

W5a.   1948 (May 22): Budapest; György Kurtág, piano.

Other selected performance

W5b.   1969 (Nov.): Kiruna, Sweden; Herba Riseber, piano.

W6.   *Invention for Piano* (1948; unpublished)
Ms. belongs to O. Nordwall. *See*: B118, App. II, p. 173.

Première

W6a.   1948 (May 22): Budapest; György Kurtág, piano.

W7.   *Régi magyar társas táncok* (1949; Editio Musica, Budapest, and
Schott; 10-11 min.)
"Old Hungarian Dances." Arrangements of 18th & 19th century
dances for string orchestra with flute or clarinet ad lib. After János
Bihari, János Lavotta, Antal Csermák and Márk Rózsavölgyi.

Première

W7a.   1950 (Feb.): Budapest: Hungarian Radio Orchestra; György Lehel,
conductor.

W8.   *Ifjúsági kantáta* (1949; unpublished)
"Youth cantata." For solo voices (SATBar), chorus, orchestra. Text by Péter Kuczka.

Première

W8a.   1949 (Aug. 18): Budapest.

W9.   *Ballada és tánc* (1950; Schott; ca. 3 min.)
"Ballade and Dance." After Rumanian folksongs, for school orchestra. Arrangement of *Baladá si joc* for 2 violins (ms. with Ligeti). Later reworked as 1st and 2nd movements of *Concert Románesc* for orchestra (1951).

Première

W9a.   1952 (Aug. 20): Győr; Úttörő zenekar; K. Fódor, conductor.

W10.   *Kállai kettős* (1950; Editio Musica, Budapest)
"Duet from Kallai." Setting of two Hungarian folksongs for 4-part mixed chorus. 1. Felűről fúj az őszi szél (The autumn wind blows from above). 2. Eb fél, kutya fél (The dog is afraid). *See:* App. II, p. 174.

Première

W10a.   1950 (Oct. 31): Budapest.

W11.   *Sonatina* (1950; unpublished; ca. 4:15)
For piano 4-hands. Three movements. Ms. at Editio Musica, Budapest. The 1st page of the ms. is reproduced in *Ligeti-dokument*. *See:* B120, App. II, p. 173.

W12.   *Haj, ifjúság* (1952; M.T. Központi Együttes Énekkarra, Budapest)
"Youth." Two pieces for 4-part mixed chorus a-cappella. *See:* App. II, p. 174.

Première

W12a.   1952 (April 8): Budapest.

W13.   *Ot Arany-dal* (1952; unpublished; 10-11 min.)
Five songs for mezzo-soprano and piano. Words by János Arany. 1. Csalfa sugár (False ray of light). 2. A legszebb virág (The prettiest flower). 3. A bujdosó (The exile). 4. A csender dalokból (From a quiet song). 5. Az ördög elvitte a fináncot (The Devil take the tax collector).

Première

W13a.   1953: Budapest; Jolán Máthé, soprano.

W14.   *Musica ricercata* (1951-53; Schott; ca. 22 min.)
11 pieces for piano. Ms. belongs to Ove Nordwall. *See:* W15-16,
B482, D48-D50, App. II, p. 170, p. 172, p. 173.

Première

W14a.   1969 (Nov. 18): Sundsvall, Sweden; Liisa Pohjola, piano.

W15.   *Six Bagatelles* (1953; Schott; ca. 11 min.)
Arranged for wind quintet from nos. 3, 5, 7, 8, 9, and 10 of *Musica
ricercata*. *See:* B415, B579, B642, D64-D71, App. II, p. 170-74.

Première

W15a.   1969 (Oct. 6): Södertälje, Sweden; Stockholm Philharmonic Wind
Quintet.

Other selected performances

W15b.   1970: Warsaw; Stockholm Philharmonic Wind Quintet; Warsaw
Autumn Festival.

W15c.   1977 (May 8): London; Stockholm Philharmonic Wind Quintet;
London Musical Digest. *See:* B291, B351, B387, B661, App. II,
p. 170.

W15d.   1981 (May 10): Munich; Syrinx Quintet; Musica Viva series. *See:*
B314, B335, B585, App. II, p. 171.

W16.   *Omaggio a Frescobaldi* (1953; unpublished)
Ricercar for organ. This was the original version of *Musica
ricercata*, no. 11. Ms. belongs to Ove Nordwall. *See:* W14, App. II,
p. 172, p. 173.

Première

W16a.   1978: Bremen; Karl-Erik Welin, organ.

W17.   *Sonata for Violoncello* (1st mvt. 1948, 2nd mvt. 1953; Schott; ca. 9
min.)
For solo cello. "Dialogo e capriccio." Ms. belongs to O. Nordwall.

Première

W17a.   1979: London; Rohan de Saram, violoncello. *See:* B385.

W18. *Pápainé* (1953; Schott; ca. 3 min.)
"Widow Pápai." For 4-8 part mixed a cappella choir. Based on a
popular Hungarian ballad. German translation by Hilger Schallen;
English by Desmond Clayton. Ms. belongs to Ove Nordwall. 1st
page of ms. reproduced in *Det omöjligas konst* & *Ligeti-dokument*.
See: App. II, p. 171.

Première

W18a. 1967 (May 16): Stockholm; Radio Chamber Choir; Eric Ericson,
conductor.

W19. *String Quartet No. 1* (1953-54; Schott; ca. 20-21 min.)
"Métamorphoses nocturnes." 1st page of ms. reproduced in *Ligeti-
dokument*. Ms. belongs to Ove Nordwall. *See*: Analysis: B118.
Record reviews: B332, B557, B639. Performances: B349, B474,
B494, B507. Recordings: D72-D74.

Première

W19a. 1958 (May 8): Vienna; Rámor Quartet.

Other selected performances

W19b. 1970 (Oct. 5): Berlin; Drolc Quartet.

W19c. 1977 (May 8): London; Arditti Quartet; London Musical Digest.
See: B291, B351, B387, B661, App. II, p. 170.

W19d. 1981 (May 10): Munich; Arditti Quartet; Musica Viva series. *See*:
B314, B335, B585, App. II, p. 171.

W20. *Éjszaka; Reggel* (1955; Schott; ca. 5 min.)
"Night; Morning." 2 pieces for 3-part mixed a cappella choir. Words
by Sándor Weöres. German and English translations by György
Ligeti. A partly autograph copy of the score belongs to John S.
Weissmann. Ms. belongs to the composer. *See*: D25-D27, App. II,
p. 173, p. 174.

Première

W20a. 1968 (March 16): Stockholm; Stockholm Radio Choir, Eric
Ericson, conductor.

W21. *Mátraszentimrei dalok* (1955; Schott; ca. 4:30)
"Songs from Mátraszentimre." For 2 and 3-part children's or
women's chorus a cappella. After Hungarian Folksongs. German
translation by Hilger Schallen; English by Desmond Clayton. Ms.
belongs to Ove Nordwall.

W22. *Chromatische Phantasie* (1956; unpublished)
For piano. Ms. belongs to Ove Nordwall.

II. Complete Works, 1956-1989

W23. *Glissandi* (1957; 7:30)
Electronic, 1 channel. Realized in the Electronic Studio of the West German Radio, Cologne. Ms. belongs to Ove Nordwall. *See:* D30.

W24. *Pièce électronique no. 3* (1957-58; 8:00) not realized
Electronic, 4 channel. Originally entitled "Atmosphères". Score published in *Ligeti-dokument*. Ms. belongs to Ove Nordwall. *See:* B9.

W25. *Artikulation* (1958; 3:50)
Electronic, 4 channel. Typed ms. at Schott. Realized in the Electronic Studio of the West German Radio, Cologne. Ms. belongs to Ove Nordwall. A listening score was designed by Rainer Wehinger. *See:* B126, B130, B243, B654, B675. Analysis: B120, B152, B212, B700. Reviews: B334, B349, B494, B614, Recording: D2.

Première

W25a. 1958 (March 25): Cologne, in the concert series, "Musik der Zeit" of the West German Radio.

W26. *Apparitions* (1958-59; Universal; ca. 9 min.)
For large orchestra. Originally, *Víziók* (1956) was a single movement work. This work was left behind when Ligeti fled Budapest. Ligeti reconstructed this movement and added a second and third (unfinished) movement to form *Apparitions* for chamber orchestra (1957). Finally, a revised version of *Víziók* was coupled with a new second movement to form the final version. Ms. at Universal Editions, Vienna. Ms. of 1957 version belongs to Ove Nordwall. *See:* Ligeti's comments: B26, B29, B42, B45, B56, B66, B98, B175. Analysis: B120, B124, B142, B143, B707. Teaching method: B280. Performances: B491, B569, B674. Recording: D1.

Première

W26a. 1960 (June 19): Cologne; North German Radio Orchestra; Ernest Bour, conductor, at the International Society for Contemporary Music festival. *See:* B397, B413, B601, B602.

W27. *Atmosphères* (1961; Universal; 9 min.)
For large orchestra without percussion. Ms. lost. *See:* Ligeti's comments: B21, B29, B33, B36, B56, B66. Analysis: B118, B124, B143, B193, B234, B254, B259, B266, B270, B279. General discussion: B120, B135, B142, B197, B262-3, B714, B729. Program

notes: B646, B664, B710. Teaching methods: B267. Performances: B296, B312, B433, B537, B562, B583. Recordings: D3-D5.

Première

W27a.   1961 (Oct. 22): Donaueschingen; South West German Radio Symphony Orchestra; Hans Rosbaud, conductor; Donaueschingen Music Festival. *See*: B410-412, B484, B568, B612.

Other selected performances

W27b.   1964 (Jan. 2-5): New York; New York Philharmonic; Leonard Bernstein, conductor (first U.S. performance). *See*: B406, B521.

W27c.   1969 (Oct. 23-31): New York; New York Philharmonic; Seiji Ozawa, conductor. *See*: B404.

W27d.   1971 (March 17): San Francisco; San Francisco Symphony; Seiji Ozawa, conductor.

W27e.   1980 (Jan. 9): San Francisco; San Francisco Symphony; Edo de Waart, conductor.

W28.   *Fragment* (1961, slightly revised, 1964; Universal; ca. 7-10 min.) For chamber ensemble. Ms. belongs to Mr. Alfred Schlee. *See*: B702, App. II, p. 173.

Première

W28a.   1962 (April): Munich; Members of the Munich Philharmonic Orchestra, conducted by the composer; "Neue Musik" concert series. *See*: B570.

W29.   *Die Zukunft der Musik: Eine kollektive Komposition* (1961; dé/collage no. 3 (Cologne, 1962); ca. 10 min.) The Future of Music: a Collective Composition. "Musical provocation" for lecturer and audience. See also entry under Writings by Ligeti: Commentaries on his own works (B27) for information on translations. *See*: B27, B120, B173, B528.

Première

W29a.   1961 (Aug.): Alpbach, Austria, at the "European Forum."

W30.   *Trois Bagatelles for Piano* (1961; Fluxus; ca. 5 min.) "Musical ceremonial" for pianist. Ms. belongs to Ove Nordwall and was reproduced in *Ligeti-dokument*. *See*: B120, D89, D90.

Première

W30a. 1962 (Sept. 26): Wiesbaden; Karl-Erik Welin; "Fluxus Festival."

Other selected performance

W30b. 1979 (Oct.): Cleveland; Eva Nordwall, harpsichord.

W31. *Volumina* (1961-62; revised, 1966; Peters; 16 min.)
For organ. Ms. of the original version belongs to C.F. Peters; Ms.
of the revised version belongs to Ove Nordwall, Stockholm. *See:*
Ligeti's comments: B39, B65, B120. Analysis: B240, B285. General
discussions: B190, B191, B207, B268, B269. Teaching methods:
B273. Performances: B482, B534, B580, B642, B709. Record
reviews: B389, B402. Recordings: D94-D100.

Premières

W31a. 1962 (May 4): Bremen; Karl-Erik Welin.

W31b. 1968 (March 8): Kiel; Karl-Erik Welin. (rev. version)

W32. *Poème symphonique* (1962; 20-100 min.)
"Musical ceremonial" for 100 metronomes (played by 10 musicians
directed by a conductor). Ms. belongs to Ove Nordwall. See also
entry under Writings by Ligeti: Commentaries on his own works
(B40) for information on translations. *See:* B33, B40, B215, B657.
Performances: B462, B614, App. II, p. 170.

Première

W32a. 1963 (Sept. 13): Hilversum, Netherlands; conducted by the
composer. *See:* B215, B347.

Other selected performances

W32b. 1965 (March 4): Buffalo; Lukas Foss, conductor. First U.S.
performance. *See:* B423.

W32c. 1969: Bratislava; Smolenice Festival. Ligeti was present at this
performance with a reduced number of metronomes. It was his
first visit to an East European country since 1956. *See:* B490.

W32d. 1980 (Oct. 26): Second German Television program entitled
"Spielwiese - Experimente - Improvisationen - Spielereien."
(16:11).

W32e. 1989 (Oct. 29): London; "Ligeti by Ligeti" festival. *See:* B638,
App. II, p. 174.

W33. *Aventures* (1962; slightly revised, 1963; Peters; ca. 11 min.)
For three singers (SABar) and seven instrumentalists. Ms. at the
North German Radio, Hamburg, who commissioned the work. *See*:
Ligeti's comments: B56, B72. Analysis: B143, B152, B171, B204,
B231, B236. General discussion: B160, B176, B195, B227, B237,
B250, B288, B677, B700. Score reviews: B247, B253. Performances
(*Aventures* alone): B453, B518, B591, B629. (With *Nouvelles
Aventures*): B292, B293, B303, B337, B341, B358, B425, B430,
B452, B457, B465, B467, B473, B487, B493, B498, B511, B535,
B545, B579, B603, B613, B626, B642, B647, B695. Record reviews:
B402, B631, B634. Recordings: D6-D9.

Première

W33a. 1963 (April 4): Hamburg; Gertie Charlent, Marie-Thérèse Cahn,
William Pearson, soloists; Die Reihe Ensemble; Friedrich Cerha,
conductor; Concert series "Das Neue Werk" of the North
German Radio. *See*: B295.

Other selected performances (see also performances listed under
W36)

W33b. 1966 (Oct. 19): Stuttgart; Württemberg State Theater; Gertie
Charlent, Marie-Thérèse Cahn, William Pearson, soloists;
members of the Stuttgart Opera Orchestra, Friedrich Cerha,
conductor. Rolf Scharre, director. (This was a "pantomime
version" not authorized by the composer). *See*: B428, B442,
B444, B567.

W33c. 1970 (Feb.): Darmstadt; Gertie Charlent, Marie-Thérèse Cahn,
William Pearson, soloists; Bruno Maderna, conductor; Harro
Dicks, director. *See*: B460, B463, B486, B599, B624.

W33d. 1972 (Nov. 11): San Francisco; Phyllis Bryn-Julson, Jan
DeGaetani, Richard Frisch, soloists; members of the San
Francisco Symphony Autumn Orchestra; Leon Fleisher,
conductor.

W33e. 1986 (May 21): New York; Karen Beardsley, Joyce Castle, John
Brandstetter, soloists; Zoltán Peskó, conductor; scenario and
stage direction by Ian Strasfogel. Concert series: "Horizons
'86." *See*: B417, B447.

W34. *Nouvelles Aventures* (1962-65; Peters; ca. 12:30)
Same performers as *Aventures*. Ms. at the Norddeutscher
Rundfunk, Hamburg, who commissioned the work. Ove Nordwall
has the complete sketches. *See*: Ligeti's comments: B72. Analysis:
B123, B143, B152, B200, B223, B231, B236. General discussion:
B195, B227, B237, B250, B288, B677, B700. Score reviews: B247,
B253. Performances: B292, B293, B303, B337, B341, B358, B425,
B430, B452, B457, B465, B467, B473, B487, B493, B498, B511,
B535, B545, B579, B603, B613, B626, B642, B647, B695. Record
reviews: B402, B631, B634. Recordings: D6-D9.

Première

W34a.   1966 (May 26): Hamburg; Gertie Charlent, Marie-Thérèse Cahn,
William Pearson, soloists; North German Radio Ensemble;
Andrzej Markowski, conductor; concert series "Das Neue Werk"
of the North German Radio. *See:* B418, B487, B616.

Other selected performances

W34b.   1966 (Oct. 19): Stuttgart; Württemberg State Theater; Gertie
Charlent, Marie-Thérèse Cahn, William Pearson, soloists;
members of the Stuttgart Opera Orchestra, Friedrich Cerha,
conductor. Rolf Scharre, director. (This was a "pantomime
version" not authorized by the composer). *See:* B428, B442,
B444, B567.

W34c.   1970 (Feb.): Darmstadt; Gertie Charlent, Marie-Thérèse Cahn,
William Pearson, soloists; Bruno Maderna, conductor; Harro
Dicks, director. *See:* B460, B463, B486, B599, B624.

W34d.   1986 (May 21): New York; Karen Beardsley, Joyce Castle, John
Brandstetter, soloists; Zoltán Peskó, conductor; scenario and
stage direction by Ian Strasfogel. Concert series: "Horizons
'86." *See:* B417, B447.

W35.   *Requiem* (1963-65; Peters; ca. 27 min.)
For soprano, mezzo soprano, two 5-part mixed choruses and
orchestra. 1. Introit. 2. Kyrie. 3. Dies irae. 4. Lacrymosa. The
original title was *Fyra satser ur Requiem* (Four movemnts from
Requiem)-- originally a setting of the complete liturgical text was
planned. Commissioned by the Swedish Radio for the 10th
anniversary of the concert series "Nutida Musik." Ms. belongs to
C.F. Peters. *See:* Ligeti's comments: B34, B41, B56, B113.
Analysis: B124, B143, B233. General discussion: B146, B249.
Performances: B297, B311, B336, B458, B490, B506, B523, B592,
B647, B709. Record reviews: B401, B575. Recordings: D59, D60.

Première

W35a.   1965 (March 14): Stockholm; Liliana Poli, sop.; Barbro Ericson,
mz.; Swedish Radio Orchestra and Chorus; Oratorio Chorus;
Michael Gielen, conductor; concert series "Nutida Musik" of the
Swedish Radio. *See:* B497.

Other selected performances

W35b.   1967 (Jan.): Cologne; Liliana Poli, sop.; Barbro Ericson, mz.;
Hamburg and Cologne Radio Choirs; Cologne Radio Symphony
Orchestra; Andrzej Markowski, conductor. 1st performance in
Germany. *See:* B344, B478, B530.

W35c.   1971 (Nov.): London; Liliana Poli, sop.; Anna Malewicz-Madey, mz.; BBC Symphony and Chorus; Michael Gielen, cond. *See*: B501.

W36. *Aventures et Nouvelles Aventures* (1966; Peters; 30-40 min.) Theatre piece to the two earlier works, in 14 scenes. *See*: B32, B72.

Première

W36a.   1970 (Oct. 16): Graz; Gertie Charlent, Marie-Thérèse Cahn, William Pearson, soloists; Die Reihe Ensemble; Friedrich Cerha, conductor; Hans Neugebauer, director. Part of the "Styrian Autumn" Festival. *See*: B525, B548.

Performances of other stage versions

W36b.   1966 (Oct. 19): Stuttgart; Württemberg State Theater; Gertie Charlent, Marie-Thérèse Cahn, William Pearson, soloists; members of the Stuttgart Opera Orchestra, Friedrich Cerha, conductor. Rolf Scharre, director. (This was a "pantomime version" not authorized by the composer). *See*: B428, B442, B444, B567.

W36c.   1968 (March 11): London; Focus Opera Group; Michael Graubart, director. *See*: B539, B574.

W36d.   1970 (Feb.): Darmstadt; Gertie Charlent, Marie-Thérèse Cahn, William Pearson, soloists; Bruno Maderna, conductor; Harro Dicks, director. *See*: B460, B463, B486, B599, B624.

W36e.   1971 (March 3): Film version produced by Klaus Lindemann and broadcast on Second German Television (26:39). Soloists, Gertie Charlent, Marie-Thérèse Cahn, William Pearson. Die Reihe Ensemble, Friedrich Cerha, conductor. *See*: B316, B459, B529.

W36f.   1972 (Oct. 26): Stuttgart; Württemberg State Theater; Gertie Charlent, Elke Estlinbaum, Klaus Hirte, soloists; Bernard Kontarsky, conductor; Ernst Poettgen, director. *See*: B430, B467, B498.

W36g.   1986 (May 21): New York; Karen Beardsley, Joyce Castle, John Brandstetter, soloists; Zoltán Peskó, conductor; scenario and stage direction by Ian Strasfogel. Concert series: "Horizons '86." *See*: B417, B447.

W37. *Lux aeterna* (1966; Peters; ca. 9 min.)
    For 16-part a cappella choir, or 16 solo voices. Ms. belongs to Dr. Clytus Gottwald. Sketches belong to Ove Nordwall. *See*: Ligeti's comments: B22, B111. Analysis: B118, B133, B143, B152, B201, B203, B206, B224, B245, B248, B251, B264, B265. General discussions: B160, B226, B230, B257, B271. Performances: B311,

B322, B562, B614, B709. Record reviews: B389, B403. Recordings: D37-D41.

Première

W37a.   1966 (Nov. 2): Stuttgart; Schola Cantorum Stuttgart; Clytus Gottwald, conductor. *See*: B394.

Other selected performance

W37b.   1977 (May 1): San Francisco; San Francisco Symphony Chorus; Louis Magor, conductor.

W38.   *Concerto for Violoncello* (1966; Schott; ca. 16 min.)
For violoncello and orchestra. Commissioned by the Sender Freies Berlin. Ms. at C.F. Peters. *See*: Ligeti's comments: B30, B56, B111. Analysis: B143, B171, B213, B272, B274, B275, B277. Performances: B297, B493, B513, B562, B564, B579. Program notes: B642, B656, B702. Recording: D16.

Première

W38a.   1967 (April 19): Berlin; Siegfried Palm, cello; Berlin Radio Symphony Orchestra; Henryk Czyż, conductor. *See*: B471.

Other selected performances

W38b   1969: London; Camden Music Festival; Göran Holmstrand; Musica Nova Ensemble; Siegfried Naumann, conductor. 1st U.K. performance? *See*: B330, B580.

W38c.   1971 (Oct. 28-Nov. 1): New York; Siegfried Palm, cello; New York Philharmonic; Michael Gielen, conductor. 1st U.S. performance? *See*: B470.

W39.   *Lontano* (1967; Schott; ca. 11 min.)
For large orchestra; Ms. at Schott. *See*: Ligeti's comments: B21, B66. Analysis: B133, B143, B210, B211, B228, B246, B255, B260, B261. Program notes: B659. Performances: B379, B489, B503, B582. Recordings: D35, D36.

Première

W39a.   1967 (Oct. 22): Donaueschingen; Southwest German Radio Symphony; Ernest Bour, conductor; Donaueschingen Music Festival. *See*: B355, B485, B608.

Other selected performance

W39b.   1972 (Sept.): Berlin; Berliner Festwochen; Berlin Philharmonic; Christoph von Dohnányi, conductor. *See*: B323.

W40. *Study for Organ No. 1* "Harmonies" (1967; Schott; ca. 6-9 min.) *See*:
Analysis: B190, B191, B207, B216. Performances: B482, B637,
B642, B709. Record reviews: B389, B402, B515, B516. Recordings:
D78-D83.

Première

W40a.   1967 (Oct. 14): Hamburg; Gerd Zacher, in the Lutherkirche,
Hamburg-Wellingsbüttel. *See*: B643.

W41. *Continuum* (1968; Schott; ca. 4 min.)
For harpsichord; Ms. in the Paul-Sacher-Stiftung, Basel. There are
also versions for 2 harps 1974), and for barrel-organ. *See*:
Analysis: B117, B133, B143, B171, B278, B286. General discussion:
B150, B258. Performances: B302, B482, B483, B600, B637 (organ),
B642. Record review: B401. Recordings: D17-D21.

Première

W41a.   1968 (Oct.): Basel; Antoinette Vischer, harpsichord.

Other selected performance

W41b.   1977 or 78: Sweden; Eva Nordwall, classical harpsichord.

W42. *String Quartet No. 2* (1968; Schott; ca. 23 min.)
Ms. belongs to the composer. Sketches belong to Ove Nordwall.
See: Ligeti's comments: B80. Analysis: B143, B205, B232. Score
reviews: B208, B282. General discussion: B168, B728.
Performances: B349, B374, B386, B393, B494, B507, B510, B573.
Record reviews: B332, B389, B557. Recordings: D75-D77.

Première

W42a.   1969 (Dec. 14): Baden-Baden; LaSalle Quartet. *See*: B333, B455,
B594, B625.

Other selected performances

W42b.   1977 (May): London; Arditti Quartet; London Musical Digest. *See*:
B291, B351, B387, B661.

W42c.   1981 (May 10): Munich; Arditti Quartet; Musica Viva series. *See*:
B314, B335, B585.

W43. *Ten Pieces for Wind Quintet* (1968; Schott; ca. 15 min.)
Ms. at Schott. *See*: Analysis: B123, B143, B239, B244, B256, B287.
Performances: B307, B330, B390, B416, B435, B493, B522, B573,
B580, B614, B642. Recordings: D85-D88.

Première

W43a.   1969 (Jan. 20): Malmö, Sweden; Stockholm Philharmonic Wind
Quintet.

Other selected performances

W43b.   1977 (May 8): London; Stockholm Philharmonic Wind Quintet;
London Musical Digest. See: B291, B351, B387, B661.

W43c.   1981 (May 10): Munich; Syrinx Quintet; Musica Viva series. See:
B314, B355, B585.

W44. *Ramifications* (1967-69; Schott; ca. 8:30)
For string orchestra or 12 solo strings. See: Analysis: B143, B238.
Performances: B388, B462, B472, B531, B553. Record reviews:
B631, B634. Recordings: D54-D58.

Premières

W44a.   1969 (April 23): Berlin; Berlin Radio Symphony Orchestra; Michael
Gielen, conductor (orchestral version). See: B508.

W44b.   1969 (Oct. 10): Saarbrücken; Saar Radio Chamber Orchestra;
Antonio Janigro, conductor (solo version).

Other performance

W44c.   1983 (May 18): Stuttgart; Concert celebrating Ligeti's 60th
birthday; Stuttgart Radio Symphony Orchestra; Pierre Boulez,
conductor. See: B360, B466.

W45. *Study for Organ No. 2* "Coulée" (1969; Schott; ca. 3:30) See:
Analysis: B190, B191, B207. Performances: B320, B482, B637,
B642. Record reviews: B389. Recording: D81.

Première

W45a.   1969 (Oct. 23): Graz; Seckau Basilica; Gerd Zacher; Styrian
Autumn Festival.

W46. *Chamber Concerto* (1969-70; Schott; 21 min.)
Four movement work for flute (piccolo), oboe (oboe d'amore, cor
anglais), 2 clarinets (bass clar.), horn, trombone, piano (celesta),
harpsichord (hammond organ), 2 violins, viola, cello, bass. Ms. at
Schott. See: Analysis: B118, B202, B252. Performances:
B342,B353, B409, B436, B536, B556, B563, B642. Record reviews:
B517, B631, B634. Program notes: B653, B667. Recordings: D10-
D13.

Premières

W46a.   1970 (May 11): Vienna; Die Reihe Ensemble; Friedrich Cerha,
         conductor (movements 1-3). *See*: B321, B476..

W46b.   1970 (Oct. 1): Berlin; Die Reihe Ensemble; Friedrich Cerha,
         conductor (4th movement); Berliner Festwochen. *See*: B590.

Other selected performances

W46c.   1971 (Jan. 13): London; London Sinfonietta; David Atherton,
         conductor. *See*: B376, B502.

W46d.   1974 (May 3): New York; members of the New York Philharmonic;
         Pierre Boulez, conductor. Concert series: "Prospective
         Encounters."

W46e.   1981 (Dec. 3): Vienna; Concert series "Wege in unsere Zeit." Die
         Reihe Ensemble; Friedrich Cerha, conductor. *See*: B393, B510.

W46f.   1983 (May 13): Stuttgart; Concert celebrating Ligeti's 60th
         birthday; Stuttgart Radio Symphony; Pierre Boulez, conductor.
         See: B302, B360, B466.

W46g.   1986 (March 7): New York; Ensemble InterContemporain, Pierre
         Boulez, conductor.

W47. *Melodien* (1971; Schott; ca. 13 min.)
      For orchestra. Ms. at Schott. *See*: Ligeti's comments: B50.
      Analysis: B242. Performances: B390, B393, B488, B493, B510,
      B562, B596, B642. Program notes: B691, B696. Record review:
      B517. Recordings: D43, D44.

      Première

W47a.   1971 (Dec. 10): Nuremberg Philharmonic Orchestra; Hans
         Gierster, conductor. *See*: B364, B571, B595, B606.

Other selected performances

W47b.   1972 (April 13): Los Angeles; Los Angeles Philharmonic; Zubin
         Mehta, conductor. 1st U.S. performance. *See*: B434, B514.

W47c.   1972 (May 17): San Francisco; San Francisco Symphony; Seiji
         Ozawa, conductor. *See*: B328.

W47d.   1972 (June 24): Amsterdam; Concertgebouw Orchestra; Michael
         Gielen, conductor. *See*: B399, B589.

W47e.   1972 (Oct. 16): Graz; 46th Festival of the International Society for
         Contemporary Music.

W48. *Double Concerto* (1972; Schott; 15-17 min.)
For flute, oboe and orchestra. Ms. at Schott. *See*: Ligeti's
comments: B175. Performances: B339, B348, B390, B421, B562,
B577. Record reviews: B517. Recordings: D22, D23.

Première

W48a. 1972 (Sept. 16): Berlin; Berliner Festwochen; Karlheinz Zöller,
flute; Lothar Koch, oboe; Berlin Philharmonic; Christoph von
Dohnányi, conductor. *See*: B323, B593.

Other selected performances

W48b. 1973 (April 18): Royan; Festival International d'Art Contemporain;
Karlheinz Zöller, flute; Maurice Bourgue, oboe; Orchestre
Philharmonique de l'ORTF; Gilbert Amy, conductor. 1st French
performance.

W48c. 1973 (May 28): Vienna; Karlheinz Zöller, flute; Maurice Bourgue,
oboe; Austrian Radio Symphony Orchestra; Friedrich Cerha,
conductor. 1st Austrian performance.

W48d. 1973 (Sept. 22): Glasgow; "Musica Nova" festival; William Bennett,
flute; Michael Dobson, oboe; Scottish National Orchestra;
Alexander Gibson, conductor. 1st British performance. *See*:
B327.

W48e. 1973 (Oct. 17): Eindhoven, The Netherlands; Paul Verhey, flute;
Werner Herbers, oboe; Concertgebouw Orchestra; Bernard
Haitink, conductor. 1st Dutch performance.

W49. *Horizont* (1972; unpublished)
For solo recorder. Realized by Michael Vetter after an idea by
Ligeti. Strictly speaking this is not a composition of Ligeti's. It is
included here because it has been attributed to him.

Première

W49a. 1972: Graz; Performed by Michael Vetter. *See*: B294.

W50. *Clocks and Clouds* (1972-73; Schott; ca. 13 min.)
For 12-part women's chorus and orchestra. Ms. at Schott. *See*:
Analysis: B152. Performance: B297. Recordings: D14, D15.

Première

W50a. 1973 (Oct. 15): Graz; Styrian Autumn Festival; Austrian Radio
Chorus and Orchestra; Friedrich Cerha, conductor. *See*: B319,
B549, B559, B577.

Other selected performances

W50b.   1973 (Nov. 15): Frankfurt a.M.; Schola Cantorum Stuttgart;
          Frankfurt Radio Symphony Orchestra; Clytus Gottwald,
          conductor. 1st performance in Germany.

W50c.   1974 (May 7): London; London Symphony Orchestra; Women of
          the BBC Singers; English Bach Festival. 1st British
          performance. *See:* B348, B390, B435, B694, App. II, p. 170.

W50d.   1989 (Oct. 19): London; "Ligeti by Ligeti" festival. London
          Sinfonietta Chorus; The Philharmonia; Esa-Pekka Salonen,
          conductor. *See:* App. II, p. 174.

W51.   *San Francisco Polyphony* (1973-74; Schott; 11:30)
          For large orchestra. Ms. at Schott. A sketch was published in
          Miscellanea del Cinquantenario (Milan: Suvini Zerboni, 1978), p. 59.
          See: Analysis: B134. General discussion: B648. Performances:
          B426, B475, B500. Program notes: B673, B711. Recording: D61.

Première

W51a.   1975 (Jan. 8): San Francisco; San Francisco Symphony; Seiji
          Ozawa, conductor. *See:* B329.

Other selected performances

W51b.   1977: Stuttgart; Stuttgart Radio Symphony; Elgar Howarth,
          conductor. *See:* B300, B340, B367.

W51c.   1987 (April 22): San Francisco; San Francisco Symphony; Andrew
          Massey, conductor.

W52.   *Monument-Selbstportrait-Bewegung* (1976; Schott; 16 min.)
          Three pieces for two pianos. "Monument," "Self Portrait with Reich
          and Riley (and with Chopin in the Background)," and "In Gently
          Flowing Movement." Ms. belongs to the composer. *See:* Ligeti's
          comments: B64, B134, B698. Analysis: B118, B123, B192, B219,
          B221. Performances: B292, B462, B482, B573, B615. Record
          reviews: B306, B350, B372, B630. Recordings: D45-D47.

Première

W52a.   1976 (May 15): Cologne; Alfons and Aloys Kontarsky. *See:* B427,
          B456.

Other selected performance

W52b.   1977 (May 8): London; Bruno Canino and Antonio Ballista;
          London Musical Digest. 1st performance in England. *See:*
          B291, B351, B387, B661.

W53. **Rondeau** (1976; Schott; ca. 30 min.)
Theater piece for one actor and tape. See: B715. Performance:
B605.

Première

W53a. 1976 (Feb. 26): Stuttgart; Wolfgang Höper, performer.
See: B301, B340, B440.

W54. **Le Grand Macabre** (1974-77; Schott; 2 hours)
Opera in 2 acts (4 scenes). Libretto by Michael Meschke and Ligeti,
based on the play "La Balade du Grand Macabre" by Michel de
Ghelderode. Commissioned by the Royal Swedish Opera. See:
Ligeti's comments: B28, B31, B35, B43, B44, B51, B59, B62, B70,
B73, B74, B81, B720. Analysis: B218, B229, B283. General
discussion: B146, B209, B217, B241, B683, B704, B712.

Premières

W54a. 1978 (April 12): Stockholm; Swedish Royal Opera; Cast: Sven-Erik
Vikström, Elisabeth Söderström, Kerstin Meyer, Erik Sæden,
Arne Tyrén, Barbro Ericson, Monika Lavén, Ulla Blom, Kerstin
Wiberg, Gunilla Slättegård; Elgar Howarth, conductor; Michael
Meschke, director; Aliute Meczies, set designs and costumes;
Swedish version by Michael Meschke. See: B308, B317, B324,
B352, B356, B363, B369, B371, B375, B377, B408, B420, B438,
B505, B509, B519, B547, B558, B598, B610, B622, B627, B641,
B649, B660, B662, B690.

W54b. 1978 (Oct. 15): Hamburg; Hamburg State Opera; Cast: Hildegard
Uhrmacher, Inga Nielsen, Olive Fredricks, Deborah Browne,
Kevin Smith, Peter Haage, Dieter Weller, Ude Krekow; Elgar
Howarth, conductor; Gilbert Deflo, director; Ekkehard Grübler,
set designer; Günther Schmidt-Bohländer, chorus director;
Norddeutscher Kinderchor Hamburg; Jürgen Luhn, director;
Hamburg Philharmonic State Orchestra. See: B309, B354,
B357, B365, B370, B395, B400, B419, B437, B439, B445, B468,
B479, B492, B520, B550, B560, B572, B576, B587, B609, B619,
B621, B632, B665, B719.

W54c. 1979 (May 5): Bologna; Teatro Comunale di Bologna; Cast:
Dorothy Dorow, Slavka Taskova, Fiorella Pediconi, Rosa
Laghezza, Elena Zilio, Deborah Browne, Oslavio Di Credico,
Mario Basiola, Ugo Trama; Zoltán Peskó, conductor; Giorgio
Pressburger, director; Roland Topor, set designer; Leone
Magiera, chorus director; Italian version by Sylvia Suighi;
adapted by Maurizio Benini, Paola Molinari, and Vincenzo
Morreale. See: B125, B326, B392, B396, B448, B495.

W54d. 1981 (March 23): Paris; Elgar Howarth, conductor; Daniel
Mesguich, director. See: B331, B362, B381, B405, B446, B544,
B546, B565, B584, B604, B652.

W54e.   1983 (Dec. 2): London; Elgar Howarth, conductor; Elijah
Moshinsky, director; Timothy O'Brien, set designer; English
version by Geoffrey Skelton. *See*: B325, B346, B380, B384,
B499, B555, B623, B723.

Other selected performances

W54f.   1979 (May 3): Saarbrücken; Saarland State Theater; Cast: Roderic
Keating, Annemonika Meusel, Susanne Klare, Angelika Nowski,
Eelco von Jordis, Barbara Egel, Manfred Bertram, Elena
Marinescu, Waltraud Kromer; Matthias Kuntzsch, conductor;
Christof Bitter, director; Walther Jahrreiss, set designer. *See*:
B310, B398, B495, B628.

W54g.   1980 (Feb. 2): Nuremberg; Wolfgang Gayler, conductor; Götz
Fischer, director; Marco Arturo Marelli, set designer. *See*: B289,
B318, B450, B526, B581, B607.

W54h.   1984 (March 1): Freiburg; Eberhard Kloke, conductor; David
Freeman, director; David Roger, set design and costumes. *See*:
B299, B461, B464, B469, B586.

W54i.   1989 (Oct. 30): London; "Ligeti by Ligeti" festival. Elgar Howarth,
conductor; Concert performance in a revised English version.

W55.   *Scenes and Interludes from Le Grand Macabre* (1978; Schott; ca. 47
min.)
A two-movement work consisting of selections from the opera, for
solo voices (SMzTB), mixed chorus ad lib., and orchestra. *See*:
Performances: B462, B543. Record reviews: B345, B454.
Recordings: D62, D63.

Première

W55a.   1978 (Dec. 21): Berlin; Inga Nielsen, Olive Fredricks, Peter Haage,
Dieter Weller, soloists; Berlin Radio Symphony; Elgar Howarth,
conductor. *See*: B496.

Other selected performances

W55b.   1979 (Jan. 19): Copenhagen; Inga Nielsen, Olive Fredricks, Peter
Haage, Dieter Weller, soloists; Chorus and Orchestra of the
Danish Radio Copenhagen; Elgar Howarth, conductor. *See*:
D62.

W55c.   1983 (Dec. 2): Munich; Musica Viva Festival; Alison Hargan,
Cynthia Buchan, Roderic Keating and Fabio Giongo, soloists;
Bavarian Radio Symphony; Elgar Howarth, conductor. *See*:
B315, B338, B441.

W55d.   1986 (May 21): New York; Yoko Kawahara, Olive Fredricks, Peter
         Haage, and Dieter Weller, soloists; members of the New York
         Philharmonic; Zoltán Peskó, conductor. Concert series:
         "Horizons '86." *See*: B417, B447.

W56. *Hungarian Rock* (1978; Schott; ca. 5 min.)
      For harpsichord. *See*: Performances: B302, B466, B483, B600,
      B642. Recordings: D31-D33.

      Première

W56a.   1978 (May 20): Cologne; Elisabeth Chojnacka, harpsichord.
         Other selected performances

W56b.   1979 (Oct.): Toronto, Cleveland; Eva Nordwall, harpsichord. First
         Canadian and U.S. performances.

W56c.   1981 (May 11?): Munich; Elisabeth Chojnacka, harpsichord;
         Musica Viva series. *See*: B314, B335, B585.

W57. *Passacaglia ungherese* (1978; Schott; ca. 4 min.)
      For harpsichord. *See*: Score review: B225. Performances: B302,
      B466, B483, B600, B642. Recordings: D51-D53.

      Première

W57a.   1979 (Feb. 2): Lund, Sweden; Eva Nordwall.

      Other selected performances

W57b.   1979 (Oct.): Toronto, Cleveland; Eva Nordwall, harpsichord. First
         Canadian and U.S. performances.

W57c.   1981 (May 11?): Munich; Elisabeth Chojnacka, harpsichord;
         Musica Viva series. *See*: B314, B335, B585.

W58. *Duo for Violin and Violoncello* (1982)
      Written as an hommage to Swedish composer Hilding Rosenberg
      on his 90th birthday. Facsimile of the ms. published in the
      periodical *Tonfallet*, June 3, 1982, p. 12-13.

      Premiére

W58a.   1982 (May 2): Stockholm; Mats Zetterquist and Ewa Forsberg of
         the Gotland String Quartet.

W59. *Trio for Violin, Horn and Piano* (1982; Schott; 22 min.)
      Ms. belongs to the composer. *See*: Ligeti's comments: B60.
      Analysis: B214, B284. Score review: B235. General discussions:

B683, B716. Performances: B349, B360, B466, B481, B494, B600.
Record reviews: B373, B449, B588. Recordings: D91, D92.

Première

W59a.   1982 (Aug. 7): Hamburg-Bergedorf; Saschko Gawriloff, violin;
Hermann Baumann, horn; Eckart Besch, piano. *See*: B578,
B620, B636.

Other selected performances

W59b.   1985 (Oct.): New York; Rolf Schulte, violin; William Purvis, horn;
Alan Feinberg, piano. 1st U.S. performance. *See*: B554.

W59c.   1986 (Nov. 12): New York; Saschko Gawriloff, violin; Robin
Graham, horn; Volker Banfield, piano. Concert associated with
the giving of the Grawemeyer Award. *See*: B552.

W60.   *Den Stora Sköldpadda- Fanfaren från sydkinesiska havet* (1982;
Universal)
"The Big Turtle- Fanfare from the South China Sea." Fanfare for
solo trumpet, written for Martin Nordwall.

Première

W60a.   1984 (April 1): Stockholm; Stockholm Konserthuset; Martin
Nordwall, trumpet.

W61.   *Drei Phantasien nach Friedrich Hölderlin* (1983; Schott; 11 min.)
For 16 voices (SSSSAAAATTTTBBBB) a cappella. 1. Hälfte des
Lebens. 2. Wenn aus der Ferne. 3. Abendphantasie. *See*: Analysis:
B222. Performance: B477. Recording: D24.

Première

W61a.   1983 (Sept. 26): Stockholm; Swedish Radio Chorus; Eric Ericson,
conductor.

W62.   *Magyar Etüdök* (1983; Schott?; 5:30)
For 16 voices a cappella. Words by Sándor Weöres. Ms. belongs
to the composer. *See*: Ligeti's comments: B52, B60. Analysis:
B117, B281. Recording: D42.

Premières

W62a.   1983 (May 18): Stuttgart; Schola Cantorum Stuttgart; Clytus
Gottwald, conductor (no. 1-2). *See*: B302, B466.

W62b.   1983 (Nov. 8): Metz; Schola Cantorum Stuttgart; Clytus Gottwald,
conductor (no. 3).

W63. *Etudes for Piano*. Book 1 (1985; Schott; ca. 20 min.)
1. Désordre. 2. Cordes vides. 3. Touches bloquées 4. Fanfares. 5. Arc-en-ciel. 6. Autonme à Varsovie. *See*: Ligeti's comments: B37, B67. Score review: B276. Performances: B484, B483, B538, B552. Recordings: D28, D29.

Premières

W63a. 1985 (April 20): Zagreb (no. 1-2); Herbert Henck, piano; 13th Muzički biennale Zagreb.

W63b. 1985 (Sept. 24): Warsaw (no. 3 and 6); Volker Banfield, piano; Warsaw Autumn Festival.

W63c. 1985 (Nov. 1): Hamburg (no. 4-5); Volker Banfield, piano. *See*: B480, B617.

W64. *Piano Concerto* (1986-88; Schott; ca. 22 min.)
For piano and chamber orchestra. Originally three movements were completed in 1986, then two more were added in 1988. Ms. belongs to Mario di Bonaventura, who commissioned the work. *See*: Ligeti's comments: B38, B46, B48, B67, B71. Performances: B290, B474, B551.

Premières

W64a. 1986 (Oct. 23): Graz (movements 1-3); Anthony di Bonaventura, piano; members of the Vienna Philharmonic; Mario di Bonaventura, conductor. Styrian Autumn Festival.

W64b. 1988 (Feb. 29): Vienna (movements 4-5); Anthony di Bonaventura; Austrian Radio Symphony; Mario di Bonaventura, conductor.

Other selected performances

W64c. 1989 (Feb.): Tour in Sweden; Hubertus Dreyer, piano; The Chamber Ensemble; Ausgar Krook, conductor.

W64d. 1989 (Nov. 6): London. Volker Banfield, piano; "Ligeti by Ligeti" festival. British première of the final 5-movement version. *See*: App. II, p. 174.

W65. *Nonsense Madrigals* (1988)
1. Two Dreams and Little Bat. 2. Cuckoo in the Pear-Tree. 3. The Alphabet. 4. Flying Robert. 5. Lobster Quadrille. AATBarBarB. Ms. of no. 1 (1 leaf) reproduced in *Sonus* 9, no. 1 (fall 1988): 15.

Premières

W65a. 1988 (Sept.): Berlin; Berliner Festwochen. The King's Singers. (nos. 1-4). *See*: App. II, p. 174.

W65b.   1989 (Oct. 28): London; "Ligeti by Ligeti Festival." The King's
         Singers. (no. 5). At this performance the madrigals were
         interspersed with movements of Machaut's *Messe de Nostre
         Dame*. *See*: B527, App. II, p. 174.

W66.   *Etudes for Piano*. Book 2 (1988-)
        7. Galamb borong. 8. Fém. 9. Vertige.

        Première

W66a.   1989 (Sept. 23): Berlin (no. 7-8); Volker Banfield, piano; Berliner
         Festwochen.
         Other selected performance

W66b.   1989 (Nov. 6): London. Volker Banfield, piano; "Ligeti by Ligeti"
         festival. British première of nos. 7-8. *See*: App. II, p. 174.

3

Writings by Ligeti

I. Theoretical Writings

B1. "Aspekte der Webernschen Kompositionstechnik." In *Anton Webern II*, Musik Konzepte, Sonderband, 51-104. Munich: Edition Text + Kritik, 1984. 427 p.

Four parts of a ten-part series of radio lectures originally broadcast on Southwest Geman Radio in 1963-64. 1. Webern und die Romantik. 2. Weberns Harmonik. 3. Webern und die Zwölftonkomposition. 4. Weberns komplexe Kompositionstechnik.

B2. "Computer und Komposition: Subjektive Betrachtungen." In *Tiefenstruktur, Musik, Baukunst: Festschrift Fritz Winckel zum 80. Geburtstag am 20. Juni 1987*, 22-30. Berlin: Technischen Universität Berlin, 1987.

The most important aspect of computer music for Ligeti is that the experience of working with computers can allow composers to think about musical forms, structures and processes differently. For example Ligeti's exposure to computer music in 1972 influenced some of his work in the 1980s such as the *Etudes for Piano* (especially nos. 1 and 6), sketches for his opera based on Shakespeare's *Tempest*, and the fourth movement of the *Piano Concerto*.

"Den elektroniske musiks historie." *See*: B10.

B3. "Die Entdeckung des Raumes in der Musik." *Forum* 7 (1960): 152-54.

Originally titled "Die Funktion des Raumes in der Musik." A Swedish translation by Ove Nordwall appeared as "Rummets funktion i musiken." *Studiekamraten* (Lund) no. 6 (1966): 119-121, *Origo* (Stockholm) no. 4 (1966): 28-30, and *Hufvudstadsbladet* (Helsinki), May 21, 1967, p. 9-10. The (re)discovery of "space" in music followed the breakdown of tonality and was also influenced by the development of electronic music and stereo technology. The concept of space in music can be compared to the concept of time in painting. One possibility which can be explored is the creation of imaginary space within real space.

"Form in der Neuen Musik." *See*: B14.

"Die Funktion des Raumes in der Musik." *See*: B3.

B4.   *A Klasszikus harmóniarend I-II.* Budapest: Zeneműkiadó, 1956.

A two-volume collection of examples of classical harmony.

B5.   *Klasszikus összhangzattan.* Budapest: Zeneműkiadó, 1954.

A textbook on classical harmony.

B6.   "Die Komposition mit Reihen und ihre Konsequenzen bei Anton Webern." *Österreichische Musikzeitschrift* 16 (1961): 297-302.

Ligeti observes that Webern's use of free atonality led easily into the use of 12-tone rows. Webern organized his rows into three or four groups each of which contained four or three tones. These smaller groups were organized to emphasize minor seconds, major sevenths and minor ninths. Webern's compositional technique reveals many extensions to serialism, such as series of tone colors in which none is repeated. Thus Webern's music was the starting point of the new serialism.

B7.   "Kompositorische Tendenzen heute." *Neue Musik* 1 (1960).

The entire issue is devoted to this text. Swedish translation by Bo Alphonce: "Aktuella kompositionstendenser." *Nutida Musik* 4, no. 3 (1960/61): 2-4. This is a condensation of a number of ideas presented in other articles written around the same time, most notably "Wandlungen der Musikalische Form." *See:* B16.

B8.   "Megjegyzések a bartóki kromatika kialakualásának egyes felteteleiröl." *Új Zenei Szemle* no. 9 (Sept. 1955): 41-44.

"Remarks on Several Conditions for the Development of Bartók's Chromaticism."

"Metamorphoses of Musical Form." *See:* B16.

B9.   "Musik und Technik: Eigene Erfahrungen und subjektive Betrachtungen." In *Rückblick in die Zukunft: Beiträge zu Lage in den achtziger Jahren,* Hans Rössner, ed., 297-324. Berlin: Severin und Siedler, 1981.

Ligeti recounts the theory and methods used in electronic music of the 50s. Gottfried Michael Koenig's *Essay* and his own *Pièce electronique no. 3* serve as examples. He then shows how the technique used in electronic music were carried over into instrumental and vocal music. Sections of *Apparitions* and *Requiem* illustrate this. Ligeti offers some observations on the work of the Studio for Electronic Music of the West German Radio, Cologne, and other studios, as well as electronic music in general. He comments on the differences (and similarities) between "acoustic" and electronic sound, on the use of computers in composition, and on the discrepancy between the "imaginary space" of electronic music and the real space in which the music is heard. *See:* W24.

B10.   "Musik von anderen Planeten: zur Geschichte und Gegenwart der elekronischen Musik." *Forum* 8 (1961): 292-95.

Translated by Ove Nordwall as "Den elektroniske musiks historie." *Dansk Musiktidsskrift* 41 (1966): 113-17. Also appeared as "Den elektrofoniska musikens historia och nuvarande situation." *Musik och Ljudteknik* 8, no. 2 (1966): p. 10-14, no. 3, p. 18-20, and no. 4, p. 12-14. The distinction between electronic and acoustic or "natural" music is misleading. All music is artificial because nature contains only individual sounds without context. The real distinction between electronic and traditional music is that in electronic music tone color can be treated as a spectrum, rather than a set of discrete values. This quality was very important to the total serialists of the 50s. Another influence was electronically aided speech analysis. The work of early pioneers of electronic music is summarized.

"Det musikaliska formtänkandets förvandlingar." See: B16.

B11.   "Neue Notation: Kommunikation oder Selbstzweck?" Darmstädter Beiträge zur neuen Musik no. 9 (1965): 35-50.

Translated into Swedish in Musikern no. 6 (June 1968): 6-7, and no. 7-8 (July-Aug. 1968): 6-8. Ligeti begins by describing the difference between graphic and symbolic notation. An analogy is the difference between a picture of a house and the written word "house." The value of traditional notation is primarily practical and communicative. The value of representational notation is primarily aesthetic. Ligeti favors traditional notation when writing for traditional performing media. For new media, such as electronic music, new notation must be devised.

"Om musikalisk form." See: B14.

B12.   "Pierre Boulez: Entscheidung und Automatik in der Structure Ia." Die Reihe no. 4 (1958): 33-63.

Translated into English in Die Reihe no. 4 (1960): 32-62. The work is analyzed in detail, revealing three working stages of composition: Decision I, Automatism, Decision II. The rigid structure of the piece allows it to be used as a "textbook" example of serial construction. Ligeti shows various musical elements which permit compositional freedom of choice and others which are pre-determined. "... decisions and automatisms are not opposed principles but two aspects of the same principle."

"Remarks on Several Conditions for the Development of Bartók's Chromaticism." See: B8.

"Some Remarks on Boulez's 3rd Piano Sonata." See: B20.

B13.   "Über die Harmonik in Weberns erste Kantate." Darmstädter Beiträge zur neuen Musik no. 3 (1960): 49-64.

Based on a lecture given at the 1959 Darmstadt Ferienkurse. A section of the first movement of Webern's op. 29 is analyzed in terms of harmonic relationships. Fundamental differences between tonal and atonal harmony are illustrated.

B14.   "Über musikalische Form." Neues Forum 13 (1966): 291-95, and 419-21.

Also appeared as "Form in der Neuen Musik." Darmstädter Beiträge zur Neuen Musik no. 10 (1966): p. 23-35. Translated into Swedish by Göran Fant as "Om musikalisk form." Nutida Musik 9, no. 8 (1965-66): 28-35. Translated into Swedish again by Ove Nordwall in Ligeti-dokument (see: B120). A lecture given at the Darmstadt Summer Course, 1965. Musical form is traditionally thought of as the relation of parts to each other and to the whole. This formulation ignores some essential aspects of form. Music is presented in time; musical form may be seen as an abstraction represented in spacial terms, of the musical presentation. With new music we no longer have standard formal schemes. Each new work obeys its own rules. In new music individual events tend to be isolated and unconnected to other events. In performance however, horizontal and vertical connections emerge producing an unintentional system of references a؛d as a result, musical form. By shifting the starting point of compositional method it is possible to ensure that relationships within the compositional process correspond more closely to the relationships in the composed music.

B15.   "Ubetinget at fortælle løgne." *Dansk Musiktidsskrift* 43 (1968): 6-11.

This improvised lecture was given in Helsinki, March 31, 1967 in German. It was transcribed and translated into Swedish by Ove Nordwall. This is a Danish translation from the Swedish by Birthe Hedegaard Larsen. Ligeti comments on the relationship of words and music, and on the role of the modern composer. A composer today must steer a course between the extremes of "Daedelus" (becoming so cerebral as to be incomprehensible to anyone but himself), and "Golem" (trying to please everyone, and producing bathos).

B16.   "Wandlungen der musikalischen Form." *Die Reihe* no. 7 (1960): 5-19.

An English translation by Cornelius Cardew appeared as "Metamorphoses of Musical Form." In *Form--Space*, 5-19. Die Reihe, no. 7. Bryn Mawr, Pa.: T. Presser, 1965. A Swedish translation by Ove Nordwall appeared as "Det musikaliska formtänkandets förvandlingar." in *Från Mahler till Ligeti* (*See*: B173). An Italian translation appeared in *Ligeti*, ed. by Enzo Restagno (*See*: B122). Ligeti compares the decline of serial music to the decline of tonal music. Tonality disintegrated through the growth of the leading tone. Serialism is likewise being destroyed by the effect of an absence of individual intervals. "Serial music is doomed to the same fate as all previous sorts of music: at birth it already harboured the seeds of its own dissolution." As intervals lose their individuality, the music becomes a uniform shade of grey with little contrast. This leveling out can only be avoided if "the highest possible degree of order is sought by means of decisions made by the composer in the process of composition."

B17.   "Was erwartet der Komponist der Gegenwart von der Orgel? In *Orgel und Orgelmusik heute*, edited by H. Eggebrecht, et al., 167. Stuttgart: Musikwissenschaftliche Verlags-Gesellschaft, 1968.

A paper read at a colloquium which was concerned with present problems of organ composition, organ construction, and organ playing.

B18.   "Weberns Melodik." *Melos* 33 (1966): 116-18.

Originally presented as a series of ten radio talks on Southwest German Radio, Baden-Baden. Ligeti discusses characteristics of melody in Webern's music, the effects of serial composition on melody, and changes from early to late works.

B19.   "Weberns Stil." *Gehört-Gelesen* no. 3 (1960): 187-92.

B20.   "Zur III. Klaviersonate von Boulez." *Die Reihe* no. 5 (1959): 38-40.

An English translation appeared as "Some Remarks on Boulez's 3rd Piano Sonata." *Die Reihe* no. 5 (1961): 56-58. Swedish translation by Ove Nordwall appears as "Om Boulez' tredje pianosonat." *Östersunds-Posten*, Dec. 12, 1961, p. 2. French translation appears in *Musique en jeu* 16, no. 6 (1974): 10-11. A discussion (including historical examples) of the elements which are fixed by exact notation and those which can be interpreted freely.

"Zur Geschichte und Gegenwart der elektronischen Musik." *See*: B10.

II. Commentaries on his own Works

Ligeti has written numerous program notes to accompany performances of his works. For complete details on these to 1968 see: Nordwall, Ove. *György Ligeti: eine Monographie*. Mainz: Schott, 1971. *See:* B119.

B21.   "Anlässlich Lontano." *Die Begegnung. Sonderheft, Programmheft der Donaueschinger Musiktage für zeitgenössische Tonkunst*, 1967 (unpaged).

> Program notes for Lontano. Swedish translation by Ove Nordwall: *Dagens Nyheter*, Feb. 3, 1968, p. 4; also in *Ligeti-dokument*. Ligeti describes the development of his static style in the 1950s. This development led to the composition of *Atmosphères*. The style then underwent more change to include intervallic constellations. This new kind of polyphonic-harmonic web can best be heard in *Lontano*. *See:* W39.

"Anteckningar till Volumina." *See:* B39.

B22.   "Auf dem Weg zu *Lux aeterna*." *Österreichische Musikzeitschrift* 24 (1969): 80-88.

> An exposition of the compositional ideas and techniques involved in this piece. "Vergleichen könnte man diesen Vorgang etwa mit einem Bühnenbild, das zunächst deutlich zu sehen ist, in allen seinen Einzelheiten; dann steigt Nebel auf und die Konturen des Bildes verschwimmen, bis schließlich das Bild selbst unsichtbar geworden ist; darnach verflüchtigt sich der Nebel, es tauchen zuerst nur andeutungweise neue Verschwinden auf, bis dann, mit dem völligen Verschwinden des Nebels, ein neues Bild sichtbar wirt." ["The process could be compared perhaps with a stage setting which at first is clearly seen in detail. A fog appears and blurs the contours of the set until finally the set itself is invisible. Then the fog evaporates, and the suggestion of new shapes emerge. When the fog completely disappears a new set is visible."] Also includes a brief discussion by Karlheinz Roschitz of problems of modern vocal music. *See:* W37.

B23.   "Auswirkung der elektronischen Musik auf mein kompositorisches Schaffen." In *Experimentelle Musik*, edited by Fritz Winckel. Schriftenreihe der Akademie der Künste Berlin, 7, 73-80. Berlin: Mann, 1970.

> Ligeti describes his work and influences at the Electronic Studio of the West German Radio, Cologne. He shows how this experience has influenced his non-electronic works such as *Atmosphères* and the *Requiem*. He describes his musical goals, one of the results of which is emphasis on tone color. In fact, tone color is only one of the many possibilities inherent in the network structure of Ligeti's music.

"Bemärkninger til *Volumina*." *See:* B39.

B24.   "... cellon 'talar': Dokumentation kring György Ligetis cellokonsert." *Nutida Musik* 29, no. 4 (1985-86): 9-14.

> A collection of excerpts from letters and commentary on the *Concerto for Violoncello*. Translated and edited by Ove Nordwall.

B25.   "Diskussionsprotokoll från 'Tonsättaren och samhället'." *Nutida Musik* 12, no. 2 (1968-69): 59-60.

The text of a radio program entitled "To Lie and Deceive." Ligeti presents his ideas about art in general ("Art must not be true") and about *Aventures et Nouvelles Aventures* in particular.

B26.   "Fragen und Antworten von mir selbst." *Melos* 37 (1971): 509-16.

An English translation appears in: *György Ligeti in Conversation with Peter Várnai, Josef Häusler, Claude Samuel and Himself (See:* B61). Ligeti discusses aspects of his compositional process, e.g. the relationship of "primitive," emotional raw material to systematic conscious decisions. He describes the influence serial music had on him after his emigration from Hungary in 1956. Some of his specific techniques are outlined with reference to certain of his works. He refers especially to *Apparitions. See:* W26.

B27.   "The Future of Music: a Collective Composition." *dé/collage* no. 3 (1962).

Text in English and German. The composer describes his piece in which he stood silent on a speakers platform at a convention. Timings are given and the character of each section is described. Translations appear also in Danish (*Politisk Revy* 4 (March 1966): 15), Japanese (*Shiryo Shitsy*, SAC Journal no. 32 (1963)), and Swedish (*Nutida Musik* 6, no. 8 (1962/63): 29-31). The Swedish translation was reprinted in *Från Mahler till Ligeti. See:* W29, B173.

B28.   "*Le Grand Macabre.*" *Österreichische Musikzeitschrift* 36 (1981): 569-70.

This is a brief description of the opera. *See:* W54.

"György Ligeti, *Atmosphères.*" *See:* B36.

B29.   "Kilka uwag o utworach niektórych moich kolegów i moich wlasnych." *Ruch Muzyczny* 6, no. 20 (1962): 1-2.

A transcription of a radio lecture given on Nov. 14, 1961, on Polish Radio. The lecture was presented as part of the series "Musical Horizons." Ligeti comments on *Apparitions, Atmosphères,* and works of Stockhausen, Kagel, Cerha, and König *See:* W26, W27.

B30.   "Kommentar till min violincellkonsert." *Musikern* no. 6-7 (June-July 1967): 6.

Program notes for the *Concerto for Violoncello,* translated from German by Ove Nordwall. Reprinted in *Ligeti-dokument.* (See: W38, B120).

B31.   "Langer Weg zur neuen Oper." *Neue Musikzeitung* 27, no. 3 (1978): 30.

Ligeti answers three questions relating to *Le Grand Macabre.* Several pictures relating to the Stockholm production fill the rest of the page. *See:* W54a.

B32.   "Libretto zu *Aventures et Nouvelles Aventures.*" *Neues Forum* 13 (1966): 774-79, and 14 (1967): 86-92.

The composer provides his own detailed stage directions for singers, three pantomimists, dancers, and extras, to be used in staging these works. In an afterword Ligeti explains his intentions in writing the musical works, and his thoughts on the staging of them See: W36.

B33.   "Ligeti: The CAPAC-Macmillan Lecture." edited by Michael Schulman. *The Canadian Composer* no. 83 (Sept. 1973): 16-21+.

An abridged text of a lecture given at the University of Toronto on July 13, 1973. Ligeti outlines his work from the mid-50s to the early 70s, especially *Atmosphères*, *Aventures et Nouvelles Aventures*, *Poème Symphonique* and *Continuum*. In English and French.

B34.   "Ligeti über sein *Requiem*: Zur Aufführing in der Stiftskirche." *Stuttgarter Zeitung*, July 11, 1969.

Ligeti discusses the form and musical structure of this work on the occasion of a performance at the Stuttgarter Kirchenmusiktage. See: W35.

B35.   "Meine neue Oper: eine Comic Strip: AZ-Gespräch mit dem Avantgarde-Komponisten Ligeti." *Abendzeitung*, April 10, 1978.

This brief description of *Le Grand Macabre* includes some comments by the composer, recorded by Reinhard Beuth. See: W54.

"O wlasnym utworze na organy Volumina." See: B39.

B36.   "Om *Atmosphères*." *Nutida Musik* 6, no. 1 (1962-63).

Reprinted in v. 18, no. 1 (1974-75): 10-11; and again in v. 24 (1980-81): 10-11. Translated into Swedish by Bo Ullman. Describes the style and compositional techniques of the work. See: W27.

B37.   "On My *Etudes For Piano*." *Sonus* 9, no. 1 (fall 1988): 3-7.

The music of Conlon Nancarrow and central African polyphony influenced the ideas behind these pieces. By combining hemiola with African additive rhythms a single performer is able to produce the illusion of several simultaneous layers of different tempi. See: W63.

B38.   "On My *Piano Concerto*." *Sonus* 9, no. 1 (fall 1988): 8-13.

This work represents the realization of new conceptions of harmony and rhythm. "When this music is properly performed, that is at the given speed and with the given accentuation within the separate levels, after a certain time it will 'lift off' like an aircraft." See: W64.

B39.   "Die Orgel sprengt die Tradition." *Melos* 33 (1966): 311-13.

Danish translation by Jens Brincker: Bemaerkninger til *Volumina*." *Dansk Musiktidsskrift* 40, no. 5 (1965): 147-49. Abridged Polish version appeared as "O wlasnym utworze na organy *Volumina*." *Ruch Muzyczny* 10, no. 8 (1966): 8. Swedish translation by Ove Nordwall: "Anteckningar till Volumina." *Kyrkomusikernas tidning*, Vagnhärad, no. 9 (1966): 124-125, and *Östersunds-Posten*, Jan. 19, 1967, p. 2. New Swedish translation by Nordwall: "Orgelns nya klangmögligheter." *Musikern* no. 4 (1967): 6. Also reprinted in *Ligeti-document* (See: B120). An Italian translation appeared in *Ligeti* ed. by Enzo Restagno (See: B122). Ligeti describes the musical structure of *Volumina*, and compares it to traditional works and other contemporary works. "Die Musiksprache meines Orgelwerkes ist untraditionell. Solch ein kompositorischer Standpunkt ist problematisch, wenn man bedenkt, daß die Orgel, mehr als jedes anderes Instrument, durch Tradition vorbelastet ist.... Strenge und Erhabenheit allein bleiben aus der Orgeltradition übrig; alles andere verschwindet in den weiten, leeren Räumen, den 'Volumina' der musikalischen Form." ["The language of my organ music is untraditional. Such a compositional standpoint is problematic when one considers that the organ, more than any other instrument, is burdened with tradition.... Strictness and grandeur alone remain of the organ tradition. All else vanishes in the broad, empty space, the 'Volume' of musical form."] *See:* W31.

"Orgelns nya klangmögligheter." *See:* B39.

B40.   "Poème Symphonique für 100 Metronome." *Revue Integration* 4 (1965): 137-39.

Appeared also under the title: Symphonie (für 100 Metronome)." In *Humor am Rand der Notenlinien.* Edited by Lothar Knessl, 104-108. Salzburg: Residenz Verlag, 1965. English translation by Eugene Hartzell: *Fluxus CCVTRE,* 1964. English and Spanish (Spanish translation by Ramón Barce): *Sonda* 2 (1968): 19-26. Swedish translation by Ove Nordwall: *Det omöjligas Konst* and *Ligeti-dokument.* A description of *Poème Symphonique* including detailed performance instructions. *See:* W32, B120, B121.

B41.   *"Requiem* von György Ligeti: Einleitung und Kommentar." *Wort und Wahrheit* 23, no. 4 (1968): 308-313.

Monika Lichtenfeld provides background on the development of the musical style of the work. Ligeti describes it movement by movement. *See:* W35.

B42.   "Spielanweisung zur Erstfassung des zweiten Satzes der *Apparitions.*" *Musica* 22 (1968): 177-79.

Some brief but detailed instructions pertaining especially to the aleatoric aspects of the original version of this piece. *See:* W26.

"Symphony (für 100 Metronome)." *See:* B40.

B43.   "Den Stora Makabern." *Musikrevy* 33, no. 3 (1978): 89-90.

A description of how the work came to be composed. Translated from conversations with the composer and the composer's introduction, by Ove Nordwall. *See:* W54.

"Tillstånd, händelser, förvandlingar." *See:* B45.

"Die Zukunft der Musik." *See:* B27.

B44.   "Zur Entstehung der Oper *Le Grand Macabre.*" *Melos/Neue Zeitschrift für Musik* 4 (1978): 91-93.

Ligeti describes the process through which he came to compose *Le Grand Macabre,* his decision to abandon the meaningless phonetic text of *Aventures et Nouvelles Aventures,* and the selection and "Jarryfication" of a theater piece by Michel de Ghelderode. He also discusses the ambiguity of the opera's title character. *See:* W54.

B45.   "Zustände, Ereignisse, Wandlungen." *Blätter + Bilder* 11 (1960): 50-57.

Reprinted in *Melos* 34 (1967): 165-69. Slovak translation by V. Neumannová: "Apparitions: Poznámky k mojej orchestrálnej skladbe." *Slovensá Hubda* 10

(1966): 173-75. Swedish translation by Ove Nordwall: "Tillstånd, händelser, förvandlingar." *Bonniers Litterära Magasin* no. 2 (1965): 114-16, reprinted in *Från Mahler till Ligeti*. Ligeti describes the musical structure of the first movement of *Apparitions*. He begins by relating a childhood dream in which a large web is shaken back and forth and is constantly changing shape. This imagery had some influence on the structure of *Apparitions*. "Die musikalische Form, die nach den hier geschilderten Vorstellungen und Prinzipien gebaut ist, entspringt einer fortdauernden Wechselwirkung von Zuständen und Ereignissen. Die Zustände werden dabei von plötzlich auftauchenden Ereignissen unterbrochen und verändern sich unter deren Einfluß; und umgekehrt: die veränderten Zustände haben auch eine gewisse Wirkung auf die Art der Ereignisse; denn diese müssen immer von neuartiger Prägung sein, um den veränderten Zustand weiter verändern zu können. Auf diese Weise entsteht eine unablässige Wandlung: die schon dagewesenen Zustände und Ereignisse schalten gegenseitig ihr nochmaliges Auftreten aus, sind also unwiederbringbar." ["The musical form which is designed according to these ideas and principles, springs from a continuing interaction of states and events. The states are interrupted by suddenly emerging events and are changed by this influence. Conversely, the altered states have a certain influence on the sort of events which occur, because the events must always have a new character in order to be able to further change the states. In this way, there is constant change. The former states and events mutually compensate for their renewed appearances, and are therefore irretrievable."] *See*: W26, B173.

III. Interviews

B46.   "Back to the Future." *The Observer*, May 31, 1987, p. 18.

> This brief interview with Nicholas Kenyon focuses on Ligeti's views on other composers past and present. Ligeti also comments on his latest works including the *Piano Concerto* which was performed at the Almeida Festival in June, 1987. *See*: W64.

B47.   *Beszélgetések Ligeti Györggyel*. Budapest: Zeneműkiadó, 1979. 126 p.

> English translation in *György Ligeti in Conversation with Peter Várnai, Josef Häusler, Claude Samuel, and Himself*. Reviewed in *Magyar Zene* 20 (1979): 435-36. An extensive interview in three parts with Peter Várnai. The first part consists of general comments on Ligeti's various techniques: micropolyphony, "cooled expressionism" and the sound of malfunctioning machinery. All of his styles and influences of Bartók, Stravinsky, and Berg can be found in the *String Quartet No. 2*. The second part is a more detailed discussion of each work, taken chronologically from *Atmosphères* to *Le Grand Macabre*. The composer comments on his notational practices. An interesting description of San Francisco is also included. In part three, Ligeti discusses his educational ideas, the state of contemporary music, and his thoughts on past composers, especially Schumann and Mahler. *See*: B61.

B48.   "A Budapest Interview with Ligeti." *New Hungarian Quarterly* 25 (summer 1984): 205-10.

> Reported by István Szigeti. Ligeti recounts the major events of his life and also discusses his musical style. He comments in detail on his current ideas with regard to his *Piano Concerto*. *See*: W64.

B49.   "Computer-Musik als Kreativer Dialog zwischen Musiker und Maschine? Gespräch mit dem Komponisten György Ligeti." *Musik + Medizin* 2, no. 5 (1976): 43-45.

> In this interview with Lutz Lesle, Ligeti discusses the implications of computer-aided composition. He suggests the possibility that Hamburg may become a center for computer music.

B50.   "Conversation with Ligeti at Stanford." *Numus West* No. 2 (1972): 17-20.

> An interview with Louis Christensen. Ligeti discusses the difference in cultural climate between central Europe and the American west coast, the possibilities of computer music, and his recently completed *Melodien*. *See*: W47.

"D'Atmosphères á Lontano." *See*: B66.

B51.   *Entretien avec György Ligeti*. Paris: Hubschmid & Bouret, 1981.

> An interview with Claude Samuel, given on the occasion of the Paris production of *Le Grand Macabre*. Ligeti relates the history of how his opera came to be composed, comments on his musical style, and his dramatic goals. He also comments on operatic tradition and 20th century opera in general. An English translation appears in *György Ligeti in conversation with Peter Varnai, Josef Häusler, Claude Samuel, and Himself*. *See*: W54d, B61.

B52.   "Gespräch mit György Ligeti." *Melos* 38 (1971): 213-14.

> An interview with Walter Bachauer, reprinted from *Die Welt*, March 13, 1971. Ligeti discusses some general thoughts about musical style and composition, including the influence of popular music in his work.

B53.   "Gespräch mit György Ligeti." *Neue Zeitschrift für Musik* 145, no. 1 (1984): 8-11.

> A conversation with Monika Lichtenfeld which took place on May 18, 1983 in Stuttgart on the occasion of a concert celebrating Ligeti's 60th birthday. Ligeti discusses his unproductive period (1978-82), the *Horn Trio, Magyar Etüdök, Three Fantasies*, and his plans for a new opera based on *The Tempest*.

B54.   "Gustav Mahler und die musikalische Utopie: ein Gespräch zwischen György Ligeti und Clytus Gottwald." *Neue Zeitschrift für Musik* 135 (1974): 7-11, 288-95.

> In three parts: I. Musik und Raum. II. Collage. III. Die Achte--Epilog zu den Gesprächen mit György Ligeti. A discussion taped in 1972 for the South German Radio, and broadcast in Jan. 1974. Ligeti relates the concepts of space and collage to Mahler's music, referring sometimes to other composers including himself. In part III. Gottwald comments on Mahlers Eighth Symphony.

B55.   "György Ligeti." In *Was ist Musikalische Bildung?*, by Werner Klüppelholz, 66-75. Musikalische Zeitfragen, 14. Kassel: Bärenreiter, 1984.

> This interview focuses on educational aspects of music and art. Ligeti discusses the concept of a qualified or ideal listener with regard to his own music. His music can be appreciated at different levels, but a well educated listener can appreciate the many extramusical associations present in the music. He also comments on the place of modern music in society. The book was reviewed in *Musica* 39 (1985): 301-2.

B56.   "György Ligeti." In *Werkstattgespräche mit Komponisten*, by Ursula Stürzbecher, 32-45. Cologne: Gerig, 1971.

> An interview. The composer describes his early years in Transylvania and Budapest, the development of his musical style, and his work since 1956. He comments specifically on *Apparitions, Atmosphères, Aventures*, the *Cello Concerto*, and the *Requiem*. See: W26, W27, W33, W38, W35.

B57.   "György Ligeti: Distinguished and Unpredictable." *Musical America* 107, no. 4 (Sept. 1987): 12-15+.

> This interview with Dorle J. Soria took place in New York during the composer's visit to receive the Grawemeyer Award. Ligeti comments on his most current influences, including fractal geometry and Central African polyphony. He also discusses literature, architecture and his family. He reports that he is working on additional movements for his piano concerto, a violin concerto for Saschko Gawriloff, and continues to plan an opera based on Shakespeare's *The Tempest*.

B58.   "György Ligeti gibt Auskunft: ein Gespräch mit Monika Lichtenfeld." *Musica* 26 (1972): 48-50.

> Ligeti discusses his new teaching position in Hamburg and plans to visit San Francisco as Composer-in-Residence at Stanford University. He also talks about

the development of his musical style leading up to *Melodien*, and his plans for future works.

B59.   "György Ligeti--illusions et allusions." *Interface* 8 (1979): 11-34.

Includes a summary in English. An interview which traces the background of *Le Grand Macabre. See:* W54.

B60.   "György Ligeti im Gespräch mit Denys Bouliane." *Neuland Jahrbuch* 5 (1984-85): 72-90.

This interview originally appeared in French in *Sonances* 3, no. 1 (Oct. 1983): 8-27. Ligeti comments on his early choral music in Hungary, on Kodály and Hungarian folk music, on poet Sandor Weöres, and on his *Magyar Etüdök* and *Horn Trio. See:* W62, W59.

B61.   *György Ligeti in conversation with Peter Varnai, Josef Häusler, Claude Samuel and Himself.* London: Eulenburg Books, 1983, 140 p.

English translations of interviews published originally in Hungarian, German and French. Reviewed in *Brio* 21 (1984): 26-27, *Times*, no. 4236, p. 646, and *Music and Letters* 65 (1984): 381-82. *See:* B26, B47, B51, B66.

B62.   "György Ligeti: Mon Opéra es un Pot au Feu que Sort de la Poubelle." *Monde de la Musique* no. 32 (March 1981): 71-73.

An interview with Jean-Noël Von Der Weid, given on the occasion of the Paris production of *Le Grand Macabre*. Ligeti discusses his experience with electronic music and the philosophy behind his opera. *See:* W54d.

B63.   "'Ich will nicht kleine Ligetis heranziehen': Welt-Gespräch mit dem ungarischen Komponisten über seine künftige Lehrtätigkeit." *Die Welt*, Jan. 4, 1973.

An interview with Wolfgang Schultze in which the composer discusses his work as a teacher.

B64.   "Ich würde nie mit Computer komponieren: Gespräch mit dem Komponisten György Ligeti." *Neue Musikzeitung* 28, no. 5 (1979): 27.

A transcript of an interview given during the intermission of a concert which included *Monument-Selbstportrait-Bewegung*, performed by Erika Haase and Einar Steen-Nökleberg. Ligeti discusses his ideas about piano technique and about composition in general. *See:* W52.

B65.   "In meiner Musik gibt es keine Weltanschauung: Gespräch mit György Ligeti." *Das Orchester* 36 (1988): 885-90.

This interview with Lutz Lesle covers a wide range of topics from politics to the future of music. Ligeti tells about his early years in Hungary. He also discusses his favorite artists and writers.

B66.   "Interview mit György Ligeti." *Melos* 37 (1970): 496-507.

A transcription of a radio interview with Josef Häusler on the occasion of the première of *Lontano*. Reprinted in: Nordwall, Ove. *György Ligeti: eine Monographie*. Translated into French as "D'*Atmosphères* à *Lontano*: un entretien entre György Ligeti et Josef Häusler." *Musique en jeu* No. 15 (Sept., 1974): 110-119. Translated into English by Sarah E. Soulsby in: *György Ligeti in Conversation with Peter Varnai, Josef Häusler, Claude Samuel and Himself.* A substantial piece which includes discussions of *Lontano, Atmosphères, Apparitions,* and *Volumina.* The composer describes his work in terms of his musical ideas and in terms of the resulting effect. He also describes his stylistic development during the 1960s. *See:* W39, W27, W26, W31, B61, B119.

B67.   "Interview mit György Ligeti. *Zeitschrift für Musikpädagogik* 11, no. 37 (Nov. 1986): 3-11.

In an interview with Hans Joachim Erwe which took place in Hamburg on July 16, 1986, Ligeti discusses briefly the development of his style. He comments extensively on the *Etudes for Piano* and the *Piano Concerto.* Polyrhythm and polymeter play a significant role in his present style. Influence on his work in the eighties has come from the music of Conlon Nancarrow, Bantu music of central and eastern Africa, and fractal geometry. Finally he makes some remarks about aspects of listener qualification with regard to his music. There exist many subcultures within the present European tradition. Ligeti's music is accessible to anyone familiar with the general musical language of the culture, who is open to things outside the "official" and "avant-gardist" subcultures. *See:* W63, W64.

B68.   "'The Island is full of noise': György Ligeti im Gespräch mit Sigrid Wiesmann." *Österreichische Musikzeitschrift* 39 (1984): 510-14.

An interview given in preparation for the Styrian Autumn festival in Graz which was devoted to Ligeti's works. The composer discusses his relation to tradition and to present trends. He also describes the work on a libretto for an opera based on Shakespeare's "The Tempest." His collaborator in this project is Geoffrey Skelton. Finally, he comments on his lack of recent theoretical writing, his students, and several recordings of his works.

"Das Komische ist Todernst." *See:* B73.

B69.   "Ligeti på svenska då ... nu ... framtiden ..." *Nutida Musik* 19, no. 4 (1975-76): 25-29.

A transcription of a spontaneous interview with Berit Berling given on Swedish Radio on Dec. 18, 1975, the day before a concert of contemporary music. The composer discusses the 1956 Hungarian uprising, and his various works.

B70.   "Ligeti talks to Adrian Jack." *Music and Musicians* 22, no. 22 (July 1974): 24-30.

Following some discussion of Ligeti's compositional methods is a fascinating preview of the composer's thoughts on the libretto of *Le Grand Macabre.* This interview took place before Ligeti began composition of the opera, and is enlightening as well as entertaining. "I don't want to ironise opera. I like very much theatre. It will be a piece for theatre, with music as an integral part--as the main part. It's not in the opera tradition. Although it has connections with Rossini--not musically, but in the tempo. But it has this connection with the movies. It is something which is done in the opera house, but it is outside the opera as a genre. Therefore there will be no expression, no opera situations." *See:* W54.

B71.   "Musik mit schlecht gebundener Krawatte." *Neue Zeitschrift für Musik* 143 (1981): 471-73.

An interview with Monika Lichtenfeld on the occasion of a concert sponsored by the Bavarian Radio, and featuring both string quartets, both wind quintets, and three harpsichord solos. Ligeti speaks mostly about future projects and plans including the *Piano Concerto*, and a new stage work." *See*: W64.

B72.   "Musik zwischen Konstruktion und Emotion: Gespräch mit György Ligeti." *Musik und Gesellschaft* 34 (1984): 472-77.

An interview with Mathias Hansen on the occasion of a visit by the composer to the Dresden Music Festival. Ligeti discusses his compositional philosophy with regard to constructivism and emotionalism. He discusses *Aventures et Nouvelles Aventures* in particular. *See*: W33, W34, W36.

B73.   "Musikdramatische Comics aus "Breughelland." *Die Deutsche Bühne* 49, no. 10 (1978): 10, 39-41.

An interview with Jochem Wolff which also appeared as "Das Komische ist todernst ... *Le Grand Macabre*--Abbilder unserer heutigen Welt. György Ligeti im Gespräch mit Jochem Wolff." In *Programmheft der Hamburgischen Staatsoper*, edited by Peter Dannenberg and Jochem Wolff. Ligeti describes the development of the work from 1965 to its completion. He comments on the philosophical implications of the libretto and music. He also discusses the development of his own musical style. *See*: W54b.

B74.   "Nach der ersten Oper weitere Opernpläne: Imre Fabian sprach mit dem Komponisten György Ligeti." *Opernwelt* 19, no. 6 (1978): 29-30.

Ligeti comments on his relationship with tradition and with the avant-garde. He also discusses absurd theater and current directions in music theater. The interview focuses especially on *Le Grand Macabre*. *See*: W54.

B75.   "Nedokončený rozhovor." *Hudebný život* 1 (1969): 3.

An interview in Slovak with Naďa Herčková on Ligeti's opinions about music, interpretation, the audience, and his own work.

B76.   "Neue Musik lebt, solange man über sie schreibt: György Ligeti will künftig mit dem Computer komponieren." *Die Welt*, July 13, 1973.

A summary of a conversation with Lutz Lesle on the occasion of the composer's 50th birthday.

B77.   "Swedish Music of Today: Conversation between György Ligeti and Ulla-Britt Edberg (1970)." in *Tradition and Progress in Swedish Music*. Special ed. of *Musikrevy*, 1973. p. 64-66.

The composer remarks on the avant-garde musical climate in Stockholm and the world in general. Translated from *Musikrevy: Sonderheft in deutscher Sprache*, Stockholm, 1970.

B78.   "Tendenzen der neuen Musik in den USA: György Ligeti im Gespräch mit Clytus Gottwald." *Melos/Neue Zeitschrift für Musik* 1 (1975): 266-72.

Reprinted in *Music und Bildung* 8 (Feb. 1976): 56-61. A transcript of an interview broadcast on South German Radio in 1973. Ligeti remarks on American culture in general, and on the works of composers Terry Riley and Harry Partsch in particular.

B79.　"... wenn etwas das gewisse Etwas hat: ein Gespräch mit dem Komponisten György Ligeti." *Musik + Medizin* 3, no. 12 (1977): 57-58, 62-64.

The interviewer is Wolfgang Sandner. Most of this conversation concerns popular music. Ligeti believes pop music is too commercial, yet it has produced works of high art, for example the work of the Beatles with George Martin, and the work of Miles Davis.

B80.　"Wenn man heute ein Streichquartett schreibt." *Neue Zeitschrift für Musik* 131 (1970): 378-81.

A transcript of an interview with Josef Häusler, broadcast on Southwest German Radio on the occasion of the première of the *String Quartet No. 2*. Reprinted in: Nordwall, Ove. *György Ligeti: eine Monographie*. Translated into Swedish as "Att skriva straakkvartett idag." *Nutida Musik* 14, no. 3 (1970-71): 2-6. Ligeti discusses the history of the string quartet, and specific influences on his quartet composition. *See*: W42, B119.

B81.　"'Wie Reste aus einem Mülleimer'." *Die Welt*, Oct. 7, 1978.

A very brief interview with Hans Otto Spingel, given on the occasion of the German première of *Le Grand Macabre*. Ligeti comments on the staging, musical aspects of his opera, and his views on Hamburg. *See*: W54b.

IV. Minor Writings

B82.   "17 Komponisten schreiben zum Schott-Jubilaeum." *Melos* 37
(1970): 227.

A brief paragraph commemorating the 200th anniversary of Schott.

B83.   "Apropos Musik und Politik." In *Ferienkurse '72*, 42-46. Darmstädter
Beiträge zur neuen Musik, no. 13. Mainz: Schott, 1973.

A transcription of remarks made spontaneously in Darmstadt in 1972. An
English translation appeared as "On Music and Politics." *Perspectives of New
Music* 16, no. 2 (1978): 19-24. Ligeti stresses that musical structure is on a
different plane than political or social meaning. He also argues against the idea
that music which is intended for only a few people is reactionary or elitist and
therefore should be eliminated."

B84.   "Bartók: Medvetánc (1908) (Elemzés)." *Zenei Szemle* 5 (1948): 251-
55.

An analysis of Bartók's "Bear Dance."

B85.   "Bartóks fünftes Streichquartett: Einführung und Formanalyse." In
Philharmonia Taschenpartitur no. 167. Vienna: Universal Edition,
1957.

In German, French and English. This introduction to the fifth string quartet by
Bartók appears untitled (title cited here is from Nordwall, *György Ligeti: eine
Monographie*, p. 171). Swedish translation by Ove Nordwall appears as
"Introduktion och analys av Bartóks femte stråkkvartett." *Musik-kultur* no. 2
(1966): 6-7.

B86.   "Béla Bartóks Werk." *Melos* 16 (1949): 153-55.

Ligeti revised this work catalog originally compiled by Erich Doflein.

B87.   "Carl Orff zum Gedenken." *Neue Zeitschrift für Musik* 143 (1982): 27.

Ligeti, among other musicians, offers a brief memorial to Carl Orff.

B88.   "Contemporary Music: Observations from Those Who Create It."
Music & Artists 5, no. 3 (June-July 1972): 21.

Some brief but entertaining comments on the state of music.

B89.   "Egy aradmegyei román együttes." In *Emlekkönyv Kodály Zoltán 70.
születésnapjára*, 399-404. Budapest: Zenetudományi tanulmányok
Akadémia kiadó, 1953.

"A Rumanian Ensemble from the Arad District," in "Festschrift for Zoltán Kodály's
70th birthday.

B90.   "Einführung zu Friedrich Cerha: Relazioni fragili." Program notes for
the concert series "die reihe" (Vienna, May 16, 1960).

Swedish translation by Ove Nordwall: "Introduktion till Cerha: Relazioni Fragili." *Musik-kultur* no. 2 (1966): 7, and *Dansk Musiktidsskrift* 41 (1966): 161. An introduction this work by Cerha.

B91. "Försvar för orkestern (ur ett brev fraan György Ligeti 18/9 1969)." *Musikrevy* 29 (1974): 238-39.

This is a translated section of a letter from the composer to Ove Nordwall. Ligeti gives some insight into his attitudes toward orchestral composition.

B92. "Gát József: Kottaolvasás." *Zenei Szemle* 5 (1948): 277.

A score review.

B93. "György Ligeti." In *Mein Judentum*, edited by Hans Jürgen Schultz, 234-247. Stuttgart: Kreuz Verlag, 1978.

This book is based on a series of talks broadcast on the South German Radio. Ligeti describes his life as a Jew, especially during his childhood and youth. The anti-semitism in pre-war eastern Europe is described, as well as the terrible persecution suffered during the Second World War.

B94. *György Ligeti: from sketches and unpublished scores 1938-56 from the collection of Ove Nordwall.* Publications issued by the Royal Swedish Academy of Music, 16. Stockholm: Norstedts, 1976.

Miniature facsimiles of mss. with introduction and comments by Ove Nordwall. Excerpted from "Tre texter." *Artes* 2, no. 3 (1976): 83-98. *See:* B684.

B95. "Járdányi Pál és Szervánszky Endre fuvolaszonatinái." *Uj Zenei Szemle* no. 12 (1954): 26-28.

"The Flute Sonatas of Pál Járdányi and Endre Szervánszky."

B96. "Járdányi Pál: Szonáta két zongorara." *Zenei Szemle*, Aug. 1949, p. 103.

A review of Járdányi's sonata for two pianos.

B97. "Kották." *Zenei Szemle* 6 (1948): 337.

Includes short reviews of two works by Ferenc Farkas: *Régi magyar táncok* and *12 Weöres Sándor dal*.

Ligeti-Dokument. See B120.

B98. "Ligeti über Lutoslawski." *Musica* 22 (1968): 453.

An excerpt of a letter Ligeti wrote to Ove Nordwall clarifying his relationship to Lutoslawski with respect to *Apparitions. See:* W26.

B99. "'Meine Musik ist elitäre Kunst'--György Ligeti antwortet Lutz Lesle." *Musica* 28 (1974): 39-40.

Ligeti discusses some of his musical goals and ideas briefly and comments on the usefulness of musical criticism. "Ich will mit meiner Musik niemanden beeinflussen, nicht die Gesellschaft ändern." ["I don't wish to influence anyone with my music, or to change society."]

B100. "Min utveckling some tonsättare." *Dagens Nyheter*, Feb. 3, 1968, p. 4.

A summary of the composer's work since the early 1950s, translated by Ove Nordwall.

B101. "Möte med Kurtág i efterkrigstidens Budapest." *Nutida Musik* 29, no. 2 (1985-86): 31.

The composer relates his experiences after the war when he and György Kurtág were students in Budapest. He also tells about their common backgrounds and political beliefs and what happened after they finished school.

B102. "Musikalische Erinnerungen aus Kindheit und Jugend." In *Festschrift für einen Vertreger: Ludwig Strecker, zum 90. Geburtstag*, edited by Carl Dahlhaus, 54-60. Mainz: Schott, 1973.

A fascinating and entertaining account of Ligeti's early years in Transylvania. Ligeti relates anecdotes illustrating the influence of the gypsies, of his parents' gramophone, of early visits to the opera, and of his first piano teacher on his musical development. Swedish translation in "Tre texter." *Artes* 2, no. 3 (1976): 83-98 (*See*: B684). Excerpts of the Swedish translation appear as "Om min Barndom." *Musikern* no. 4 (April 1977): 10-11. An Italian translation appeared in *Ligeti* ed. by Enzo Restagno. *See*: B122.

B103. "Népzenekutatás Romániában." *Uj Zenei Szemle* no. 3 (Aug. 1950): 18-22.

"Folk Music Research in Rumania."

B104. "Neue Musik in Ungarn." *Melos* 16 (1949): 5-8.

Ligeti describes the social conditions and musical life in Hungary, and comments on the work of the most prominent Hungarian composers.

B105. "Neues aus Budapest: Zwölftonmusik oder 'Neue Tonalität'?" *Melos* 17 (1950): 45-48.

This is another summary of musical life in Hungary. Ligeti especially noted the controversy over which musical language will take the place of tonality: serialism or a "new tonality."

B106. "Om Ligeti some folkmusiksamlare." *Nutida musik* 20 (1976-77): 15-16.

These excerpts from a personal letter to Ove Nordwall were translated by the recipient. They deal with the work of Ligeti and other ethnologists in Rumania.

"On Music and Politics." *See*: B83.

B107. "Österreichische Musikzeitschrift." *Zenei Szemle* 5 (1948): 284-85.

Short reports written in Hungarian, on articles published in Österreichische Musikzeitschrift between July 1947 and Jan. 1948.

B108. "Sugár: Vonóstrio." *Zenei Szemle*, Aug. 1949, p. 105-6.

A review of Rezsö Sugár's string trio.

B109.   "Szervánszky Endre: Vonósnégyes." *Zenei Szemle*, Aug. 1949, p. 102-3.

A review of Szervánszky's string quartet.

B110.   "Über neue Wege im Kompositionsunterricht." In *Three Aspects of New Music*, 9-44. Publications of the Royal Academy of Music and the Royal Swedish College of Music, 4. Stockholm: Nordiska, 1968 (New ed., 1971).

Reviewed in: *Nutida Musik* 12 (1968-69): 61-62, *Music in Education* 33 (1969): 199, *Musical Times* 110 (1969): 1043, and *The World of Music* 13, no. 2 (1971): 54-57. Describes two composition courses taught by Ligeti at the Royal Swedish College of Music, Stockholm. The text was written in 1963.

B111.   "Ur två brev från György Ligeti till en svensk forskare." *Konsertnytt* 2 (1967): 12-13.

Excerpts of letter to Ove Nordwall, dealing with *Lux aeterna* and the *Concerto for Violoncello*. *See*: W37, W38.

B112.   "Veress Sándor: Billegeto muzsika." *Zenepedagógia* 2, no. 3 (March 1948): 43.

A review of Veress' "Finger Larks."

B113.   "Viele Pläne, aber wenig Zeit." *Melos* 32 (1965): 250-52.

Selections from letters to Ove Nordwall. The composer reports on his work on the *Requiem* and several other projects. *See*: W35.

B114.   "A Viennese Exponent of Understatement: Personal Reflections on Friedrich Cerha." *Tempo* no. 161-62 (June-Sept. 1987), p. 35.

Comments given when Friedrich Cerha was awarded the Austrian State Prize on Oct. 26, 1986. English translation by Inge Goodwin.

B115.   "Weberns fein gesponnener Kosmos." *Frankfurter Allgemeine Zeitung*, Sept. 14, 1965.

4

Writings about Ligeti

I. Books

Beszélgetések Ligeti Györggyel.
See entry under "Writings by Ligeti. Interviews" (B47).

Entretien avec György Ligeti.
See entry under "Writings by Ligeti. Interviews." (B51).

B116. Griffiths, Paul. György Ligeti. Contemporary composers. London: Robson Books, 1983. 128 p.

This is the only book length biography to appear in English so far. It begins with an interview covering the composer's life up to 1956. The bulk of the volume surveys the composer's post-1956 works up to the Horn Trio. The style is non technical and captures a sense of the joy of Ligeti's music. Includes a discography and short bibliography. Reviewed in:
Brio 21 (1984): 26-27.
Times of London, no. 4236, p. 646, J. Deathridge
Music and Letters, 65 (1984): 381-82, A. Whitall.
New Statesman, Nov. 25, 1983, p. 22.
Central Opera Services Bulletin 27, no. 3 (1986-87): p. 66.

György Ligeti in Conversation with Peter Varnai, Josef Häusler, Claude Samuel and Himself. London: Eulenburg Books, 1983, 140 p.
See entry under "Writings by Ligeti. Interviews." (B61).

B117. Kolleritsch, Otto, ed. György Ligeti: Personalstil-Avantgardismus-Popularität. Studien zur Wertungsforschung, Heft 19. Graz: Universal, 1987. 237 p.

This is the proceedings of a symposium held as part of the Ligeti Festival at the 1984 Styrian Autumn. Contents: "Ligeti und die elektronische Musik" by Gottfried Michael Koenig; "'Ein weitverzweigtes Spinnennetz'" by Christoph von Blumröder; "Musik - Klang - Farbe. Zum Problem der Synästhesie in den frühen Kompositionen Ligetis" by Elmar Budde; "Zum Aspekt des musikalischen Raums bei Ligeti" by Christian Martin Schmidt; "Allusion - Illusion? Überlegungen anläßlich Continuum" by Hartmuth Kinzler; "Wertherarchie und Negationslust. Kompositions-psychologische Aspekte bei Ligeti" by Ulrich Dibelius; "'... und alles Schöne hatt' er behalten...' Fragmente zu Ligetis Ästhetik" by Monika

Lichtenfeld; "Clocky Clouds and Cloudy Clocks: Europäisches Erbe in beschmutzter Zeitlupe" by Hermann Sabbe; "'Die ich rief, die Geister/Werd ich nun nicht los' Zum Problem von György Ligetis Avantgarde-Konzeption" by Martin Zenck; "Personalstil und Musiksprach. Anmerkungen zur Positionsbestimmung György Ligetis" by Rudolf Frisius; "Ligetis *Magyar Etüdök* (1983)" by Clytus Gottwald; "Die Orgelwerke von György Ligeti" by Zsigmond Szathmáry; "Über Klang-Verästelungen und über die Form-Bewegung" by Ivana Stoïanova. Each contribution is followed by a discussion among the other participants including Ligeti himself. *See*: W41, W62, App. II, p. 172.

B118.   Michel, Pierre. *György Ligeti: Compositeur d'aujourd'hui*. Musique ouverte. Paris: Minerve, 1985. 246 p.

The first part of this volume is a critical biography through 1983, ending with the *Drei Phantasien nach Friedrich Hölderlin*. Many musical examples are included. The second part consists of a series of interviews with the composer which took place on Dec. 29-30, 1981. Ligeti discusses the political situation in Hungary, the influence of many composers from Bartók to Nancarrow, his thoughts on electronic music, and many other topics. The third part consists of six analyses of works by Ligeti: *Invention for Piano* (1948), *String Quartet No. 1* (1954), *Atmosphères* (1961), *Lux aeterna* (1966), *Chamber Concerto* (1970) and *Monument for Two Pianos* (1976). Includes substantial work list, bibliography, and discography. *See*: W6, W19, W27, W37, W46, W52.

B119.   Nordwall, Ove. *György Ligeti: eine Monographie*, translated from Swedish by Hans Eppstein. Mainz: Schott, 1971. 229 p.

This is basically a German translation of *Ligeti-dokument* (*See*: B120), without some of the reproductions of scores, but with additional material including two interviews with Josef Häusler (originally broadcast on Southwest German Radio, Baden-Baden, July 19 and 26, 1968, shortly before the première of *Lontano*, and Dec. 14, 1969, shortly before the première of the *String Quartet No. 2*. Includes an extremely complete list of writing and .musical works to 1970. This is the only complete published list of pre-1956 works. A revision by Fred Sallis of this list is forthcoming. Reviews:
Musik und Bildung 4 (1972): 257. Siegfried Borris.
Die Musikforschung 27 (1974): 244-45. Reinhold Brinkman.
Numus West no. 2 (1972): 21-22. Louis Christensen "Ligeti Literature."
Melos 40 (1973): 150-51. Hanspeter Krellmann.
Neue Zeitschrift für Musik 133 (1972): 354-55. Monika Lichtenfeld.
Musical Times 113 (1972): 870. Roger Smalley.

B120.   --------. *Ligeti-dokument*. Stockholm: Norstedt, 1968. 318 p.

In Swedish. A collection of essays describing *Atmosphères, Apparitions, Artikulation, Volumina, String Quartets Nos. 1 and 2, Aventures, Die Zukunft der Musik, Fragment, Requiem, Concerto for Violoncello*, together with excerpts from letters to Nordwall commenting on works between 1966 and 1969. Also includes sketches and scores by Ligeti. Includes a lists of Ligeti's writings and musical works. Reviewed by Louis Christensen in *Numus West* no. 2 (1972): 21.

B121.   --------. *Det omöjligas Konst: anteckningar kring György Ligetis Musik*. Stockholm: Norstedt, 1966. 118 p.

Includes descriptions of Ligeti's compositions with examples from the scores, a bibliography, and a short biographical sketch. Reviews:
Nutida Musik 10 (1966-67): 56-57. Göran Fant.
Svensk Tidskrift för Musikforskning 49 (1967): 230-31. Sten Anderson.
Dagens Nyheter, Feb. 21, 1968. Lennart Hedwall,
Numus West no. 2 (1972): 21-22. Louis Christensen.

B122.   Restagno, Enzo, ed. *Ligeti*. Bibliotheca di cultura musicale. Autori
e opere. Turin: Edizioni di Torino, 1985. 265 p.

A collection of essays published on the occasion of the Settembre Musica
Festival in Turin in 1985. Some of the essays are translated from previously
published sources, including five selections by the composer himself:
"Volumina." translated by David Urman from "Bemerkungen zu meinem
Orgelstück Volumina (*See*: B39); "Monument, Selbstportrait, Bewegung."
translated by David Urman; "Memorie musicali dell'infanzia e della giovinezza."
translated from the German by Laura Patriarca (*See*: B102), and "Metamorfosi
della forma musicale." translated from German (*See*: B16). A number of new
writings are included as well, especially studies of several individual works.
Contributions are divided into three parts: Musical language, Works, and the
composer's own writings. The volume is completed by a selective work list,
bibliography and discography. Reviewed in:
    Revista Musical Italiana 20 (1986): 455-56.
    Neue Zeitschrift für Musik 147, no. 4 (April 1986): 75.

B123.   Sabbe, Hermann. *György Ligeti: Studien zur Kompositorischen
Phänomenologie*, Musik-Konzepte, 53. Munich: Edition Text +
Kritik, 1987. 110 p.

This book attempts to develop special methods for the analysis of Ligeti's works
by focusing on psychological and sociological aspects. *Bewegung* for two
pianos (*See*: W52), and the first of the *Ten Pieces for Wind Quintet* (*See*: W43)
are described. Methods of describing *Nouvelles Aventures* (*See*: W34) are also
discussed. A review by Sigrid Wiesmann appears in *Österreichische
Musikzeitschrift* 42 (1987): 480.

B124.   Salmenhaara, Erkki. *Das musikalische Material und seine
Behandlung in den Werken "Apparitions", "Atmosphères", und
"Requiem" von György Ligeti*. Translated from Finnish by Helke
Sander. Acta Musicologica Fennica, 2. Helsinki: Suomen
Musiikkitieteellinen; Forschungsbeiträge zur Musikwissenschaft, 19.
Regensburg: G. Bosse, 1969. 203 p.

Originally the author's doctoral dissertation. These analyses focus on
compositional techniques and relationships between structural levels.
Appendices include textual sketch material from the composer (*See*: W26, W27,
W35). Reviews:
    Die Musikforschung 27 (1974): 244-45, Reinhold Brinkmann.
    Svensk Tidskrift för Musikforskning 26 (1971): 138-39, Jørgen Lekfeld.

B125.   Topor, Roland. *Le Grand Macabre, dessins des décors et costumes
de l'opéra de György Ligeti*. Zürich: Diogenes, 1980. 75 p.

A collection of sketches for the costumes and scenery for the Bologna
production of the opera. Includes a preface by Topor and four photographs of
the production. *See*: W54c.

B126.   Wehinger, Rainer. *György Ligeti: Artikulation. elektronische Musik,
eine Hörpartitur*. Mainz: Schott, 1970.

Reviewed in *Musikrevy* 26 (1971): 33-34, and *Numus West* no. 2 (1972): 21-22.
A visually delightful colored listening score with sound disc and analysis. *See*:
W25, B150, B243, B654, B675.

II. Journal Issues devoted to Ligeti

B127.   *Artes* 2, no. 3 (1976)
        See: B684.

B128.   *Musik und Bildung* 7, no. 10 (Oct. 1975)
        See: B136, B149, B152, B210, B270, B678.

B129.   *Numus West* no. 2 (1972)
        See: B50, B119, B120, B121, B126, B139, B654.

B130.   *Nutida Musik* 19, no. 2 (1975-76)
        See: B175.

B131.   *Sonus* 9, no. 1 (fall 1988)
        See: W65, B37, B38, B216, B240, B252.

III. General Studies

B132. Bernard, Jonathan W. "Inaudible Structures, Audible Music: Ligeti's Problem, and his Solution." *Music Analysis* 6, no. 3 (1987): 207-36.

Analyses of sections from several of Ligeti's micro-canonic works shed light on the role of micro-polyphony in his music. The canonic details, though hidden, reveal a reciprocal relationship with the perceived form and texture of the resulting music. The contrapuntal procedures used in these works serve as an alternative to serial techniques. This allows the composer freedom to determine the final details, but provides a consistent structure for the work.

B133. Beyer, William Huntley. "Compositional Principles in Three Works of György Ligeti." DMA diss., University of Washington, 1975.

Examines *Lux aeterna, Lontano,* and *Continuum* in terms of the concepts of stasis and change as compositional principles. *See:* W37, W39, W41.

B134. Bodman, Christopher. "Darmstadt International Summer Course for New Music, 1976." *Composer* 59 (winter 1976-1977): 31-32 + .

A report of the meeting from the point of view of one composition student. "Georgy [sic] Ligeti, who was very critical of the closed argument of West German musical reviews described himself as walking on a tightrope between atonal music and tonal, but nevertheless writing out of his own choice of criteria. He concentrated in his seminars on two works; *Three Pieces for Two Pianos,* comprising Monument, Self-portrait with Reich and Riley, and 'in zart fliessender Bewegung'; and the orchestral work *San Francisco Polyphony.* He explained the general concept of overlaying grids, which, one after the other gradually changed across the parameters of pitch, tempo, dynamic and register." *See:* W52, W51.

B135. Bonnet, Antoine. "Sur Ligeti." *Entretemps* 1 (1986): 5-15.

This study of Ligeti's music concentrates on his static style of the sixties and in particular on *Atmosphères.* Comparisons are made with the work of Boulez, Cage and Stockhausen. *See:* W27.

B136. Borris, Siegfried. "Das kalkulierte Labyrinth: Betrachtung zur Musik Ligetis." *Musik und Bildung* 7 (1975): 481-89.

A study of the works of Ligeti and the various phases through which he has passed.

B137. Bosseur, Jean-Yves. "György Ligeti." *Musique de Notre Temps* 1 (1973): 135-39.

A general survey of Ligeti's works from *Atmosphères* to the *Chamber Concerto.*

B138. Bossin, Jeffrey. "György Ligeti's New Lyricism and the Aesthetic of Currentness: The Berlin Festival's Retrospective of the Composer's Career." *Current Musicology* 37 (1984): 233-39.

This report on the 33rd Annual Berliner Festwochen (Sept. 1983) focuses on works by Ligeti which were presented in a series of four concerts commemorating the composer's sixtieth birthday. Ligeti himself delivered extended commentaries. A summary of Ligeti's career and artistic development occupies the bulk of the report. "Just as the tone-carpet compositions of the early sixties could be viewed in part as a protest against serialism and what Ligeti calls the 'clique in Cologne and Darmstadt,' so the style of the Trio for Violin, Horn, and Piano represents a protest against the tabu of melody and other traditional features; the composer himself described his use of ABA form as resulting from sheer audacity, for example." See: App. II, p. 172.

B139.   Christensen, Louis. "Introduction to the Music of György Ligeti." *Numus West* No. 2 (1972): 6-16.

An illustrated survey of Ligeti's post-Hungary work to 1972.

B140.   Clendinning, Jane Piper. "Contrapuntal Techniques in the Music of György Ligeti." Ph.D. diss., Yale University, 1989.

Ligeti's use of micropolyphony can be divided into two subcategories: microcanonic compositions, in which a single melodic line is set against itself in canon; and pattern-meccanico compositions, in which lines formed from repeated patterns with a gradually changing pitch content are combined in counterpoint. Works are examined which use one of these techniques or a combination of the two.

B141.   Commanday, Robert. "The Composer Ligeti: Always Thinking in Terms of the Future." *San Francisco Chronicle*, May 21, 1972, "This World," p. 45.

A discussion of Ligeti's development as seen in the style of works produced during the sixties and early seventies. "'Each new piece is a step in a direction (without a goal)'."

B142.   Dibelius, Ulrich. *Moderne Musik 1945-1965*. München: Piper, 1966. 392 p.

Ligeti's life and works up to 1965 are discussed on p. 183-193. *Apparitions* and *Atmosphères* are examined in some detail. See: W26, W27.

B143.   -------. "Reflexion und Reaktion über den Komponisten György Ligeti." *Melos* 37 (1970): 89-96.

Examines the development of Ligeti's style by means of analyses of: *Requiem, Lontano, Atmosphères, Lux aeterna, Ten Pieces for Wind Quintet, Cello Concerto, Aventures et Nouvelles Aventures, Apparitions, Continuum, Ramifications*, and the *String Quartet No. 2. See*: W35, W39, W27, W37, W43, W38, W33, W34, W41, W44, W42.

B144.   Dobson, Elaine. "The Music of György Ligeti from 1958 to 1968: Form, Notation and the Concept of Illusion." M.M. Thesis, University of Queensland, 1973. 199 p.

A study of the ways Ligeti's control over form, formlessness, and an exacting notation produce the phenomenon of illusion.

B145.   Fabian, Imre. "Jenseits von Tonalität und Atonalität: Zum 50. Geburtstag von György Ligeti." *Österreichische Musikzeitschrift* 28 (1973): 233-38.

A brief survey of the composer's career and works.

B146.   Fischbach, Lars. "Ligetis histrioner." *Musikrevy* 29, no. 3 (1974): 122.

This brief discussion of *Requiem* and *Le Grand Macabre* asserts that evidence of indirect knowledge of Nazi death camps can be found in Ligeti's music. It compares the *Requiem* to the film "M.A.S.H." *See*: W35, W54.

B147.   Fischer, Kurt von. "Transzendenz in der modernen Musik?" *Reformation* 2 (1980): 87-94.

Discusses utopian elements in works composed around 1970 by Ligeti and others.

B148.   Floros, Constantin. "György Ligeti: Prinzipielles über sein Schaffen." *Musik und Bildung* 10 (1978): 484-88.

Translated into Swedish as "György Ligeti, principiellt om hans skapande." *Nutida Musik* 24, no. 3 (1981-82): 3-7. Discusses Ligetis's style and compositional techniques. Also considers his relationship with new music and with tradition.

B149.   Frisius, Rudolf. "Tonal oder postseriell?" *Musik und Bildung* 7 (1975): 490-501.

A study which attempts to show that Ligeti's music restores some characteristics of tonal musical language through a negation of serial techniques.

B150.   Goebels, Franzpeter. "Gestalt und Gestaltung musikalischer Grafik." *Melos* 39 (1972): 23-34.

Discusses aspects of musical graphics. Includes references to Ligeti's *Continuum* and Rainer Wehinger's listening score to *Artikulation*. *See*: W25, W41, B126.

B151.   Gruhn, Wilfried. "Avantgarde - auf der Suche nach einer neuen Form." *Musik und Bildung* 2 (1970): 481-84.

Reprinted in *Orchester* 19 (1971): 5-8. An examination of several of Ligeti's orchestral works in light of the composer's statements in "Metamorphosis of Musical Form" (*See*: B16). The author finds that both content and form is indeterminate. This is an evasion of rather than a solution to the problem of form in modern music.

B152.   -------. "Textvertonung und Sprachkomposition bei György Ligeti." *Musik und Bildung* 7 (1975): 511-19.

The author examines the relationship of music and language in contemporary music by means of analyses of four works by Ligeti: *Artikulation* (an imaginary language), *Aventures et Nouvelles Aventures*, *Lux aeterna*, and *Clocks and Clouds* (*See*: W25, W33, W34, W37, W50).

B153.   Häusler, Josef. "György Ligeti, oder, Die Netzstruktur." *Neue Zeitschrift für Musik* 144, no. 5 (1983): 18-21.

Just as the term "network" is used to describe the structure of some of Ligeti's works, Häusler compares Ligeti's career to a network of ideas and styles which form threads and periodically come together in knots. All of Ligeti's major works from *Apparitions* to the *Horn Trio* are discussed.

B154.   ‑‑‑‑‑‑‑. *Musik im 20. Jahrhundert.* Bremen: Schünemann, 1969. 441
p.

Pages 259-269 consist of an introduction to Ligeti's works from 1958
(*Artikulation*) to 1967 (*Lontano*).

B155.   Hinz, Klaus-Michael. "Bitte keine Expressionisten: Porträt von
György Ligeti." *Neue Musikzeitung* 32 (Aug.-Sept. 1983): 4.

A brief discussion of Ligeti's life and musical style, with extensive quotes from
the composer. "Wissen Sie, ich gehöre noch so zur Darmstädter Avantgarde.
Mir ist nicht die Tonalität, sondern nur der expressionistische Gestus fremd."
["You know, I still belong to the Darmstadt Avantgarde. Tonality is not foreign to
me, but only the expressionistic gesture."]

B156.   Ibarra Groth, Federico. "Ligeti y Globokar." *Heterofonia* 5, no. 26
(1972): 22+

English summary, p. 46-47. Ligeti's work can be divided into three phases. The
first is represented by works such as *Artikulation* and *Aventures et Nouvelles
Aventures*. The second phase includes *Atmosphères*, *Lontano*, the *Requiem*,
Lux aeterna and *Volumina*. The third phase was initiated by *Continuum*.

B157.   Jöckle, Rudolf. "Die mitkomponierte Aura: Requiem und Orgelwerke
von György Ligeti." *Schallplatte und Kirche* (suppl. to *Musik und
Kirche* vol. 40) 1 (1970): 57-59.

Examines Ligeti's relation to traditions of church music on the basis of two
recordings: Candide CE1009, and Wergo 60045. Ligeti always chooses to follow
tradition.

B158.   Keller, Hans. "The Contemporary Problem." *Tempo* no. 89 (summer
1969): 25-28.

Keller discusses Ligeti's place in the question of musical meaning or sense:
"sense in sound which, for the hearing listener doesn't need verbal explanations
or justifications." Ove Nordwall responded to this article in "Letters to the
Editor." *Tempo* no. 90 (autumn 1969): 36. *See:* B179.

B159.   ‑‑‑‑‑‑‑. "Music 1975." *The New Review* 2, no. 24 (March 1976): 17-
53.

A discussion of modern music with several paragraphs on Ligeti. "His is the
only meaningless--or at least truthless--music that deserves unreserved
acceptance, the only chaos that is not empty, the only place outside of heaven
and earth that is not hell."

B160.   Kneif, Tibor. "Typen der Entsprachlichung in der neuen Musik." In
*Über Musik und Sprache: Sieben Versuche zur neueren
Vokalmusik*, edited by Rudolf Stephan, 20-33, Veröffentlichungen
des Instituts für neue Musik und Musikerziehung, 14. Mainz:
Schott, 1974.

Discusses *Lux aeterna* and *Aventures* with regard to linguistic content. *See:*
W37, W33.

B161.   Koch, Gerhard R. "Rückzug nach vorn: Nostalgie und Regression in der neuen Musik." *Musica* 27 (1973): 433-37.

In this discussion of several differing styles of modern music, several of Ligeti's works are mentioned. "Freilich erreicht Ligeti in einigen seiner neueren Werke bisweilen die Region jener Schwelle an der Künstlichkeit und Kunstgewerblichkeit nicht mehr allzu weit voneinander entfernt zu liegen scheinen." ["In some of his latest works, Ligeti has indeed occasionally reached that middle ground in which artificiality and craftsmanship no longer seem so removed from each other."]

B162.   Kropfinger, Klaus. "Ligeti und die Tradition." In *Zwischen Tradition und Fortschritt*, edited by Rudolf Stephan, 131-42. Veröffentlichungen des Instituts für neue Musik und Musikerziehung, 13. Mainz: Schott, 1973. 142 p.

The author uses the concepts of "involuntary memory" (Adorno) and "aura" to discuss Ligeti's relationship to musical tradition."

B163.   Lackner, Erna. "György Ligeti." *Frankfurter Allgemeine Magazin*, Sept. 11, 1987, p. 10-20.

This introduction to Ligeti focuses on insights into the composer's compositional attitudes and processes. Ligeti is quoted extensively, commenting on the situation in music today, and on factors that have influenced his work. His experiences during the Second World War are described. Four interesting photographs by Jürgen Röhrscheid are included.

B164.   Lichtenfeld, Monika. "György Ligeti oder das Ende der seriellen Musik." *Melos* 39 (1972): 74-80.

Ligeti will be thought of as the composer who destroyed serial music, or at least subdued it. A number of works are surveyed.

B165.   -------. "György Ligeti: Portret." *Ruch Muzyczny* 28, no. 19 (Sept. 16, 1984): 3-6.

A survey of Ligeti's career assembled and translated from several articles published in German. Includes extensive quotes from the composer's comments on his own works.

B166.   "Ligeti: Sehr gehässig." *Der Spiegel* 21, no. 45 (Oct. 30, 1967): 202-204.

A brief survey of the composer's career and works.

B167.   Lobanova, Marija. "Technika es Stilus Probematikaja a 60-as--80-as Evek Zene Toerekvesei Koezoett." *Magyar Zene* 26 (1985): 255-70.

Translation of title: "Problematics of Style and Technique in the Music of the 60s--80s: Parallels Between the Music of György Ligeti and New Soviet Music."

B168.   McCabe, John. "The Condition of Music." In *The Black Rainbow: Essays on the Present Breakdown of Culture*, edited by Peter Abbs, 114-33. London: Heinemann, 1975.

An attack on the growth of internationalism in 20th century music. The author defends regional attachments as an essential basis of musical life, and ascribes what he finds to be superficiality in the music of such composers as Ligeti, Penderecki and Stockhausen to their efforts to satisfy "international" or "metropolitan" trends. Describes the *String Quartet No. 2* as "among the masterpieces of twentieth-century music" *See*: W42.

B169.   Meyer, Heinz. "Wie komponieren Sie eigentlich." *Musik und Bildung* 13 (1981): 30-35.

This article contains a fictitious conversation between Ligeti, Handel and Ravel, intended to introduce Ligeti's musical style to beginners.

B170.   Monpoël, Marie. "La Démarche compositionelle de György Ligeti et son application à quelques oeuvres pour clavier." Master's thesis, University of Rouen, 1980. 119 p.

This study is divided into four parts: 1. Influences (Bartók, electro-acoustic, and repetitive music). 2. Ligeti's principles and methods of composition. 3. The auditive result (the phenomenon of illusion). 4. Detailed descriptions of five of Ligeti's works.

B171.   --------. "Micropolyphonie obligée dans l'oeuvre de Ligeti." In *Min(Max)imalismes et Musique*. Les Cahiers du Crem, No 8-9 (June-Sept. 1988), p. 87-99.

This study of the technique of micropolyphony examines sections of the *Concerto for Violoncello*, *Aventures*, and *Continuum*. This technique allows the composer to obliterate the melodic, harmonic and rhythmic aspects of the music in order to work with a sonoral fabric. In later works Ligeti allowed certain intervals, and melodic and rhythmic aspects to play a part. *See*: W38, W33, W41.

B172.   Nordwall, Ove. "Alice im Streichquartett." *Stuttgarter Zeitung*, Nov. 2, 1968.

Nordwall describes Ligeti's development since coming to the west, and also describes his major works. Includes numerous quotes from the composer, and a facsimile of a sketch of the *String Quartet No. 2*.

B173.   --------, ed. *Från Mahler till Ligeti: en antdogi om vår tids musik*. Stockholm: Orion/Bonniers, 1965.

A collection of essays, in Swedish translation, with commentary by Nordwall. Includes "Metamorphoses of Musical Form," "Zustände, Ereignisse, Wandlungen," and "Die Zukunft der Musik." *See*: B16, B27, B45.

B174.   --------. "György Ligeti 1980." *Österreichische Musikzeitschrift* 35, no. 2 (1980): 67-78.

A survey of several major works. Includes a work list and comments by Ligeti and Stockhausen.

B175.   -------. "György Ligeti. Dokumentation." *Nutida Musik* 19, no. 2 (1975-76): 5-17.

A selection of comments by the composer on *Apparitions*, *Lontano*, the *Double Concerto*, and *San Francisco Polyphony*. Includes a work list and discography.

B176.   -------. "György Ligetis musik." *Nutida Musik* 7, no. 6 (1963-64): 1-12.

This survey of the composer's life and works deals especially with *Aventures*. *See*: W33.

B177.   -------. "Der Komponist György Ligeti." *Musica* 22 (1968): 173-77.

Nordwall describes Ligeti's post-1956 career and his major works. There is also some discussion of the opera which was at that time in progress.

B178.   -------. "Monument-självporträtt-roerelse." *Nutida Musik* 20, no. 4 (1976-77): 12-14.

A survey of works including commentary by the composer. *See*: W52.

B179.   -------. "Two Hungarians abroad: (2) György Ligeti." *Tempo* no. 88 (1969): 22-25.

A brief survey of Ligeti's post-emigration career to 1968. Discusses the major works from *Artikulation* to *Continuum*. Hans Keller responded to some of his comments in "The Contemporary Problem." *Tempo* no. 89 (summer 1969): 25-28 (*See*: B158). A similar survey appeared in: *Ruch Muzyczny* 12, no. 17 (1968): 21-22.

B180.   Oehlschlägel, Reinhard, and Erhard Karkoschka. "Briefwechsel über die Form in der Musik." *Melos* 35 (1968): 103-6.

Oehlschlägel refers to the writings of Ligeti on the subject of musical form.

B181.   Rijavec, Andrej. "Susret sa Györgyom Ligetijem." *Zvuk* no. 2 (summer 1985): 22-25.

This survey of Ligeti's career was originally presented as the opening talk at the 22nd Chamber Music of the 20th Century Festival held in Radenci, Yugoslavia. This festival was dedicated to Ligeti's music. *See*: App. II, p. 173.

B182.   Rochelt, Hans. "György Ligeti." *Neues Forum* 17 (1970): 475.

A very general and philosophical discussion of Ligeti's ideas and musical style.

B183.   Salmenhaara, Erkki. "György Ligeti." In *Vuosisatamme musiikki*, 204-7. Helsinki: Otava, 1968. 239 p.

A general survey.

B184.   Sandner, Wolfgang. "Kleine Gesten--machtvolle Musik: zum sechzigsten Geburtstag des Komponisten György Ligeti." *Frankfurter Allgemeine Zeitung*, May 28, 1983, p. 23.

A celebratory essay which mentions an all Ligeti concert organized by Stuttgart Radio. "György Ligeti ist nie eine kolossale Nachtigall gewesen. Näher stand ihm schon immer der Mozartsche Geist, 'aus kleinen Gesten die machtvollste Musik zu erschaffen'." ["György Ligeti has never been a colossal nightingale. He is closer to the spirit of Mozart 'making the most powerful music from small gestures'."]

B185.   -------. "Der Kunstanspruch der Rockmusic - Beziehungen zwischen populärer' und 'ernster' Musik." *Universitas* 32 (1977): 1185-90.

This discussion of connections between Rock music and certain elements in contemporary art music touches on Ligeti's work.

B186.   Schmidt, Christian Martin. *Brennpunkte der Neuen Musik: Historisch-Systematisches zu wesentlichen Aspekten.* Musik-Taschen-Bücher. Theoretica, 16. Cologne: Gerig, 1977. 166 p.

Pages 106-14 consist of a discussion of Ligeti's theoretical writings and his musical style. The concept of "musical space" serves as a focal point in this discussion, which makes use of numerous quotes from the composer himself.

B187.   Soria, Dorle J. "Artist Life." *High Fidelity/Musical America* 23 (Dec. 1973): MA2+

A relatively substantial survey of Ligeti's life and career, with some interesting quotes.

B188.   Steinitz, Richard. "Connections with Alice." *Music and Musicians* 22 (1973): 42-47.

An excellent introduction to Ligeti, including several quotes and anecdotes, and describing the essential features of his music. Steinitz brings out Ligeti's good-humored yet vigorous attitudes toward music.

B189.   -------. "The Music of György Ligeti." *The Listener* 91 (1974): 577-78.

An introduction which concentrates on Ligeti's concern with texture.

B190.   Thomas, Janet Owen. "Contemporary Music and the Avant-Garde: An Introduction." *Organists Review* 69, no. 279 (1985): 31-37.

Ligeti's three organ works, *Volumina, Harmonies,* and *Coulée* are described on p. 33-35. *Harmonies* is summarized as "a very straightforward piece to be attempted by someone of more adventurousness than skill!" *Coulée* is described as "music of a machine over-running crazily" *See*: W31, W40, W45.

B191.   -------. "Ligeti's Organ Music." *Musical Times* 124 (1983): 319+.

A somewhat detailed survey of Ligeti's organ writing, and of three pieces for organ, *Volumina, Harmonies,* and *Coulée.* "His organ works do not follow in either the French colouristic tradition nor the German contrapuntal one; they exist *per se* as realized examples of his own radically individual musical mind...." *See*: W31, W40, W45.

B192.   Vermeulen, Ernst. "Ligeti's 'Amerikaans' Zelfportret." *Mens en Melodie* 33 (1978): 212-17.

A description of *Monument-Selbstportrait-Bewegung,* with some discussion of Ligeti's place in the history of modern music. *See*: W52.

B193.   Vogt, Hans. "György Ligeti: *Atmosphères*." In *Neue Musik seit 1945*. 3rd ed., 307-14. Stuttgart: Philipp Reclam, 1982.

Briefly sketches Ligeti's work from 1958 to 1978. Includes a more detailed discussion of *Atmosphères*. See: W27.

B194.   Weissmann, John S. "Guide to Contemporary Hungarian Composers." *Tempo* no. 47 (spring 1958): 28-29.

A brief look at Ligeti at an early stage of his western career. "A fundamental stylistic reorientation is ... likely."

B195.   Whittall, Arnold. *Music Since the First World War*. London: Dent, 1977. 277 p.

Includes a discussion of Ligeti's music (p. 242-46). Fairly objective descriptions except for a reference to *Aventures et Nouvelles Aventures* as "scrappy and monotonous studies in vocal agility." See: W33, W34.

B196.   Wiesmann, Sigrid. "Eine dritte Wiener Schule?" *Melos/Neue Zeitschrift für Musik* 4 (1978): 475-76.

A brief argument to the effect that one might speak of a third Viennese school of composition represented by György Ligeti, Roman Haubenstock-Ramati, and Friedrich Cerha. Whereas the first school was concerned with form, and the second with structure, this new school is concerned with sound and color.

B197.   Williams, Alastair. "Music as Immanent Critique: Stasis and Development in the Music of Ligeti." In *Music and the Politics of Culture*, edited by Christopher Norris, 187-225. London: Lawrence & Wishart, 1989.

The first half of this study outlines the work of Theodor Adorno and Jacques Derrida in attempting to establish a model of the contemporary interaction between music and politics. The second half consists of an examination of Ligeti's music with reference to this model. Art can be aware of itself and critique itself. For example, "*Atmosphères*' much acclaimed negation of serialism is both a rupture, and abandonment of serial procedures, and a realisation of the potential for obsessive organisation of musical parameters to result in their very dissolution." The author concludes that "Ligeti's musical development emerges as an enormous ongoing constellation which transmutes itself from within, and accretes new ideas to itself on its path, but in which no previous discovery becomes entirely submerged." See: W27.

B198.   Winkler, Gerhard E. "György Ligetis Metapherwelt und ihre strukturellen Bezüge." *Noema* 1 (1984): 42-48.

Ligeti often uses metaphors in describing his music. Although visual and tactile comparisons are common, this music could not be called programmatic. A brief examination of the use of a few of these metaphors (e.g. windows, faery lands, infinity) uncovers structural interrelationships in Ligeti's music. Some of these metaphors were inspired by John Keats, Lewis Carroll and Franz Kafka.

B199.   Wojnowska, Elzbieta. "Ligetiego wyrok na serializm." *Ruch Muzyczny* 17, no. 20 (1973): 6-7, and no. 21: 12-13.

This survey of Ligeti's career focuses on his musical philosophy, with frequent quotes from his theoretical writings. His comments on serialism are one aspect of the discussion.

IV. Analyses of Individual Works

Included here are detailed analyses as well as shorter discussions and score reviews of individual works.

B200.   Anhalt, Istvan. "Ligeti's *Nouvelles Aventures*: A Small Group as a Model for Composition." In *Alternative Voices: Essays on Contemporary Vocal and Choral Composition*, 41-92. Toronto: University of Toronto Press, 1984.

This analysis focuses on the sociolinguistic meaning of the work. Although there is no explicit plot, the affects expressed are specific. The characters have personalities and interact with one another. The piece can serve as a model of social and linguistic evolution. *See*: W34.

B201.   Bauer, Hans-Joachim. "Statistik, eine objektive Methode zur Analyse von Kunst? Die Leistungsfähigkeit statistischer Methoden für die Analyse von Kunstwerken am Beispiel von György Ligetis *Lux aeterna*." *International Review of the Aesthetics and Sociology of Music* 7 (1976): 249-63.

Summary in English. An examination of *Lux aeterna* with reference to Wilhelm Fucks' book, *Nach allen Regeln der Kunst* (According to all the rules of Art). Also discusses statistical methods of analysis in general. *See*: W37.

B202.   Bernager, Olivier. "Autor du Concerto de chambre de Ligeti." *Musique en jeu*, no. 15 (Sept. 1974): 99-101.

The *Chamber Concerto* is examined briefly in terms of compositional techniques which can be found in Ligeti's other works. *See*: W46.

B203.   Beurle, Hans Michael. "Nochmals: Ligetis *Lux aeterna*: eine Entgegnung auf Clytus Gottwalds Analyse." *Musica* 25 (1971): 279-281.

This analysis offers an alternative to the conclusions reached by Gottwald (*See*: B224). Gottwald's analysis is seen as too performance oriented and therefore not objective. *See*: W37.

B204.   Beurle, Jürgen. "*Aventures von György Ligeti*." In *Analyse: Neue Musik*, 53-56. Herrenberg: Döring, 1976.

This brief article describes the work in terms of seven structural levels and discusses its social implications. There are six accompanying graphic illustrations. *See*: W33.

B205.   Borio, Gianmario. "L'Eredità Bartókiana nel Secondo Quartetto de G. Ligeti: Sul Concetto di Tradizione nella Musica Contemporanea." *Studi Musicali* 13 (1984): 289-307.

A study of the *String Quartet No. 2* within the framework of string quartet tradition and musical aesthetics. Ligeti's connection to Bartók is to be understood in terms of gestures rather than musical morphology. *See*: W42.

B206. Cogan, Robert. "György Ligeti: *Lux aeterna.*" In *New Images of Musical Sounds*, 39-43. Cambridge: Harvard University Press, 1984.

A spectrum photograph of a performance of *Lux aeterna* (*See:* D34) is presented along with explanatory text which reveals the shape and texture of the work. *See:* W37.

B207. Collins, Glenda Whitman. "Avant-garde Techniques in the Organ Works of György Ligeti." DMA diss., North Texas State University, 1980, 88 p.

Includes a discussion of the notation and style of *Volumina* and *Two Etudes for Organ.* A brief summary appears in *Diapason* 73 no. 1 (1982): 10-11. *See:* W31, W40, W45.

B208. Craddock, Peter. "Music Review." *The Strad* 91 (1980): 423.

A score review of *String Quartet No. 2.* "Strictly for specialist ensembles experienced in this kind of exciting modern virtuosity." *See:* W42.

B209. Dadelsen, Hans-Christian von. "An der Kette gerasselt: *Le Grand Macabre* -- Entstehung und Charakteristik eines musikalischen Stils." In *Programmheft der Hamburgischen Staatsoper*, 1978, edited by Peter Dannenberg and Jochem Wolff.

The author laments the state of modern music which either regurgitates citations from the past or is aesthetically barren. Ligeti's opera at least rattles these chains. *See:* W54.

B210. --------. "Hat Distanz Relevanz? Über Kompositionstechnik und ihre musikdidaktischen Folgen--dargestellt an György Ligetis Orchesterstück *Lontano* (1967)." *Musik und Bildung* 7 (1975): 502-6.

An analysis revealing traditional compositional techniques such as canons. The result of these techniques should not be confused with tone-cluster style. *See:* W39.

B211. --------. "Über die musikalischen Konturen der Entfernung. Entfernung als räumliche, historische und ästhetische Perspektive in Ligetis Lontano." *Melos/Neue Zeitschrift für Musik* 2 (1976): 187-90.

An analysis which centers around the concepts of musical "space" and "distance." *See:* W39.

B212. Dahlhaus, Carl. "Ästhetische Probleme der elektronischen Musik." In *Experimentelle Musik*, edited by Fritz Winckel, 81-90. Schriftenreihe der Akademie der Künste Berlin, 7. Berlin: Mann, 1970.

Includes a discussion of *Artikulation. See:* W25.

B213.   Dale, S.S. "Contemporary cello concerti; György Ligeti." *The Strad* 85 (1974): 281+.

This article introduces Ligeti and his work to the reader, and then examines the *Concerto for Violoncello*, especially with respect to performance problems. "The most striking fact which impresses the listener is Ligeti's concern with dynamics." *See*: W38.

B214.   Dibelius, Ulrich. "Ligetis Horntrio." *Melos* 46 (1984): 44-61.

A detailed analysis which focuses on Ligeti's relationship to traditional and contemporary music. Includes a chronology and a work list. *See*: W59.

B215.   -------. "Mälzel, wenn er losgelassen." *Hifi Stereophonie* 19 (1980): 168-69.

A description of *Poème symphonique*, and of the amusing circumstances of its première. Also a discussion of the ideas behind this piece. *See*: W32.

B216.   Escot, Pozzi. "Charm'd Magic Casements." In *Contiguous Lines: Issues and Ideas in the Music of the 60's and 70's*, ed. Thomas DeLio, 31-56. Lanham, Md.: University Press of America, 1985.

Reprinted in *Sonus* 9, no. 1 (fall 1988): 17-37. This is a discussion of the concept of dynamic symmetry or "hidden likenesses" in art. An analysis of *Harmonies* makes use of several diagrams which show a variety of symmetrical relationships hidden within the work. *See*: W40.

B217.   Fabian, Imre. "Ein unendliches Erbarmen mit der Kreatur: zu György Ligeti's *Le Grand Macabre*." *Österreichische Musikzeitschrift* 36 (1981): 570-72.

A brief examination of the dramatic background and implications of this opera. *See*: W54.

B218.   Fanselau, Rainer. "György Ligeti zum 60. Geburtstag: György Ligeti *Le Grand Macabre*--Gesichtspunkte für eine Behandlung im Musikunterricht." *Musik und Bildung* 15 (1983): 17-24.

The structure of the opera is viewed within the context of 20th century opera in general. The musical form of *Le Grand Macabre* can be seen as a symbol of the development of this genre. *See*: W54.

B219.   Febel, Reinhard. "György Ligeti: Monument - Selbstporträt - Bewegung." *Zeitschrift für Musiktheorie* 9, no. 1 (1978): 35-51, and 9, no. 2 (1978): 4-13.

Reprinted in *Musik für zwei Klaviere seit 1950 als Spiegel der Kompositionstechnik*. Herrenberg: Döring, 1978. 186 p. Each of the three pieces is analysed. *Monument* is constructed from six threads or layers, three in each piano. Superimposed grids of tone repetitions begin in the middle range of the instruments and move to the extreme high and low registers. The second piece combines a typical Ligeti style with the phase shifting of Reich and Riley, as well as a hint of Chopin. *Bewegung* is related to *Monument* in that both pieces use gradual changes to convey musical space. Compositional techniques are found which can also be seen in *San Francisco Polyphony*. *See*: W52.

B220.   Fischer, Erik. "Die Dissoziation der Gattungsstruktur in den musikdramatischen 'Oppositionsformen': Ligeti, *Aventures*." In *Zur Problematik der Opernstruktur: Das Künstlerische System und Seine Krisis im 20. Jahrhundert*, by Erik Fischer, 158-182. Beihefte zum Archiv für Musikwissenschaft, Bd. 20. Wiesbaden: F. Steiner, 1982.

This is a revision of the author's doctoral dissertation (Ruhr-Universität Bochum, 1980). *Aventures et Nouvelles Aventures* are analysed as examples of "anti-opera," a stage work in which there is no "subject" or causal stage action. While contemporary opera and anti-opera are based on opposing artistic goals, both remain tied to the fundamental structure of opera. *See:* W36.

B221.   Floros, Constantin. "György Ligeti, Tre stycken för två pianon." *Nutida Musik* 24, no. 3 (1981-82): 8-9.

This description of the work annotates Ligeti's commentary (*See:* B122). The work is described as "sound music" in the spirit of Debussy. *See:* W52.

B222.   -------. "Ligetis *Drei Phantasien nach Friedrich Hölderlin* (1982)." *Neue Zeitschrift für Musik* 146, no. 2 (Feb. 1985): 18-20.

This is a brief overview of this unaccompanied choral piece, including comparisons with *Lux aeterna* which is scored for the same voices. Translated into Swedish and English in *Nutida Musik* 27, no 1 (1984-85): 14-16, 18-20. *See:* W37, W61.

B223.   Gallaher, Christopher Summers. "Density in Twentieth-century Music." Ph.D. diss., Indiana University, 1975.

Studies the relationship of "vertical density" and "horizontal density" in several musical compositions of the late 50s and early 60s including *Nouvelles Aventures*. *See:* W34.

B224.   Gottwald, Clytus. "Lux aeterna: Ein Beitrag zur Kompositionstechnik György Ligetis." *Musica* 25 (1971): 12-17.

An analysis which emphasizes the way in which details combine to create unity in this work. The piece is viewed as a representation of the eternal. *See:* W37, B203.

B225.   Hannigan, Barry. "György Ligeti, *Passacaglia ungherese* for Harpsichord." *Notes* 39 (1982): 460-61.

A review of the score. "... suitable for concert fare and an excellent work for an intermediate student." *See:* W57.

B226.   Häusler, Josef. "Einige Aspekte des Wort-Ton-Verhältnisses." In *Die Musik der sechziger Jahre*, edited by Rudolf Stephan, 65-76. Veröffentlichungen des Instituts für neue Musik und Musikerziehung Darmstadt, 12. Mainz: Schott, 1972.

Describes compositional principles which were significant in vocal music during the 1960s including *Lux aeterna*. *See:* W37.

B227.   Helms, Hans G. "Voraussetzung eines neuen Musiktheaters." In
        Musik auf der Flucht vor sich selbst, edited by Ulrich Dibelius, 92-
        115. München: Hanser, 1969, 152 p.

    Includes a brief description of *Aventures et Nouvelles Aventures* within a broader
    discussion of modern musical theater. *See*: W33, W34, W36.

B228.   Hofman, Srdan. "Kompozicioni Postupak Gyorgya Ligetija u delu
        Lontano." *Zvuk* no. 1 (1980): 28-43.

    In Serbo-Croatian. The work is divided into three sections. The first is
    constructed from a series of twelve melodic formulas. The second section is
    characterized by changes in harmonic density. The third section contains the
    highest density of movable structures of harmonic color. A summary in very
    poor English is included. *See*: W39.

B229.   Howarth, Elgar. "Ligeti's *Le Grand Macabre*." *Opera* 33 (1982):
        1229-33.

    Summarizes the plot and discusses the characters and music of the opera. *See*:
    W54.

B230.   Hupfer, Konrad. "Gemeinsame Kompositionsaspekte bei
        Stockhausen, Pousseur, und Ligeti." *Melos* 37 (1970): 236-37.

    Includes a discussion of *Lux aeterna* based on a lecture given by Ligeti at the
    1967 Darmstadt Festival. *See*: W37.

B231.   Kaufmann, Harald. "Ein Fall absurder Musik: Ligetis *Aventures &
        Nouvelles Aventures*." In *Spurlinien*, 130-58. Vienna: Elisabeth
        Lafite Verlag, 1969.

    Revision of "Ein Beispiel absurder Musik." In *Protokolle '66*. Wien, 1966.
    Translated into French as "Un cas de musique absurde: *Aventures et Nouvelles
    Aventures* de Ligeti." *Musique en jeu* no. 15 (Sept. 1974): 75-98. An analysis of
    the structure and meaning of the work. A central concept of this discussion is
    that absurdity in art does not mean formlessness. The form of this work follows
    its own absurd logic. The phonetic sounds used are those found in languages
    with which Ligeti is familiar. Meaning is inherent in the phonetic values given.
    Aventures consists of five interwoven lines of expression or "stories." One story
    dominates in each of the eight sections. The individual elements of each story
    are manipulated through variation, permutation, and interpolation, making them
    difficult to follow. This is an example of the absurd logic of the work. Ligeti's
    libretto is also discussed. *See*: W33, W34, W36.

B232.   -------. "Ligetis zweites Streichquartett." *Melos* 37 (1970): 181-86.

    An analysis which relates this work to Samuel Beckett's *Endgame*. *See*: W42.

B233.   -------. "Eine moderne Totenmesse." *Neues Forum* 13 (1966): 59-61.

    Reprinted as "Betreffend Ligetis Requiem." In *Protokolle '71*, 158-68. Wien,
    1971; translated into Swedish as "Död och förnyelse: om György Ligetis
    Requiem." *Nutida Musik* 8, no. 5-6 (1964-65): 154-65. An exposition of the
    structure of the *Requiem* with some comment on Ligeti's style and means of
    expression. *See*: W35.

B234. -------. "Strukturen im Strukturlosen." *Melos* 31 (1964): 391-98.

This analysis of *Atmosphères* examines the means by which static music may be manipulated: dynamic changes, ostinatos, and canons for example. The work is divided into 22 sections, the last of which is silent. Some theoretical implications of the work are pointed out. Reprinted in *Spurlinien* (Vienna: Lafite, 1969, p. 107-17). A summary in English, French and German appears in the program notes for Wergo WER 60095. *See*: W27, D4.

B235. Kiraly, Philippa. "Music Reviews." *Notes* 43 (1986): 190.

A review of the score of the *Horn Trio*. *See*: W59.

B236. Klüppelholz, Werner. "Aufhebung der Sprache: zu György Ligetis *Aventures*." *Melos/Neue Zeitschrift für Musik* 2 (1976): 11-15.

Studies the voice parts in *Aventures*. Sounds are placed into three categories: 1. completely free of meaning, 2. conventionalized, and 3. symbolic in meaning. *See*: W33.

B237. -------. *Sprache als Musik: Studien zur Vokalkomposition seit 1956.* Herrenberg: Döring, 1976. 214 p.

The author's Ph.D. dissertation, Universität Köln, 1976. Examines text setting with regard to its semantic, syntactic, and timbral dimensions. Includes a discussion of *Aventures et Nouvelles Aventures*. *See*: W33, W34.

B238. Kričevcov, Nataša. "Ramifications." *Muzikološki Zbornik* 23 (1987): 89-97.

In English. This brief examination focuses on the relationship of linear or horizontal structures to static or vertical ones. Both elements are always present, but one or the other predominates at any given point. *See*: W44.

B239. Lichtenfeld, Monika. "*Zehn Stücke für Bläserquintett* von György Ligeti." *Melos* 39 (1972): 326-33.

A detailed examination of this work, noting the reconciliation of static and explosive styles which had previously remained separate. *See*: W43.

B240. Luchese, Diane. "Levels of Infrastructure in Ligeti's *Volumina*." *Sonus* 9, no. 1 (fall 1988): 38-58.

This analysis shows that several formal structures exist simultaneously in *Volumina*. For example, it can be viewed in terms of ABA form (based on the Golden Section), or as a sort of hidden passacaglia. Ligeti has introduced a number of new techniques in this work. *See*: W31.

B241. Lundberg, Camilla. "György Ligeti's *Le Grand Macabre*." *High Fidelity/Musical America* 28 (Aug. 1978): MA38-39.

A synopsis and discussion of the opera. "The first Absurd Opera? I mean consciously absurd? ... Absurd, no. Parodic, yes." *See*: W54.

B242.   Macaulay, Janice Michel. "Aspects of Pitch Structure in György Ligeti's *Melodien für Orchester*." DMA diss., Cornell University, 1986. 268 p.

The work has three structural planes; a foreground consisting of melodies and shorter melodic patterns, a middleground consisting of subordinate ostinato-like figuration, and a background consisting of sustained pedal tones. *See*: W47.

B243.   Miereanu, Costin. "Une Musique électronique et sa 'partition': *Artikulation*." *Musique en jeu*. 15 (Sept. 1974): 102-9.

The author discusses the problem of notation of electronic music, and Rainer Wehinger's listening score of *Artikulation* in particular. *See*: W25, B126.

B244.   Morrison, Charles D. "Stepwise Continuity as a Structural Determinant in György Ligeti's *Ten Pieces for Wind Quintet*." *Perspectives of New Music* 24 (1985): 158-82.

The work is examined in terms of pitch-class (pc) centricity. Pitch classes and pc complexes are established, approached, and prolonged by means of stepwise connections. *See*: W43.

B245.   Müller, Karl-Josef. "Bedeutende geistliche Werke der musikalischen Avantgarde. György Ligeti: *Lux aeterna*." *Musica Sacra* 95 (1975): 166-69.

An analytical study which examines Ligeti's compositional techniques. *See*: W37.

B246.   --------. "György Ligeti: *Lontano* (1967)." In *Perspektiven neuer Musik*, edited by D. Zimmerschied, 215-33. Mainz: Schott, 1974. 333 p.

Discusses the work from the standpoint of didactics. Plan: 1. Information (historical perspective), 2. Analysis, 3. Material, 4. Consideration of didactics and learning goals, 5. Bibliography. *See*: W39.

B247.   Nielsen, Niels Karl. "György Ligeti: *Aventures*." *Dansk Musiktidsskrift* 20 (1965): 69-70.

A review of the scores to *Aventures et Nouvelles Aventures*. "Don Quixote without Sancho Panza." *See*: W33, W34.

B248.   Nilsson, A. "Den vokala orkestern--finns den?" *Nutida Musik* 29, no. 3 (1985-86): 21-22.

This brief analysis of *Lux aeterna* compares Ligeti's treatment of choral voices with the principles stated in the "Singstimmen" section of Richard Strauss' edition of the Berlioz *Instrumentations-lehre*. *See*: W37.

B249.   Nordwall, Ove. "György Ligeti--introduktion till en otidsenlig modernist." *Konsertnytt* 2, no. 6 (April 1967): 6-10.

An English translation appeared as: "Sweden." *Musical Quarterly* 52 (1966): 109-13. A Czech translation appears as "Tvorba." *Slovenska Hudba* 10 (1966): 406-8. A review of the *Requiem* including a discussion of Ligeti's earlier works. "Ligeti may give the impression of a bewildering diversity of styles in his music, but that this impression is only a superficial one becomes clear upon closer analysis: at bottom there is the same strong and individual mind, capable of the most different expressions and turning the most different material into something original, important, unprecedented." *See*: W35.

B250. -------. "Klangliga Äventyr." *Musikern* no. 6 (June 1966): 8-9..

A discussion of *Aventures et Nouvelles Aventures* drawing heavily on the author's book *Det omögligas Konst. See*: W33, W34, B121.

B251. Op De Coul, Paul. "Sprachkomposition bei Ligeti: *Lux aeterna*. Nebst einigen Randbemerkungen zu den Begriffen Sprach- und Lautkomposition." In *Über Musik und Sprache*, edited by Rudolf Stephan, 59-69. Veröffentlichungen des Instituts für neue Musik und Musikerziehungen, 14. Mainz: Schott, 1974.

An analysis which contrasts the concepts of "speech composition" and "sound composition." *See*: W37.

B252. Pulido, Alejandro. "Differentiation and Integration in Ligeti's *Chamber Concerto*, III." *Sonus* 9, no. 1 (fall 1988): 59-80.

An analysis which focuses on the creation and manipulation of imaginary space. *See*: W46.

B253. Read, Gardner. "György Ligeti: Aventures for 3 singers and 7 instrumentalists." *Notes* 28 (1971): 304.

A review of the score. "... a fascinating and, at times, a hilarious series of timbral adventures lasting some eleven minutes." *See*: W33.

B254. Reeth, Michel van. "De strijkers: Herhalings en heront-dekkingsies(sen) voor (hoger) secundair." *Adem* 16 (1980): 61-67.

Practical performance technique as well as formal analysis of *Atmosphères* is dealt with in this article for young string players. Summaries in English (p. 104) and French (p. 102). *See*: W27.

B255. Reiprich, Bruce. "Transformation of Coloration and Density in György Ligeti's *Lontano*." *Perspectives of New Music* 16 (spring/summer 1978): 167-80.

A detailed examination of Ligeti's technique of micropolyphony in this orchestral work. "Extremely dense canonic counterpoint sustains a sound-mass continuum of fluctuating coloration and density." *See*: W39.

B256. Richart, Robert W. "An Analysis of György Ligeti's *Ten Pieces for Wind Quintet*." MA thesis, University of Oregon, 1982. 62 p.

Includes a biographical sketch and a survey of Ligeti's works to 1968. The analysis includes 10 color graphs representing the individual movements. *See*: W43.

B257. Richter, Christoph. "Interpretation zu *Lux aeterna* von György Ligeti." *Musik und Bildung* 4 (1972): 237-41.

Discusses the relationship of word to music in *Lux aeterna*. *See*: W37.

B258.   -------. *Theorie und Praxis der didaktischen Interpretation von Musik.* Schriftenreihe zur Musikpädagogik. Frankfurt am Main: Diesterweg, 1976. 132 p.

Continuum serves as an example of didactic interpretation. *See*: W41.

B259.   Roberts, Gwyneth Margaret. "Procedures for Analysis of Sound Masses." Ph.D. diss., Indiana University, 1978. 237 p.

A detailed analysis of *Atmosphères* is included in this study of the development of sound masses as a compositional technique. A general approach to analysis of sound-mass composition is outlined. *See*: W27.

B260.   Rollin, Robert L. "Ligeti's *Lontano*: Traditional Canonic Technique in a New Guise." *Music Review* 41 (1980): 289-96.

Reprint of: "The Genesis of the Technique of Canonic Sound Mass in Ligeti's *Lontano.*" *Indiana Theory Review* 2, no. 2 (winter 1979): 23-33. A study of the ways Ligeti uses canonic techniques to produce textural variation. The development of these techniques is traced through Ligeti's earlier works and the work of other composers. *See*: W39.

B261.   -------. "The Process of Textural Change and the Organization of Pitch in Ligeti's *Lontano.*" DMA diss., Cornell University, 1973.

An analysis which reveals a serial ordering of pitches in the overall structure of the work. *See*: W39.

B262.   Rösing, Helmut. *Die Bedeutung der Klangfarbe in traditioneller und elektronischer Musik.* Schriften zur Musik, Bd. 12. Munich: Katzbichler, 1972. 92 p.

Pages 48-52 consist of a discussion of Ligeti's use of tone color. Comments are based on a spectrographic analysis of *Atmosphères*. *See*: W27.

B263.   -------. "Über den Funktionswandel der Klangfarbe in der Music: Von Bach bis Ligeti." *HiFi-Stereophonie* 13 (1974): 632, 638.

A discussion of the use of tone color as an independent compositional dimension. Based on a spectrographic analysis of *Atmosphères*. *See*: W27.

B264.   Rummenhöller, Peter. "Möglichkeiten neuester Chormusik (Ligeti: *Lux aeterna* - Schnebel: *Deuteronomium* 31, 6)." In *Der Einfluss der Technischen Mittler auf die Musikerziehung unserer Zeit*, 311-17. Mainz: Schott, 1968.

An examination of the integration of melodic, harmonic and rhythmic materials in *Lux aeterna*. *See*: W37.

B265.   Sabbe, Hermann. "Techniques Médiévales en Musique Contemporaine: Histoire de la Musique et Sens Culturel." *Revue Belge de Musicologie* 34/35 (1981-82): 220-33.

Lux aeterna is analysed as an example of how modern avant-garde music shares some characteristics with music of the 14th century *Ars Nova*. One such characteristic is a lack of rigid periodicity. *See*: W37.

B266. Salmenhaara, Erkki. "György Ligetin *Atmosphères* ja siinä ilmenevä uusi esteettinen ja strukturaalinen ajattelu." In *Suomen Musiikin Vuosikirja 1963-64*, 7-36. Helsinki: Otava, 1964.

Includes English summary. *Atmosphères* illustrates one of the most important characteristics of avant-garde music: uniqueness. For this work Ligeti has developed special techniques for manipulating tone fields. *See*: W27.

B267. Schaarschmidt, Helmut. "Neue Musik im Musikunterricht der Sekundarstufe I: György Ligetis *Atmosphères*." *Musik und Bildung* 12 (1980): 790-92.

Describes how this work could be presented to a group of students. *See*: W27.

B268. Schmiedeke, Ulrich. *Der Beginn der neuen Orgelmusik 1961/62: Die Orgelkompositionen von Hambraeus, Kagel und Ligeti*. Berliner musikwissenschaftliche Arbeiten, Bd. 19. Munich: Katzbichler, 1981.

A discussion of *Volumina* is included on p. 46-47. The work is compared with *Atmosphères* and with *Konstellationen I* by Bengt Humbraeus. Originally presented as the author's doctoral dissertation (Technisches Universität Berlin, 1979). A review by D. Gojowy appears in *Musikforschung* 37 (1984): 237-38. *See*: W31, W27.

B269. Schnebel, Dieter. "Berichte von neuer Orgelmusik. III. György Ligetis Orgelfantasie *Volumina*." In *Walter Gerstenberg zum 60. Geburtstag*, edited by Georg von Dadelsen and Andreas Holschneider, 151. Wolfenbüttel and Zürich: Möseler, 1964.

Describes the content of the work and the new techniques it requires. *See*: W31.

B270. Schneider, Sigrun. "Zwischen Statik und Dynamik. Zur formalen Analyse von Ligetis *Atmosphères*." *Musik und Bildung* 7 (1975): 506-10.

An analysis detailing the structure of the work and the treatment of tone fields ("field technique"). *See*: W27.

B271. Schreier, Manfred. "György Ligetis *Lux aeterna*--ein Beitrag zur Praxis der Chorleitung." *Musica* 33 (1979): 371-75.

A description of the piece with suggestions and exercises for rehearsal. *See*: W37.

B272. Schubert, Giselher. "Über ein partielles Formproblem neuerer Musik." *Schweizerische Musikzeitung/Revue musicale suisse* 116 (1976): 88-90.

Investigates the relationship between large form and musical detail in the *Concerto for Violoncello*. *See*: W38.

B273.   Schuler, Manfred. "György Ligeti: Volumina. Ein Unterrichtsbeispiel für die Sekundärstufe II." *Musik und Bildung* 7 (1975): 520-23.

The author presents a lesson plan designed to introduce this work to secondary students. *See*: W31.

B274.   Schultz, Wolfgang-Andreas. "Zwei Studien über das Cello-Konzert von Ligeti." *Zeitschrift für Musiktheorie*. 6 (1975): 97-104.

Includes a summary in English. The first study, "Aesthetic Causality," applies the models used by Ligeti in "Zustände, Ereignisse, Wandlungen" (*See*: B45). The second study, "Komposition mit Mustern," is an analysis of the 2nd movement in terms of models used to structure the piece. The article concludes with some comments from the composer. *See*: W38.

B275.   Stephan, Rudolf. "György Ligeti: *Konzert für Violoncello und Orchester*. Anmerkungen zur Cluster-Komposition." In *Die Musik der sechziger Jahre*, edited by Rudolf Stephan, 117-27. Veröffentlichungen des Instituts für Neue Musik und Musikerziehung Darmstadt, 12. Mainz: Schott, 1972.

An examination of Ligeti's use of tone clusters in the *Concerto for Violoncello*. *See*: W38.

B276.   Svard, Lois. "György Ligeti: Études pour piano, premier livre." *Notes* 44 (1987-88): 578-79.

A score review. "These Etudes are marvelously inventive, carrying the polyrhythms of Stravinsky's 1908 Etudes to dizzying heights. But one has the feeling here, as with all the best piano etudes since Chopin, that the music, and not the technical wizardry, is foremost." *See*: W63.

B277.   Swift, Richard. "Ligeti: *Konzert für Violoncello und Orchester* (1966)." *Notes* 26 (1970): 620-21.

A review of the score. "It might be objected that the solo cello's role is less than concertante, but it is the chamber music scoring of the composition and the masterful control of pitch and sonority which generate the subtle but powerful expressiveness of the music." *See*: W38.

B278.   Urban, Uve. "Serielle Technik und barocker Geist in Ligeti's Cembalo-Stück *Continuum*: Untersuchung zur Kompositionstechnique." *Musik und Bildung* 5 (1973): 63-70.

An examination of the stylistic background of this piece and others works from around 1967. *See*: W41.

B279.   Van der Slice, John DeWitt. "An Analysis of György Ligeti's *Atmosphères*." DMA thesis, University of Illinois, 1980. 46 p.

Includes a graphic transcription of the piece representing pitch vertically and duration horizontally. Examines the pieces in detail and discusses its place in the development of music in the early 1960s. *See*: W27.

B280. Walgenbach, Wilhelm. "Versuche zur Bildung ästhetischer Redundanzen im Musikunterricht einer Volksschule." *Musik und Bildung* 1 (1969): 551-57.

The author demonstrates the teaching of aesthetic principles through a lesson devoted to *Apparitions*. The lesson addresses German 9th grade students. *See*: W26.

Wehinger, Rainer. *György Ligeti: Artikulation. elektronische Musik, eine Hörpartitur. See*: B126.

B281. Wells, William. "Music Reviews." *Notes* 42 (1986): 867.

A review of the score of *Magyar Etüdök. See*: W62.

B282. Whittall, Arnold. "Reviews of Music: *String Quartet No. 2.*" *Music Review* 40 (1979): 236-38.

A review of the score. "Ligeti's virtuosity as an exploiter of instrumental colour can lead him to use that colour as a substitute for more substantial content, and this work, for all the skill of its formal articulation over a span of more than 21 minutes, does seem to squander its exciting diversity of tone in a manner that prefers gesture to argument." *See*: W42.

B283. Wiesmann, Sigrid. "Bedingungen der Komponierbarkeit: Bernd Alois Zimmermanns "Die Soldaten", György Ligetis "Le Grand Macabre." In *Für und Wider die Literaturoper: Zur Situation nach 1945*, herausgegeben von Sigrid Wiesmann, 27-37. Thurnauer Schriften zum Musiktheater, Bd, 6. Laaber, West Germany: Laaber-Verlag, 1982.

Le Grand Macabre is described in dramatic as well as musical terms within a discussion of the requirements of modern music theater. "Auch er komponiert gewissermaßen nicht im direkten Zugriff, wie etwa Hindemith und auch Schönberg, sondern auf verschlungenen Umwegen (wodurch man sich an Alban Berg erinnert fühlen kann): Er braucht komplizierte Arrangements, um sich inspirieren zu lassen, braucht auch die Mühe pedantischer Kleinarbeit selbst wenn am Ende dennoch eine einfache, schlagende Wirkung resultiert." ["He does not compose in a direct seizure so to speak, as for example Hindemith or Schönberg, but rather through roundabout detours (which is reminiscent of Alban Berg). He needs complicated arrangements to inspire him. He also needs the labor of pedantic detail work, provided it results in a simple and striking effect."] *See*: W54.

B284. Wilheim, András. "Ligeti's Horn Trio." *New Hungarian Quarterly* 25 (summer 1984): 210-13.

This is an English translation of a Hungarian article which appeared in *Muzsika* 26 (May 1983): 23-27. It is a discussion of the structure and content of this work. "Of music produced recently there are only a chosen few pieces in which novelty goes hand in hand with quality, with a value such that, in T.S. Eliot's phrase, by it 'the whole existing order must be, if ever so slightly, altered' and 'the conformity between the old and the new' is established." *See*: W59.

B285.   Williamson, Beth Loeber. "Performing new organ music: Ligeti's
        Volumina." *American Organist* 13, no. 10 (1979): 32-36.

>   Reprinted in *Triangle* 76, no. 2 (1981): 22-25. An analysis and a discussion of
>   performance techniques. Includes quotes from the composer and from Karl-Erik
>   Welin, for whom the piece was composed. *See*: W31.

B286.   Wißkirchen, Hubert. "Klausurbeispiel der Aufgabenart 'Analyse und
        Interpretation' (Ligeti: *Continuum*)." *Musik und Bildung* 16 (1984):
        180-87.

>   A reproduction of two university exam essays analyzing the beginning of this
>   piece. *See*: W41.

B287.   Yannay, Yehuda. "Toward an Open-ended Method of Analysis of
        Contemporary Music: a Study of Selected Works by Edgard
        Varèse and György Ligeti." DMA diss., University of Illinois, 1974.
        163 p.

>   Outlines an analytical approach to works in which density, texture, timbre, and
>   related elements assume a structural role. An analysis of *Ten Pieces for Wind
>   Quintet* serves as an example of this approach. *See*: W43.

B288.   Zenck, Martin. "Auswirkung einer 'musique informelle' auf die Neue
        Musik: Zu Theodor W. Adornos Formvorstellung." *International
        Review of the Aesthetics and Sociology of Music* 10, no. 2 (1979):
        137-65.

>   Includes summaries in English and Croatian. Examines Ligeti's theoretical
>   writings, *Aventures et Nouvelles Aventures*, and Stockhausen's *Klavierstück I* to
>   support Adorno's idea of *musique informelle*. *See*: W33, W34.

V. Reviews

B289.   Adam, Klaus. "Nürnberg." *Oper und Konzert* 19 (1981): 18-19.

The Nürnberg production of *Le Grand Macabre* was directed by Wolfgang
Gayler. "Musikalische erscheint mir die Partitur arg mager; ein Paar bewegende
leise-traurige Augenblicke, manches brillant, insgesamt sehr fad.... Nicht
verschwiegen sei, daß diese 'Besondere Oper zu besonderem Preis' erstaunlich
viel Jugend ins Theater lockte und von den jungen Leuten auch heftig
akklamiert wurde." ["Musically the score seems severely meager to me. A
couple of moving, faintly sad moments, some brilliance, mostly quite insipid.... It
is no secret that this 'special opera at a special price' attracted an astonishing
number of young people and was highly acclaimed by them."] *See:* W54g.

B290.   Allenby, David. "The Almeida Festival." *Musical Opinion* 110 (Oct.
1987): 296-98.

This festival featured the U.K. première of the *Piano Concerto*. "Well, I must
admit I was not the only member of the audience to be taken aback by the
conventional nature of much that was offered. The shape of the work as a
whole with its three movements fast-slow-fast, is traditional in the extreme, and
although the Ligeti fingerprints of sudden outbursts and use of extreme registers
are still present, all is trapped within a forward-moving continuity that could
almost be called symphonic." *See:* W64, App. II, p. 173.

B291.   Aprahamian, Felix. "Sounds and Fury." *Sunday Times*, May 15,
1977, p. 35.

Briefly reviews a London Musical Digest concert consisting of the two string
quartets, the two wind quintets, and *Monument-Selbstportrait-Bewegung*.
"There, in the more experimental *Three Pieces for Two Pianos* and the Second
Quartet, despite Ligeti's rejection of chance elements, his precise notation
produces sounds which ultimately impinge on the ear as haphazard and
improvisatory." *See:* W15c, W19c, W42b, W43b, W52b, App. II, p. 170.

B292.   Augustyn, Rafal. "Trzy tygodnie u Ligetiego." *Ruch Muzyczny* 23,
no. 24 (1979): 12.

A report on the Centre Acanthes, a festival dedicated to the work of Ligeti, held
July 19-Aug. 6, 1979, in Aix-en-Provence. *Aventures et Nouvelles Aventures* and
Monument-Selbstportrait-Bewegung were performed, and Ligeti taught a course
in composition. The author was especially impressed by the personal contact
with the composer. *See:* W33, W34, W52, App. II, p. 171.

B293.   Bachmann, Claus-Henning. "Graz: die Unausweichlichkeit der
'Provinz' Über den Steirischen Herbst und Ligetis 'Abenteuer."
Neue Zeitschrift für Musik 131 (1970): 589-91.

A review of a performance of *Aventures et Nouvelles Aventures* Includes a
discussion of the text of the work. *See:* W33, W34, W36a.

B294.   -------. "Graz: ein Musikprotokoll-über Boulez, Eisler und den
Realismus." *Neue Zeitschrift für Musik* 133 (1972): 35.

Includes a description of the première of *Horizont* for solo recorder, composed
by the performer, Michael Vetter after an idea by Ligeti. "Minimale
Veränderungen treten als unerhörte Ereignisse ins Bewußtsein, das Artikulieren
des Tons, die Erlösung vom stimmlosen Luftstrom, wird zum Abenteuer; am
Ende bleibt nur das Atmen des Spielers, Leben-Zeichen des zu sich selbst

gekommenen Menschen." ["Minimal changes are sensed as inaudible events, the articulation of tones, the release of toneless airstreams becomes an adventure. Finally only the performer's breathing remains: a life-sign of a man who has found himself."] *See:* W49a.

B295.   ‑‑‑‑‑‑‑. "György Ligetis *Abenteuer.*" *Musica* 17 (1963): 113-14.

A review of the première of *Aventures.* "'Abenteuer der Form und des Ausdrucks' wurden verhießen, und schon dieses imaginäre Moment beschreibt nicht nur deutlich die Position Ligetis, sondern wirft auch ein Licht auf den jüngsten Stand 'absurden Komponierens -- um ein Schlagwort aus dem theatralischen Nachbarbereich auf Music anzuwenden.... Das Publikum reagierte jedenfalls bemerkenswert, genau zwischen Lachen und Nicht-Lachen." ["'Adventures of form and of expression' were promised, and indeed this imaginary factor depicts clearly not only Ligeti's position, but also throws light on the latest state of 'absurd' composition -- to borrow a word from the theater.... The public responded noteworthily in any case: exactly between laughter and non-laughter."] *See:* W33a.

B296.   ‑‑‑‑‑‑‑. "Von Ligeti bis Vivaldi." *Musica* 16 (1962): 73.

A review of a "Neue Werk" concert in Hamburg which included *Atmosphères.* *See:* W27.

B297.   Balázs, Istvan. "Ein Ligeti-Abend in Budapest." *Neue Zeitschrift für Musik* 144, no. 6 (June 1983): 34-35.

A review of a concert in the Ferenc Liszt Academy of Music featuring the Hungarian Philharmonic Orchestra and the Budapest Symphony, György Lehel, conductor, and the Hungarian Radio Choir, Ferenc Sapszon, conductor. The evening's performance consisted of *Clocks and Clouds*, *Concerto for Violoncello* (Miklós Perényi, soloist), and the *Requiem* (Júlia Pászthy, sop., and Tamara Takács, alto). *See:* W35, W38, W50, App. II, p. 171.

B298.   Barry, Malcolm. "Records, Avantgarde." *Music and Musicians* 25 (April 1977): 40-41.

A review of Decca Headline HEAD 12. "Ligeti is well served by his performers under Atherton and also by the recording engineers." *See:* D11, D22, D44.

B299.   Bartenstein, Hans. "Ligetis *Grand Macabre* in Freiburg." *Orchester* 32 (1984): 440-41.

A review. "So wurde ganzes, bis ins feinste Detail minutiös vorgeschriebenes Spektrum souverän erfüllt, von den subtilen lyrischen Klanggespinsten etwa des Liebespaares bis zur Drastik der komischen oder der Härte und Gewalt der makabren Szenen und Katastrophen." ["So the whole minutely outlined Spectrum was executed masterfully to the finest detail, from the subtly lyrical sound webs around the lovers to the vividness of the comical or the harshness and force of the macabre scenes and catastrophes."] *See:* W54h.

B300.   Baruch, Gerth-Wolfgang. "Stuttgart: Ligeti, Wittinger, Kirchenmusiktage." *Melos/Neue Zeitschrift für Musik* 3 (1977): 145-46.

A performance review of the German première of *San Francisco Polyphony.* Elgar Howarth conducted the Stuttgart Radio Symphony, and Ligeti made some preliminary remarks. "Die statistischen diffusen Klangflächen und Klangbänder früherer Werke sind hier von kontrastierenden Bewegungsabläufen abgelöst, die zu hohen Registern tendieren und somit das Klangbild aufhellen. Auch die opalisierenden Klangfarben die den Reiz von Ligetis einstigen Partituren erhöhten, sind zurückgedrängt, so daß die San-Francisco-Musik spröder, herber, quasi graphischer wirkt als die bisherigen Stücke." ["The statistically diffuse sound surfaces and sound webbing of earlier works are here replaced by contrasting courses of motion, which tend toward the high register and so brighten the sound. Also, the opalescent tone color which heightens the appeal of Ligeti's earlier scores are restrained so that the San-Francisco-Music is more brittle, harsh, and quasi graphic that previous pieces."] *See*: W51b.

B301.   -------. "Stuttgart: Neues von Ligeti, Kagel und Reutter." *Melos/Neue Zeitschrift für Musik* 3 (1977): 259-61.

A review of Ligeti's Theater piece *Rondeau* performed by Wolfgang Höper. "Was Ligeti mit diesem kurzen Bühnenstück zeigen wollte, ist meiner Meinung nach die Oberflächlichkeit heutiger Konversation, die sich häufig in Phrasendrescherei und stereotypen Redewendungen, zum Beispiel über das Wetter, erschöpft. Aber auch politische Aspekte des Exilungen Ligeti zeichnen sich ab, wenn er beispielweise seinen Schauspieler für nichts und wieder nichts erschießen läßt." ["In my opinion, what Ligeti is trying to show with this short theater piece is the superficiality of modern conversation. It exhausts itself with cliches and stereotyped expressions. But Ligeti also sketches political aspects of his exile from Hungary, for example when he has his actor shot again and again for nothing."] *See*: W53a.

B302.   -------. "Ungarischer Rock aus Cembalo; Stuttgart: Geburtstagskonzert für György Ligeti mit Uraufführungen." *Die Welt*, May 20, 1983.

A review of a Ligeti concert including the *Chamber Concerto* (Pierre Boulez and the Stuttgart Radio Symphony), *Continuum*, *Passacaglia ungherese*, and *Hungarian Rock* (Elisabeth Chojnacka), two early choruses, and *Magyar Etüdök* (Clytus Gottwald and the Schola Cantorum Stuttgart). "Die exzellente Wiedergabe der Stücke markierte die besondere Bedeutung des Abends." ["The great significance of the evening was accentuated by the excellent performances."] *See*: W46f, W41, W56, W57, W62a, App. II, p. 171.

B303.   Baucke, Ludolf. "Bilderspiegel und Spiegelbilder: Ligeti und Vecchi im Opernstudio." *Neue Zeitschrift für Musik* 143 (1982): 58.

A review of a performance of *Aventures et Nouvelles Aventures* in Braunschweig. "In nur fünfwöchiger Probenarbeit glückte dem Trio Kirsten Harms, Christian Hechler und Matthias Kaiser ein erfrischend komödiantisches und vielschichtiges Musiktheater, das bei nahezu allen Beteiligten -- auch das Publikum gehört dazu -- wie eine Vitaminspritze gegen die Opernroutine wirkte." ["In only five weeks of rehearsal the trio of Kirsten Harms, Christian Hechler and Matthias Kaiser produced a refreshingly comical and multi-layered music theater which for all the participants, including the audience, worked as a vitamin shot against opera routine."] *See*: W33, W34, W36.

B304.   -------. "Telefongespräche mit Paul Klee." *Hannoversche Allgemeine Zeitung*, Feb. 21, 1985.

A record review of Wergo WER 60095. "Das resultat dieser Bemühungen ist so gut gelungen, daß wohl selbst noch die anspruchsvollere Compact disc davon zehren kann." ["The result of this effort is so successful that it could possibly compete with the demanding compact disc."] *See*: D2, etc.

B305.   Bayer, Hans. "Lesefrucht. Witzig unterhaltsam und abstrus
        knautschend: zwei 'Anti-Opern' in Stuttgart uraufgeführt."
        Gottesdienst und Kirche no. 1 (1967): 22.

   Review of the Stuttgart staging of *Aventures et Nouvelles Aventures*. *See*:
   W36b.

B306.   Becker, Wolfgang. "Zimmermann *Perspectiven und Monologe*, Ligeti
        Monument, Selbstporträt, Bewegung." *Neue Zeitschrift für Musik*
        141 (1980): 576.

   A review of Deutsche Grammophon DG-2531-102. "Die Bruder Kontarsky
   spielen diese Musik mit der Sicherheit der Interpreten, von denen alle drei Werke
   inspiriert wurden: intelligent, ohne die Emphase pianistischer Virtuosität." ["The
   Kontarsky brothers play this music with the sureness of interpreters by whom
   the three works were inspired: without emphasis on pianistic virtuosity."] *See*:
   W52, D45.

B307.   Bernheimer, Martin. "Encounter with Ligeti at Caltech." *Los Angeles
        Times*, March 10, 1972, sec. IV, p. 1.

   A review of a lecture/performance featuring *Ten Pieces for Wind Quintet* played
   by members of the Stanford Contemporary Performing Group. "[He] spent two
   hours discussing less than 20 minutes of music.... 'I am very serious, I do not
   make jokes in the music'." *See*: W43.

B308.   Beuth, Reinhard. "Piet ist ewig besoffen: György Ligetis erste große
        Oper wurde in Stockholm uraufgeführt." *Abendzeitung*, April 14,
        1978, p. 9.

   A review of the première of *Le Grand Macabre*. Another version appeared
   under the title "Nonsens unter der Gürtellinie" in *Hannoversche Allgemeine
   Zeitung*, April 14, 1978. "Im Zentrum des Stücks klafft ein etwa einstündiges
   musikalisches Loch.... Ligetis entscheidender Fehler ist wohl, daß er sich allzu
   bald festrennt in die Textbrüllerei, ins Buchstabieren des Librettos, statt der
   Musik freien Lauf zu lassen." ["A musical hole about an hour long, yawns in the
   center of the piece.... Ligeti's crucial failure is surely that he too quickly
   surrenders to the bellowing text, the spelling out of the libretto, rather than
   giving free rein to the music."] *See*: W54a.

B309.   -------. "Der Sensenmann selber beißt hier ins Gras: György Ligetis
        Oper *Le Grand Macabre* an der Hamburgischen Staatsoper
        erstaufgeführt." *Die Welt*, Oct 17, 1978.

   A review of the German première. "Man langweilt sich. Man gähnt. Man fragt
   sich, was der fäkalische Unfug auf der Bühne soll." ["One is bored. One yawns.
   One questions the purpose of the scatological mischief onstage."] *See*: W54b.

B310.   Bitz, Albert-Peter. "Ein Comic Strip vom Tod: *Le Grand Macabre*
        von György Ligeti im Saarländischen Staatstheater." *Saarbrücker
        Zeitung*, May 5, 1979.

   A review of this performance. "Nach der Generalprobe sagte Ligeti, er sei
   'überwältigt vom Niveau der Aufführung'." ["After the dress rehearsal, Ligeti said
   that he was 'overwhelmed by the quality of the performance.'"] *See*: W54f.

B311.   Böhmer, Helga.   "XXX. Festival für zeitgenössische Musik in
         Venedig." *Melos* 34 (1967): 411-14.

A review of a performance of *Lux aeterna* and the *Requiem* performed by
Musica Viva Pragensis under Zbyněk Vostřák, and the Orchestre des Teatro
Fenice under Ettore Gracis. *See*: W37, W35.

B312.   Bortolotto, Mario. "Italy: New Music at Palermo." *Perspectives of
         New Music* 2 (1964): 160.

A review of the "Settimana per la Nuova Musica" conducted by Daniele Paris,
which featured *Atmosphères*. "... a piece that is weakened by merely auditory
preciosities." *See*: W27.

B313.   Boulay, Jean-Michel. "György Ligeti." *Sonances* 6, no. 2 (Jan.
         1987): 46-47.

Record review of Wergo WER 60100 (CD: WER 60100-50). "C'est sans
hésitation que je le recommande à tous nos lecteurs, même ceux qui ont un peu
peur de la musique contemporaine." ["I recommend this to all our readers
without hesitation, even to those with a little fear of contemporary music."] *See*:
D21, D30, D53, D46.

B314.   Brachtel, Karl Robert. "Geniale Verbindung von Intellekt und
         Intuition: Musica Viva-Matinee mit Ligeti im Funkhaus." *Münchner
         Merkur*, May 12, 1981.

A review of a concert which consisted of both wind quintets (Syrinx Quintet),
both string quartets (Arditti Quartet), *Passacaglia ungherese* and *Hungarian
Rock* (Elisabeth Chojnacka, harpsichord). Ligeti also spoke. "Ligetis
Ideenreichtum fand in diesen Werken eine geniale Realisierung, eine seltene
Verbindung von Intellekt und künstlerischer Intuition." ["Ligeti's resourcefulness
found in these works a brilliant realization, a rare combination of intellect and
artistic intuition."] *See*: W15d, W42c, W19d, W43c, W56c, W57c.

B315.   -------. "Ligeti im Herkulessaal: Todesangst -- aus ironischer Distanz
         abgehandelt." *Münchner Merkur*, Dec. 5, 1983.

A review of the "Musica Viva" concert which featured a concert performance of
scenes and interludes from *Le Grand Macabre*. Elgar Howarth conducted the
Orchestra of the Bavarian Radio, with soloists Alison Hargan, Cynthia Buchan,
Roderic Keating and Fabio Giongo. Ligeti himself introduced the performance.
"Und dann war man sogleich von der Aussagekraft, der Bildhaftigkeit, der
Bedeutung dieser Musik gefangen, die gerade hier, in einem souveränen
Einbeziehen der Musik anderer Epochen, einen Verfügen über deren stilistische
Eigenheiten mit den Mitteln der Gegenwart ihre eigene Größe erweist." ["And
then one was immediately captivated by the expressive power, the vividness, the
significance of this music, which proves its greatness by a masterly inclusion of
the music of other epochs, the stylistic peculiarities of which are used through
modern methods."] *See*: W55c.

B316.   Brasch, Alfred. "Musik für Zuschauer -- die Oper auf dem
         Bildschirm." *Neue Zeitschrift für Musik* 132 (1971): 323-25.

A review of several vocal works produced for German television including
Aventures et Nouvelles Aventures, produced by Klaus Lindemann. "Lindemann
führt in viel stärkerem Maß, als das den bisherigen Versuchen einer szenischen
Aufführung des Werkes möglich war, auf menschliches Grundverhalten zurück.
Vor allem sind es panische Situationen, Szenen der Furcht, der Flucht, die da in
absurden Bildern erscheinen. Sie sind besetzt nicht nur mit den Solisten des

Stücks, sondern vor allem mit einer großen Schar von Laiendarstellern, die willig vor der Kamera auf dem Bauche kriechen, sich in Sand hineinwühlen und mit Spinat bekleckern lassen." ["Lindemann reduces the work to basic human behavior to a much greater degree than previous stagings. Above all there are panicky situations, scenes of fear, of flight, which appear in absurd images. The production includes not only the soloists, but a large crowd of extras, who are willing to crawl on their bellies, bury themselves in sand, and spatter themselves with spinach in front of the camera."] *See:* W36e.

B317.   Briner, Andres. "Stockholm: ein Ende, das nicht stattfindet. Ligetis *Le Grand Macabre* an der königlichen Oper." *Melos/Neue Zeitschrift für Musik* 4 (1978): 226-27.

Reprinted from the *Neue Zürcher Zeitung*, April 15/16, 1978. "Ligeti schreibt: 'Ich entschied mich für die Abänderung der Ghelderodeschen Version: Es bleibt völlig offen, ob der Große Makabre (Nekrotzar) der Tod ist oder ein kleiner, wenn auch durch dein Sendungsbewußtsein ins Heroische verklärter und gesteigerter Gaukler, und die Handlung wird mit einer Art Triumph des Eros beschlossen: Der Tod und die ganze dunkle Zukunft ist uns egal, es gibt nur "hier und jetzt".' Das wird in dieser Inszenierung, die Zweideutigkeiten bis zum Schluß bestehen läßt, nicht sinnfällig. Daß jenes Ende, das Nekrotzar der Welt bereiten möchte, nicht stattfindet, vermag Meschke deutlich zu machen, aber 'eine Art Triumph des Eros' aufzupfropfen." Oder ist dies, bei der Anlage des Stücks, schlechterdings unmöglich?" ["Ligeti writes, 'I determined to revise the Ghelderode version. It remains completely open whether the Great Macabre (Nekrotzar) is Death or a lesser (though more clearly and greatly heroic through his sense of mission) charlatan, and the story ends with a sort of triumph of Eros: death and the dark future are equal to us. There is only here and now.' These ambiguities remaining at the end are not evident in this production. Meschke can make it clear that Nekrotzar's End of the World doesn't happen, but he is no longer in a position to graft a 'sort of triumph of Eros' onto the work. Or is this, given the structure of the work, impossible?"] *See:* W54a.

B318.   Bronnenmeyer, Walter. "Comics aus Breughelland: Ligetis *Le Grand Macabre* in Nürnberg." *Opernwelt* 21 (March 1980): 38.

A performance review which also appeared in: *Oper und Konzert* 18, no. 5 (1980): 22. "Es zeugt vielmehr von der wiedergewonnenen Erkenntnis, da Musiktheater auch etwas mit Unterhaltung zu tun habe...." ["It speaks rather, of the recovered knowledge that music theater also has something to do with entertainment."] *See:* W54g.

B319.   Brunner, Gerhard. "Musikprotokolle 73." *Musica* 28 (1974): 28-30.

A review of the "Styrian Autumn" festival, including the première of *Clocks and Clouds* performed by the Orchestra and Chorus of the Austrian Radio under Friedrich Cerha. "*Clocks and Clouds*, deren fahles, diffuses, von den jeweils fünf Flöten und Klarinetten bestimmtes Klangkolorit an mikrobiologische Verwesungs- und Entstehungsprozesse denken läßt, festigen die beim *Doppelkonzert* doch ziemlich deutlich gewordene Überzeugung, daß augenblicklich auf der Stelle tritt." ["*Clocks and Clouds*, whose pale, diffuse tone color (determined at times by the five flutes and clarinets), was reminiscent of microbiological decomposition and regeneration processes. This piece strengthens the conviction (made rather clear by the *Double Concerto*) that, for the present, Ligeti is marking time."] *See:* W50a.

B320.   -------. "Schubert-Uraufführung und viel Modernes." *Musica* 24 (1970): 27-29.

A review of a performance by Gerd Zacher of *Etude no. 2* for organ (Coulée). "Ligeti meint daß auch 'Coulée' an eine zwecklos in Gang gehaltene Maschine denken lasse." ["Besides a 'coulée' Ligeti intends to evoke a machine working steadily to no purpose."] *See:* W45.

B321.   -------. "Viel neue Musik." *Musica* 24 (1970): 357-58.

Includes a brief review of the *Chamber Concerto* premiered by the die Reihe Ensemble. "... selbständiger, klarer, konturierter löst sich die Einzelstimme aus den harmonischen Feldern." ["... independent, clear, contoured parts resolve themselves out of the harmonic field."] *See:* W46a.

B322.   Buck, Ole. "Darmstadt." *Dansk Musiktidsskrift* 43 (1968): 14-15.

A review of a performance of *Lux aeterna*. Ligeti's style is compared to Zen Buddhism. *See:* W37.

B323.   Burde, Wolfgang. "Berlin: Glätte und Routine bei den Festwochen." *Neue Zeitschrift für Musik* 133 (1972): 637-41.

A review of the Berliner Festwochen which included performances of *Lontano* and the *Double Concerto*. The Ligeti portion of the review also appeared in *Der Tagesspiegel*, Sept. 19, 1972. Christoph von Dohnányi directed the Berlin Philharmonic with soloists Lothar Koch (oboe) and Karlheinz Zöller (flute). "... schien aus dem tastenden, verhaltenen Sprechen Ligetis ein akzentuierendes gestalten zu wollen, aus der musikalischen Atmosphäre ein Konzertstück, angereichert mit brillanten Effekten." ["... out of Ligeti's tentative, halting speech, an emphatic form seemed to be willed, out of the musical atmosphere a concert piece, enriched with brilliant effects."] *See:* W39b, W48a.

B324.   Cadieu, Martine. "D'un espace imaginaire." *Musique en jeu* no. 32 (Sept. 1978): 123-25.

A review of the world première of *Le Grand Macabre* which discusses similarities between Ligeti and Michel de Ghelderode. *See:* W54a.

B325.   Casken, John. *"Le Grand Macabre* (at the Coliseum)." *Musical Times* 124 (1983): 111.

A review of the British première. "The set is a section of the M4 motorway, and Prince Go-Go parodies 'recent Thatcherisms'.... An intriguing evening and a superb performance...." *See:* W54e.

B326.   Celli, Teodoro. "Coito Continuo." *Il Messagero*, May 7, 1979, p. 7.

A review of the Bologna production of *Le Grand Macabre*. "Allestimento di straordinario rigore, e di matematica efficacia ...." ["A production of extraordinary rigor and mathematical efficacy."] *See:* W54c.

B327.   Coates, Leon. "First Performances: Musica Nova 1973." *Tempo* No. 107 (Dec. 1973): 24-25.

A review of this contemporary music festival which featured the British première of the *Double Concerto* with William Bennett and Michael Dobson, soloists, and the New Music Group of Scotland directed by Alexander Gibson. Ligeti was present to lecture at the festival as well. "Both the ethereal first movement, and the brisk rippling second (a variation of the first), came across vividly in this performance...." *See:* W48d.

B328.   Commanday, Robert. "An Exquisite Ligeti Performance." *San Francisco Chronicle*, May 19, 1972, p. 50.

A review of a performance of *Melodien* by the San Francisco Symphony, conducted by Seiji Ozawa. "Ligeti's finest work to date, a gracious and delighting experience." *See:* W47c.

B329.   --------. "Symphony's Own 'Special'." *San Francisco Chronicle*, Jan. 10, 1975, p. 42.

A review of the première of *San Francisco Polyphony* by the San Francisco Symphony, conducted by Seiji Ozawa. Translated into German in *Melos/Neue Zeitschrift für Musik* 1 (1975): 118. "That it was so constantly absorbing is proof of the work's qualities. That it was so pellucid in realization is tribute to Seiji Ozawa's expert realization with the orchestra." *See:* W51a.

B330.   Cook, Nick. "Camden." *Musical Times* 110 (1969): 762.

A review of the Camden Music Festival which included a performance of the *Concerto for Violoncello* played by Göran Holmstrand and Musica Nova of Stockholm; and *Ten Pieces for Wind Quintet* played by the Stockholm Philharmonic Wind Quintet. *See:* W38, W43.

B331.   Crepaz, Gerhard. "György Ligeti, *Le Grand Macabre* in Paris." *Orchester* 29 (1981): 554.

A review. "Eine sehr unterhaltsame, vielleicht sogar populäre Oper." ["A very entertaining, possibly even popular opera."] *See:* W54d.

B332.   Dadelsen, Hans-Christian. "Konzentration und Anspruch." *Musica* 33 (1979): 485.

A record review of Wergo 60079. "Fast zehn Jahre sind seit der berühmten LaSalle-Einspielung des 2. Quartetts vergangen. Und das technische äußerst perfekte Arditti-Quartett hält dem einmalig hohen Vergleichs-Anspruch der LaSalle-Aufnahme nicht nur stand; es fügt einige Aspekte hinzu: Das Unterkühlt-Mechanische der Musik tritt zugunsten des Expressiv-Subjektiven etwas zurück." ["Nearly ten years has passed since the celebrated LaSalle performance of the second quartet. And the technically perfect Arditti Quartet does not only hold its ground against the singularly high standard of the LaSalle recording. It adds some aspects. The mechanical coolness of the music steps back somewhat in favor of expressive subjectivity."] *See:* W19, W42, D73, D77.

B333.   Damm, H. "LaSalle in Switzerland." *American Musical Digest*, 1, no. 4 (1970): 26.

Review of the première of *String Quartet no. 2* broadcast by the Southwest German Radio on Dec 27, 1969. Translated and abridged from *Basler Nachrichten*, Dec. 29, 1969. "Ligeti has enriched new music with a work of grandeur and validity. However, interpretation by the LaSalle Quartet was so breathtaking that the fascinated listeners were pressed to concentrate on the piece itself." *See:* W42a.

B334.   Daniel, Oliver. "Loops and Reels (Recordings)." *Saturday Review*, April 12, 1969, 67.

A review of the recording "Electronic music, vol 1" (Mercury Stereo SR-9123), which includes *Artikulation*. "His procedures are complex, but the results are simply effective.... His tape music is good, but hardly distinguishable from hundreds of others similar essays." *See:* W25, D2.

B335. Danler, Karl-Robert. "György Ligeti in Münchens Musica Viva." *Das Orchester*, 29 (1981): 647.

A review of a concert which consisted of both wind quintets (the Syrinx Quintet), both string quartets (Arditti Quartet), and *Passacaglia ungherese* and *Hungarian Rock* (Elisabeth Chojnacka, harpsichord). Ligeti also spoke. "'Meine Stücke sind nicht unausführbar', sagte Ligeti schmunzelnd, 'sondern sie sind *fast* ausführbar.'" ["My pieces are not impossible', said Ligeti grinning, 'rather, they are *nearly* performable.'"] *See*: W15d, W43c, W19d, W42c, W56c, W57c.

B336. -------. "Ligetis Requiem." *Musica* 22 (1968): 94.

A review of the second Munich Musica Viva concert, with soloists Liliana Poli, Barbro Ericson, the Bavarian Radio Choir and Symphony, Francis Travis, conductor. "Es ist ein Werk, das durch die Konsequenz seiner Konzeption fasziniert." ["It is a work which fascinates through the consistency of its conception."] *See*: W35.

B337. -------. "Musica Viva auf zwei Ebenen." *Musica* 21 (1967): 280.

A review of a concert performance of *Aventures et Nouvelles Aventures* in Munich, given by Gertie Charlent, Marie-Thérèse Cahn, and William Pearson under Bruno Maderna. "Eines aber sind Ligetis *Aventures* nicht, sie sind nicht langweilig." ["But one thing Ligeti's *Aventures* are not: they are not boring."] *See*: W33, W34.

B338. -------. "Ur- und Erstaufführung in Münchens Musica Viva: György Ligeti persönlich anwesend." *Orchester* 32 (1984): 111-12.

A review of a concert performance of scenes and interludes from *Le Grand Macabre*. Elgar Howarth conducted the Orchestra of the Bavarian Radio, with soloists Alison Hargan, Cynthia Buchan, Roderic Keating and Fabio Giongo. Ligeti himself introduced the performance. "Die Aufführung wurde in exemplarischer Weise den Intentionen des Komponisten gerecht, ja man kann die Besetzung optimal nennen." ["The performance did justice to the composer's intentions in a exemplary manner. One could call the casting optimal."] *See*: W55b.

B339. Dannenberg, Peter. "Hamburger schmähen einen Hamburger: Ligeti-Erstaufführung im 1. Philharmonischen Konzert unter Horst Stein." *Die Welt*, Sept. 18, 1974.

A review of a performance of the *Double Concerto* with soloists Claude Gérard and Winfried Liebermann. The performance was not well received by the public. "... zählt gewiß nicht zu den zentralen Werken Ligetis. Es ist eine heiter-virtuose Marginalie seines orchestralen Oeuvres eher." ["... certainly not one of Ligeti's central works. It is rather, a bright virtuosic admargination to his orchestral works."] *See*: W48.

B340. -------. "Zentrales und Marginales von Ligeti." *Neue Musikzeitung* 26, no. 2 (1977): 4.

These reviews are based on articles which appeared on Oct. 11, 1976 and Feb. 28, 1977 in the *Stuttgarter Zeitung*. The first reported the West German première of *San Francisco Polyphony* performed by the South German Radio Orchestra under Elgar Howarth. "In dem Werk, das Ligeti weiter auf dem Wege vom Statischen zum Dynamischen zeigt, gibt es, mit einer Ausnahme, keine abrupten Brüche. Alles entwickelt sich ... sehr organisch...." ["In this work, Ligeti moves further away from the static, towards the dynamic. There are, with one exception, no sudden breaks. Everything develops ... very organically."] The second review is of a performance of *Rondeau*. "Dieses *Rondeau* ist so gut wie sein Interpret. Was wir darum im Stuttgarter Kammertheater gesehen haben, ist das Stück Wolfgang Höpers so gut wie das György Ligetis." ["This *Rondeau* is as good as its interpreter. What we saw in the Stuttgart Chamber Theater is as much the work of Wolfgang Höper as of György Ligeti."] *See*: W51b, W53a.

B341.   Davis, Peter G. "Opera: Experiments in Brooklyn." *New York Times*, Feb. 20, 1977, p. 59.

A review of a staging by the New Opera Theater, Brooklyn Academy of Music, of *Aventures et Nouvelles Aventures*. "Mr. Ligeti's open-ended exercise came off best, probably because a director is free to do most anything he wants with this plotless game of sounds. Here Mr. [Ian] Strasvogel has devised some clever complements to the singers' nonverbal eruptions, and he had three talented and uninhibited performers with whom to work, Richard Barrett, Susan Kay Peterson, and Phyllis Hunter." The accompanying ensemble was Speculum Musicae, directed by David Gilbert. *See*: W33, W34, W36.

B342.   DeRhen, A. "Speculum Musicae." *High Fidelity/Musical America* 22 (May 1972): MA21-22.

A review of a performance of the *Chamber Concerto* by the ensemble Speculum Musicae. "... a bleary exercise is *déjà entendu*." *See*: W46.

B343.   Dettmer, Roger. "Ligeti." *Fanfare* Sept.-Oct. 1982, p. 263.

A record review of Deutsche Grammophon 2530 392. "The sonic brilliance and superbly quiet surfaces ... surpass Candide 31009." *See*: D35, D75, D95.

B344.   "Deutsche Erstaufführung von György Ligetis Requiem in Köln." *Melos* 34 (March 1967): 92-93.

A review of this performance featuring soprano Liliana Poli, mezzo-soprano Barbro Ericson, the radio choirs of Hamburg and Cologne, and the Cologne Radio Symphony Orchestra. "Die Kölner Aufführung hatte Präzision und entschiedene Anschaulichkeit in der mikropolyphonen wie architektonische Klangbewegung, trotz der zwar sehr intensiven, aber auch cheironomisch schweifenden Geste des Dirigenten Andrzej Markowski." ["The Cologne performance had precision and clearly displayed the micropolyphony in spite of the very intense but chironomically wandering gestures of the director Andrzej Markowski."] *See*: W35b.

B345.   Ditsky, John. "Ligeti." *Fanfare*, Nov.-Dec. 1981, p. 185.

A review of Wergo WER 60085 (*Scenes and Interludes from Le Grand Macabre*). "And I can't begin to understand why the excellent German firm of Wergo which has done so much for the Ligeti reputation should have journeyed to Denmark only to take down parts but not all of a major composition. ... give us the all, I say." *See*: W55, D62.

B346.   Driver, Paul. "A bungled Apocalypse: György Ligeti, *Le Grand Macabre*." *Times Literary Supplement*, Jan. 7, 1983, p. 12.

A review of the opera's English première. "Loftiness of statement and depth of poetry somehow do not issue in *Le Grand Macabre*.... It should be conceded also that the jokiness of the action, the madness of the antics, are mirrored by and embodied in the fabric of the music.... It is when such musical point making is allowed to flourish ... that Ligeti's artistic stature is remembered." *See*: W54e.

B347.   Du Bois, Rob. "Gaudeamus fällt aus dem Rahmen des
holländischen Musiklebens." *Melos* 30 (1963): 422-24.

Reports the première performance of *Poème symphonique* for 100 metronomes,
directed by the composer. Also describes the angry reaction of the audience.
See: W32a.

B348.   "Editorial Notes." *The Strad* 85 (June 1974): 67-69.

A review of the English Bach Festival which featured a visit by Ligeti and
performances by the London Symphony Orchestra of the *Double Concerto* and
Clocks and Clouds. "The bounder actually has the enthusiastic effrontery to
believe in old-fashioned concepts like harmony and communication." *See*: W48,
W50c.

B349.   Einemann, Marita. "György Ligeti zu gäst beim 'Bremer Podium'."
Neue Zeitschrift für Musik 144 (Nov. 1983): 26.

A review of a workshop and concert sponsored by Radio Bremen, and featuring
both string quartets, the *Horn Trio*, and *Artikulation*. "Das Bremer Podium mit
György Ligeti dürfte alle Erwartungen erfühllt, wenn nicht übertroffen haben, was
auch der frenetische, mit Bravo-Rufen gespickte Beifall erkennen ließ." ["The
Bremen Podium with György Ligeti may have fulfilled all expectations if not
exceeded them, as indicated by the frenetic applause garnished with cries of
'Bravo'."] *See*: W19, W42, W59, W25, App. II, p. 172.

B350.   Elder, Dean. "Recent Records." *Clavier* 20, no. 3 (1981): p. 10.

A review of Deutsche Grammophon DG-2531-102 (*Monument-Selbstportrait-
Bewegung*). "Although way-out in their originality and alienation from mass-
media music, I found them enjoyable and effective for recital." *See*: W52, D45.

B351.   Emmerson, Simon. "Xenakis, Ligeti and Stockhausen." *Music and
Musicians* 26 (Oct. 1977): 48-49.

A review of a London Musical Digest program devoted to Ligeti, including both
string quartets (the Arditti Quartet), both wind quintets (the Stockholm
Philharmonic Wind Quintet), and the British première of *Monument-
Selbstportrait-Bewegung* (Canino and Ballista). "[The Ten Pieces and the
Second Quartet] represent Ligeti's most refined and succinct utterances." *See*:
W19c, W42b, W15c, W43b, W52b, App. II, p. 170.

B352.   Endler, Franz. "Der Tod kann auch in Grabgewölbe sehr süß sein:
György Ligetis Oper *Le Grand Macabre* in Stockholm erfolgreich
uraufgeführt." *Die Presse*, April 14, 1978.

A review. "Wo mir ein Widerspruch zwischen den Intentionen Ligetis und der
Aufführung deutlich wird, da setzt die Hoffnung ein, daß es bei der für den
Herbst angesetzen Hamburger Erstaufführung noch besser gehen wird. Weder
die Szene noch die Aktionen sind so komisch und streng, wie Ligeti sich das
gewünsch hat. Die Farben sind blaß, die Personen keine Karikaturen. Es
scheint, man wollte in Stockholm zuletzt das Deftige in Breughel-Land
verstecken und hat dabei einige erschütternde Szenen verwässert, um ihre
Wirkung gebracht. Immerhin Jubel in Stockholm. Wenn man will: für einen
österreichischen Komponisten. Für ein Werk, das zu allen anderen Vorteilen
auch den hat, daß man es eigentlich an vielen Opernhäusern aufführen könnte,
weil es keine überdimensionale Besetzung verlangt. Ich hoffe, und das ist ein
Gefühl, das ich selten nach einer Uraufführung in den letzten Jahren hatte, *Le
Grand Macabre* bald wieder zu hören." ["Where I saw a conflict between Ligeti's
intentions and the performance, there is hope that the Hamburg production,

scheduled for the fall will go even better. Neither the scenery nor the actions are as comical and austere as Ligeti wished. The colors are pale, the people are not caricatures. It seems that in Stockholm they wanted to conceal the solidity of Breughel-Land and thus watered down the effect of some deeply moving scenes. Nonetheless, there is rejoicing in Stockholm. For an Austrian composer, if you will. For a work which, apart from all its other strengths, can be performed in many opera houses because it does not demand an oversized cast. I hope (and this is a feeling I have seldom had after recent premières) to hear *Le Grand Macabre* again soon."] *See*: W54a.

B353.   Ericson, Raymond. "Accent on Music of 20th Century." *New York Times*, Feb. 2, 1972, p. 32.

A review of a Speculum Musicae performance featuring the *Chamber Concerto*. "It is characteristic in style, setting up its own sound-scape, its twitterings so delicate at times as to become insubstantial. But there were surprising strengths this time, the sudden flare of a melodic phrase across muted sounds...." *See*: W46.

B354.   Erni, Jürg. "György Ligetis *Grand Macabre* in Hamburg: Absurdes Theater meisterlich komponiert." *Basler Zeitung*, Oct. 31, 1978.

A review. "... vermutlich nach Alban Bergs Opern bedeutendsten Musik-Theaters...." ["... probably [the] most significant music theater since Alban Berg's operas...."] *See*: W54b.

B355.   Evarts, J. "Donaueschingen." *World Music*, 10, no. 2 (1968): 41-42.

A review of the 1968 festival featuring the première of *Lontano*, performed by the Southwest German Radio Orchestra, Ernest Bour, conductor. "One felt ... as if one had been contemplating a glowing lamp which changed in intensity and colour and finally was extinguished." *See*: W39a.

B356.   Fabian, Imre. "Die Oper lebt: György Ligetis *Le Grand Macabre* in Stockholm uraufgeführt." *Opernwelt* 19, no. 6 (1978): 27-28.

Slightly differing versions of this review appeared in *Stuttgarter Zeitung*, April 19, 1978, under the title "Sensenmann und Don Quichotte", *Der Tagesspiegel*, April 22, 1978, and *Österreichische Musikzeitschrift* 33 (1978): 314-17. "Die spontane Zustimmung des dem Neuen gegenüber ohnehin sehr aufgeschlossenen schwedischen Publikums galt einem Werk, das sich bewußt zur Gattung Oper bekennt und ihre Möglichkeiten neu überdenkt." ["The spontaneous approval of the Swedish public (who are anyway quite open to anything new) was directed toward a work which acknowledges its awareness of the operatic genre, and reconsiders its possibilities."] *See*: W54a.

B357.   -------. "Die poetische Deutung einer makabren Parabel: Gilbert Deflo inszenierte die deutsche Erstaufführung von György Ligetis *Grand Macabre*." *Opernwelt* 19, no. 11 (1978): 29-30.

A review of the Hamburg production. "Sie ist eine echte, interessante Alternative zur Stockholmer Deutung, eine poetische Variante von den vielen Interpretationsmöglichkeiten, die das vielschichtige, doppelbödige Werk erlaubt." ["It is an authentic, interesting alternative to the Stockholm interpretation, one poetic variant of the many interpretative possibilities which this many-layered, ambiguous work permits."] *See*: W54b.

B358.   -------. "Vom Untergang des Abendlandes: Madernas *Satyricon* und Ligetis *Aventures et Nouvelles Aventures* in Amsterdam." *Opernwelt* 14 (May 1973): 30-33.

A review of a staging by Ian Strasfogel. "Dieser Interpretation fehlte es an Prägnanz, Deutlichkeit und Präzision." ["This interpretation lacked meaning, clarity and precision."] *See*: W33, W34, W36.

B359.   Fernandez, Dominique. "Ligeti." *Nouvelle Revue Française* no. 298 (1977): 161-62.

A review of Wergo WER 60076. "musique pas du tout intellectuelle, qui agit sur l'organisme avec la sorcellerie d'une drogue." ["music not at all intellectual, that excites one's system with the enchantment of a drug."] *See*: D23, D30, D61, D79, D84.

B360.   Fiedler, Helmuth. "Große musikalische Präsente: SDR-Geburtstagskonzert für György Ligeti im Funkstudio Berg." *Stuttgarter Nachrichten*, May 20, 1983.

A review of a concert celebrating Ligeti's 60th birthday. Works included the *Horn Trio, Ramifications, Chamber Concerto*, and several pieces for chorus and for solo harpsichord. The composer provided commentary. "... ein dreistündiges Programm, das sich in Werkauswahl und Interpretation dem Jubilar als überaus würdig erwies." ["... a three hour program, which in selection of works and interpretation proved worthy of the celebration."] *See*: W59, W44, W46f, App. II, p. 171.

B361.   Flandern, Wolfgang von. "György Ligeti ..." *Neue Zeitschrift für Musik* 140 (1979): 418.

Record review of Wergo 60076. "Die vierte dem Werk Ligetis gewidmete Wergo-Platte macht mit Kompositionen bekannt, in denen sich die ästhetischen Normen absoluter Musik mit einem normsprengenden, experimentellen Impetus fruchtbar verbinden." ["The fourth of the Wergo discs dedicated to Ligeti's works is composed of well-known works in which the aesthetic norms of absolute music are fruitfully combined with a norm-breaking, experimental impetus."] *See*: D23, D27, D61, D79, D84.

B362.   Fleuret, Maurice. "Ligeti se déchaîne: Il est normal que les imbéciles fassent la fine bouche devant un tel déferlement l'inventions." *Le Nouvel Observateur*, April 6, 1981, p. 18.

A review of the Paris production of *Le Grand Macabre*. "Il y a des semaines, des mois qu'on nous promet le scandale. Mais, cette fois, le vrai, l'une presse ..." ["A scandal has been predicted for weeks and months, but this time the real and only scandal, the intolerable scandal is that of the press ..."] *See*: W54d.

B363.   -------. "Le pur théâtre du son." *Le Nouvel Observateur*, May 15, 1978.

The Stockholm production of *Le Grand Macabre* is reviewed here. *See*: W54a.

B364.   Foesel, Karl. "Die letzten beiden Kompositionsaufträge des Nürnberger Dürerjahres 1971." *Melos* 39 (1972): 47-48.

A review of *Melodien* premiered by the Nuremberg Philharmonic under the direction of Hans Gierster. "Der Eindruck auf das Publikum der Stadtischen Philharmonic Konzerte war echt und stark." ["The impression left on the audience was real and strong."] *See*: W47a.

B365.   Forbes, Elizabeth. "Hamburg." *Opera News* 43 (Jan. 13, 1979): 29.

A review of the Hamburg première of *Le Grand Macabre*. "... this text, with its Latin tags, nonsense rhymes, puns, repetitions and vulgarisms, still looked daunting; but heard in the theater, spoken, declaimed, intoned and sung, the words were transmuted and Ligeti's anti-anti-opera emerged triumphantly, as a genuinely dramatic work.... The performance received a mixed reception: singers and musicians whole-heartedly applauded, composer greeted with boos as well as cheers." *See*: W54b.

B366.   Frank, Peter. "Ligeti." *Fanfare*, May-June 1980, p. 96-98.

A review of Decca Headline HEAD 12. "David Atherton and the London Sinfonietta prove more than adequate to the task of unraveling Ligeti's music without unwinding his sounds, as does Decca's production." *See*: D11, D22, D44.

B367.   Frankenstein, Alfred. "San Francisco Sym.: Ligeti prem." *High Fidelity/Musical America* 25 (April 1975): MA32-33.

A review of the première of *San Francisco Polyphony* performed by Seiji Ozawa and the San Francisco Symphony. "You can never tell if a modern piece, especially one as difficult as the Ligeti, will ever be played a second time. But one would like to hear it again, and that is an important test." *See*: W51a.

B368.   -------. "Avantgarde music for conservatives (recording)." *High Fidelity/Musical America* 21 (May 1971): 68.

A review of Deutsche Grammophone 2530 092 (i.e. 2530 392). The author erroneously refers to the music as aleatory, and compares the Ligeti quartet with Berg's *Lyric Suite*. "The whole performance is carried off with a joy and delight in music-making, an infectious dynamism and thrust that are totally irresistible." *See*: D35, D75, D78, D95.

B369.   Fuhrmann, Peter. "*Le Grand Macabre* im Herbst in Hamburg: Peter Fuhrmann über die Uraufführung der Ligeti Oper in Stockholm." *Fono Forum* 23 (1978): 680-82.

A review. "... registriert man das ganze Stück hindurch die aphoristische Prägnanz kleiner, scharf konturierter formaler Entwicklungen, eine Art musikalischer Abkurzung, wie sie bislang bei Ligeti unbekannt war." ["... one perceives the whole work through the aphoristic terseness of small, sharply contoured formal developments; a kind of musical abbreviation hitherto unknown in Ligeti's work."] *See*: W54a.

B370.   -------. "Ein Schiffbruch im Zirkuszelt: Ligetis *Le Grand Macabre* in Hamburg." *Neue Musikzeitung* 27, no. 6 (1978): 5.

A review. "Krasser konnte der Kontrast zwischen den beiden ersten Inszenierungen ... nicht sein. Was sich in der schwedischen Hauptstadt ... durchaus als doppelbödig in Ernst und Humor, in zeitloser Trauer und Freude, aber ebenso in der Lust am Leben wie an der Vernichtung von Leben bewährt hatte, das machte in Hamburg der Regisseur Gilber Deflo mit einem fundamentalen Fehlgriff zunichte." ["The contrast between the first two productions ... couldn't be more striking. In the Swedish capital ... ambiguities between seriousness and humor, eternal sadness and joy, but likewise between a pleasure in life and the negation of life proved to be entirely effective. In Hamburg, director Gilbert Deflo destroyed this ambiguity through a fundamental error."] *See*: W54b.

B371.   -------. "Zwölf Autohupen spielen die Ouvertüre: György Ligetis Oper *Le Grand Macabre* wurde in Stockholm uraufgeführt." *Neue Musikzeitung* 27, no. 3 (June/July 1978): 23.

A review. "Die Vulgarismen, das wurde schon deutlich, fielen dem Protest der Sänger (und Zensoren?) zum Opfer. Ein gewinnbringender Abend war es dennoch und sicher auch ein Einschnitt in der Opernkomposition von heute, der optimistische Zukunftschancen einräumte." ["The vulgarities clearly fell sacrifice to the protests of the singers (and censors?) It was a profitable evening, however, and surely also a turning point composition which abandons optimistic outlooks."] *See*: W54a.

B372.   Galewski, Myron. "Ligeti." *American Record Guide*, Nov. 1983, p. 29-30.

A review of Deutsche Grammophon DG 2531 102 (*Monument-Selbstportrait-Bewegung*). "I urge listeners who are interested in contemporary music not to delay acquiring this record." *See*: W52, D45.

B373.   Gann, Kyle. "Ligeti." *Fanfare*, Nov.-Dec. 1986, p. 159.

This is a record review of Wergo WER 60100. "This recording contains some of his most audacious gimmicks ...." *See*: D21, D33, D46, D53, D91.

B374.   Gaska, Rolf. "Kiel: Modernes Quartettspiel in Vollendung." *Neue Zeitschrift für Musik* 133 (1972): 92-93.

A review of a performance by the LaSalle Quartet of *String Quartet No. 2*. "Was an Ligetis Stück so überaus fesselt, daß man es geradezu zum Jahrhundertwerk auf dem Gebiet des Streichquartetts erklären möchte, ist der zauberische Umgang mit der Klangfarbe. Ohne daß die Instrumente aus ihrem traditionellen Habitus gerissen werden ... sprechen sie eine neue Sprache." ["What is so exceedingly fascinating about Ligeti's piece (one might declare it the masterpiece of the century for string quartet) is the magical dealings with the tone color. Without being torn out of their traditional character ... the instruments speak a new language."] *See*: W42.

B375.   Geitel, Klaus. "Kein Pulver mehr für den Weltuntergang: György Ligetis Oper *Le Grand Macabre* in Stockholm uraufgeführt: ein Rüpelstück wurde zum musikalischen Comic-Strip." *Die Welt*, April 14, 1978.

The première of this work is reviewed. "Ligetis Unwille, ein durchkomponiertes Stück zu schreiben, seine Absicht, sich statt dessen auf die comic-artige Schichtung und Häufung von musikalisch starkfarbigen Bildern zu verlassen, führt immer wieder zu einem Versickern der Musik, ihrem verstummen, das dem gesprochenen Wort allein unangefochten die Szene überläßt." ["Ligeti's unwillingness to write a through-composed piece, his intention instead to rely on comic-like layering and heaping of musically colorful images, leads inevitably to a trickling away of the music; its silencing; yielding the stage to the spoken word without challenge."] *See*: W54a.

B376.   Gill, Dominic. "Lazarov, Ligeti." *Musical Times* 112 (March 1971): 259.

A performance by the London Sinfonietta of the *Chamber Concerto* was conducted by David Atherton. "... held the attention more firmly ... a virtuoso piece...." *See*: W46c.

B377.   -------. "Royal Opera, Stockholm: *Le Grand Macabre*." *Financial Times*, Wed. April 19, 1978, p. 19.

A review which also summarizes Ligeti's western career. "Elgar Howarth's scrupulous preparation was clearly a fine achievement, which drew playing and singing on the first night of remarkable accuracy, clarity and conviction. He was helped by a strong cast." *See*: W54a.

B378.   Gojowy, Detlef. "Mutwillig und ungarisch: Das Beste nun gebündelt: Die G.-Ligeti-Kassette." *Die Welt*, March 15, 1985.

A record review of Wergo WER 60095. *See*: D2, etc.

B379.   Goldsmith, H. "Los Angeles Symphony (Mehta)." *High Fidelity/Musical America* 21 (Feb. 1971): MA22-23.

A review of a series of concerts in Carnegie Hall including *Lontano*. "It's first vaporous tones were promising enough, but the score as a whole reminded me of a diver poised for three hours above the water without ever quite gaining courage to jump in." *See*: W39.

B380.   Goodwin, Noel. "London." *Opera News* 47, no. 11 (Feb. 12, 1983): 36.

Reviews the London première of *Le Grand Macabre*. "... strange amalgam of musical sensibility and dramatic absurdity by György Ligeti, who was heartily cheered and booed in about equal measure...." *See*: W54e.

B381.   Grabócz Márta. "A Kókler Halál: Ligeti Operájának Párizsi Bemutatója." *Muzsika* 24, no. 8 (Aug. 1981): 12-15.

The Paris production of *Le Grand Macabre* is the subject of this article. The author contrasts the brilliance and greatness of the work with the "incredible incompetence" of Daniel Mesguich's production. *See*: W54d.

B382.   Gradenwitz, Peter. "Nebenwege, die zum Ziel führen: Hundertstes Konzert der Reihe 'Das Neue Werk' in Hamburg." *Frankfurter Allgemeine Zeitung*, Oct. 19, 1966, p. 10.

A review of a concert that also included a lecture by Ligeti concerning his philosophy of composition.

B383.   Grebe, Karl. "Wenn stille Töne sich spalten." *Die Welt*, May 3, 1975, "Die Geistige Welt, p. iv.

A review of four recordings: Wergo 60045, 60059, SHZW 900, and Deutsche Grammophon 2530 392. "Manchmal ist in seinem Werk Tradition in enormer Distanz präsent zum Beispiel im Streichquartett II. Wie eine abgeworfene Schlangenhaut, die nicht mehr lebt, in die aber neues Leben hineinwächst." ["Sometimes tradition is present in his work at an enormous distance, for example in the second string quartet, like a sloughed off snake skin that is no longer alive, but in which new life grows."] *See:* D32, D35, D54, D55, D59, D75, D78, D95.

B384.   Greenfield, E. "At ENO, a Mafia Rigoletto." *High Fidelity/Musical America*. 33, no. 7 (July, 1983): MA40.

A review of the British première of *Le Grand Macabre*. "But musically it was a thin evening--almost entirely Ligeti's fault--not helped much by the brilliant direction of Elgar Howarth. *See:* W54e.

B385.   Griffiths, Paul. "English Bach festival." *Musical Times* 120 (1979)" 590.

A performance by Rohan de Saram of the *Sonata for Solo Violoncello* is reviewed. "... humour has been a fixed characteristic of Ligeti's music from the beginning." *See:* W17a.

B386.   -------. "Gaudeamus Quartet." *Musical Times* 115 (Jan. 1974): 57+.

A review of a performance of the *String Quartet No. 2*. "The sonic nebulas-- which have got Ligeti a one dimensional if not bad, name--are a lesser feature in works of this period (1969); there are more 'clocks' than 'clouds', to use his own dichotomy. The quartet gives some impression of what the clouds may have been hiding: an inching towards tonality that is apparent not just in the out-of- the-blue diatonic chords." *See:* W42.

B387.   -------. "Ligeti: Queen Elizabeth Hall." *Times*, May 9, 1977, p. 9, col. 3-4.

A review of a London Musical Digest concert featuring both string quartets, both wind quintets and the *Monument-Selbstportrait-Bewegung*. "Ligeti was well served last night by the Arditti String Quartet and the Stockholm Philharmonic Wind Quintet, with only occasional slips to upset those stiff gestures and intricately patterned surfaces." *See:* W15c, W19c, W42b, W43b, W52b, App. II, p. 170.

B388.   -------. "Ligeti, Rands, Salzman." *Musical Times* 113 (1972): 279.

A review of a performance of *Ramifications* by the BBC Symphony with Pierre Boulez. "The musical interest is so widely spaced that the second hearing suffered from the reduction in impact, without any gains in terms of new discoveries for the listener." *See:* W44.

B389.   -------. "Ligeti *String Quartet No. 2, Lux aeterna, Volumina, Etude No. 1.*" *Musical Times* 124 (1983): 553.

A record review of Deutsche Grammophon DG 2543 818. "... it could prove useful to educational institutions wanting a sample of Ligeti's work in the 1960s." *See:* W42, W37, W31, W40, D38, D75, D78, D95.

B390.   -------. "New Music." *Musical Times* 115 (1974): 586-87.

Reports a concert of Ligeti's works, with a brief lecture by the composer. The performance consisted of *Melodien*, the *Double Concerto*, *Clocks and Clouds* (London Symphony Orchestra, Elgar Howarth), and *Ten Pieces for Wind Quintet* (Barry Tuckwell Wind Quintet). "The whole concert should have helped to establish that Ligeti, though very much a meticulous specialist, has more in him than an atmospheric film score suggested." *See:* W47, W48, W50c, W43, App. II, p. 170.

B391.   -------. "New Music." *Musical Times* 118 (1977): 575.

A review of an English Bach Festival concert. "If Pousseur finds beauty in untested harmony, Ligeti can make such commonplace things as octaves seem new and wondrous."

B392.   Gualerzi, Giorgio. "Pornopera." *Opera* 30 (1979): 796-98.

The Italian première of *Le Grand Macabre* in Bologna is reviewed. "The fact is that the imaginative spectacle made more impact than Ligeti's music.... In my opinion ... [the music] only rarely rose above the level of accompaniment to the stage action and was scarcely worth listening to, unless we mention the two preludes...." *See*: W54c.

B393.   Gürtelschmied, W. "Ligeti-Abend: Musterprozeß." *Kurier* (Vienna), Dec. 5, 1981.

This concert consisted of the *String Quartet No. 2* (Arditti Quartet), *Melodien* and the *Chamber Concerto* (die Reihe Ensemble, Friedrich Cerha). Ligeti also spoke. "Zwar entschuldigte er sich, wenn er glaubte, im Kabarett-Jargon zu sprechen, doch selten noch waren Komponisten-Worte so überschwenglich und dennoch treffend." ["He apologized when he imagined he was speaking in cabaret jargon, but seldom have composers' words been so exuberant and yet so to the point."] *See*: W42, W47, W46e, App. II, p. 171.

B394.   Gutscher, Manfred. "Uraufführungen neuer Kirchenmusik." *Musik und Kirche* 37, no. 1 (1967): 42-43.

Reports the première of *Lux aeterna*. "... hatte das Werk eine ganz unmittelbare und starke Wirkung beim Publikum." ["... the work had a very direct and powerful effect on the audience."] *See*: W37a.

B395.   "György Ligeti: *Le Grand Macabre* -- Deutsche Erstaufführung in der Hamburger Staatsoper." *Neue Zeitschrift für Musik* 140 (1979): 43-45.

Consists of extensive quotes from reviews of this performance, including this from Joachim Kaiser in the *Süddeutschen Zeitung*: "Wenn man nämlich die Augen schloß, wenn man absah, wegsah von den Zirkus-Blödsinnigkeiten, welche die Musik zur bloßen Untermalung degradierten, dann erklang eine momentweise sehr brillante, anspielungsreiche, in ihren besten Augenblicken wunderbar traurig ausgehörte Partitur! Aber wer geht zum Wegsehen und Handlungsverweigern in die Oper?" ["If one closed one's eyes, if one overlooked the circus-like idiocy which reduced the music to bland background, then one heard a very brilliant score, rich in allusions and in its best moments, wonderfully sad. But who goes to the opera to ignore the staging?"] *See*: W54b.

B396.   "György Ligeti, *Le Grand Macabre*, Italienische Erstaufführung am Teatro Communale, Bologna." *Melos/Neue Zeitschrift für Musik* 140 (1979): 378-79.

Translated from the Italian by Ingrid Hermann. A collection of excerpts from reviews of this performance. "Kontrastierender Beifall am Ende. Während der Aufführung größte Aufmerksamkeit mit kurzen schlüpfrigen Einwürfen, mehr im Geiste heiterer Kooperation als Feindseligkeit." ["Contrasting acclaim at the end. During the performance great attentiveness with brief objections, more in the spirit of cheerful cooperation than malevolence."] *See*: W54c.

B397.   Hähnel, Folke. "Virtuosens Återkomst." *Dagens Nyheter*, June 29, 1960.

A review of the 1960 International Society for Contemporary Music festival in Cologne, which included the première of *Apparitions*. *See*: W26a.

B398.   Halasz, Gabor. "Avantgarde-Opernwunder in der Provinz: Ligetis bisher einzige Oper *Le Grand Macabre*, inszeniert vom Frankfurter Operndirektor Christof Bitter." *Frankfurter Rundschau*, May 15, 1979.

A review of the Saarbrücken production. "Es begann wie ein handfester Opernskandal: Die Autohupen-Ouvertüre mit ihren schrillen, ordinären, aggressiven Klängen und irritierenden bizarren rhythmischen Modellen löste sofort heftigen Protest aus; Pfiffe und Zwischenrufe wie 'aufhören!' und 'Katzenmusik!' beschworen die Atmosphäre einer Premierenschlacht herauf. Auf es ging nur um den Überraschungseffekt dieses (übrigens ausgesprochen aparten) Ouvertürengags, der die Gemüter im Saarländischen Staatstheater erregte; der Sturm legte sich sehr schnell, und zum Schluß gab es sogar enthusiastische Ovationen für alle Beteiligten." ["It started out as a real opera scandal: the car horn overture with its shrill, vulgar, aggressive sounds and irritatingly bizarre rhythmic patterns gave immediate rise to loud protests. Whistles and heckling such as 'Stop!' and 'Caterwauling!' created the atmosphere of an opening night battle. But it lasted only during the surprise effect of the (decidedly unusual, after all) gag-overture, which aroused tempers in the Saarland State Theater. The storm died down very quickly and at the end there was even enthusiastic applause for all the participants."] A rewritten and somewhat expanded version of this review appeared in *Oper und Konzert* 17, no. 7 (1979): 23-24. *See*: W54f.

B399.   Halbreich, Harry. "Ligeti's *Melodien*." *Music and Musicians* 21 (Oct. 1972): 66, 68.

A review of a performance by the Concertgebouw Orchestra under Michael Gielen. "Ligeti--being present and rapturously acclaimed --was so overwhelmed by the performance of his work that he considered this to be its actual premiere, the Nuremberg Orchestra having been unable to cope with its great difficulties last year." *See*: W47d.

B400.   "Hamburg." *Oper und Konzert* 16, no. 11 (1978): 11-12.

The first German performance of *Le Grand Macabre* occasioned this harsh vilification of the work. "Was scheinbar als geschmackloses, fades und humorloses Stück gewirkt hatte, ist bei näherem Nachspüren in Wirklichkeit ein inhumanes, widerwärtig blasphemisches, indoktrinierendes und zerstörerisches Machwerk, verderbt, abgefeimt und pervers." ["What appeared as a tasteless, insipid and humorless piece is on closer inspection in reality an inhumane, repulsively blasphemous, indoctrinating and devastating concoction, depraved, insidious and perverse."] *See*: W54b.

B401.   Hamilton, David. "Ligeti." *High Fidelity/Musical America* 20 (Sept. 1970): 94.

Reprinted in *Records in Review, 1971 Edition*, 202-3. Great Barrington, Mass.: Wyeth Press, 1971. Heliodor 2549 003 and 2549 011 are reviewed. "... the works on the first disc ... are all duplication.... There is certainly a lot of skillful and knowledgeable writing ... but the substance of this Requiem seems to be all on its very slick surface.... If Miss Vischer can really play [Continuum] through like this without benefit of splices, she deserves some sort of prize for endurance and steadiness." *See*: W35, W41, D4, D7, D17, D35, D59.

B402.   -------. *"Aventures: Nouvelles Aventures; Volumina; Etude No. 1
'Harmonies'."* In *Records in Review, 1971 Edition*, 201-2. Great
Barrington, Mass.: Wyeth Press, 1971.

A record review of Candide CE 31009. "... intriguing and often entertaining in a
very theatrical way. The performances ... are quite good and noticeably more
accurate than those on Wergo 60022." *See*: W31, W33, W34, W40, D6, D78,
D98.

B403.   -------. "Helmut Franz: 'Modern Choral Music'," In *Records in
Review, 1970 Edition*, 478-79. New York: Scribners, 1970.

A review of Deutsche Grammophon 137004 (*Lux aeterna*). "None of the groups
has sopranos who can enter imperceptibly on a high B, but the Stuttgart group
is most successful at maintaining an essentially unarticulated continuum. The
new Hamburg disc is not far behind." *See*: W37, D38.

B404.   -------. "Music." *Nation* 209 (1969): 549.

Atmosphères was performed by the New York Philharmonic under Seiji Ozawa.
Nothing is mentioned of the performance however. "In short, *Atmosphères* is an
example of a very limited music, the single minded exploration of a particular
musical device.... The composer deserves considerable credit for his sonorous
inventiveness, but one cannot imagine that the work will retain much interest
when these ideas have become commonplace, and especially when they have
found their way into pieces with a higher level of organization." *See*: W27c.

B405.   Hargrove, Charles. "Quiet Night at the Opéra." *Times*, March 24,
1981, p. 5.

A report of an incident at the opening of *Le Grand Macabre* at the Paris Opera,
in which the composer stood and demanded that a defective loudspeaker be
shut off. "The audience, unaware of the interrupter's identity, told him to shut
up. The confusion increased until M. Ligeti at the height of exasperation left in a
huff." *See*: W54d.

B406.   Harrison, Jay S. "The New York Music Scene." *Musical America* 84
(Feb. 1964): 22.

The New York Philharmonic performed *Atmosphères* under Leonard Bernstein.
"... a work that, out of the depths of its lethargy is a strangely moving piece."
See: W27b.

B407.   Heckman, Donald and Arthur Cohn. "Two Views of the 'Avant-
garde' Repertoire at Philharmonic Hall." *American Record Guide*
32 (1965): 354-56.

Two reviews in one of Columbia ML-6133/MS-6733. "Ligeti, I would say, has
understood how to dress his ideas without considering any inherited method,
and he has produced a piece that is new.... And it jars the listener with its cold-
sweated message." *See*: D3.

B408.   Heikinheimo, Seppo. "The Grand Macabre." *Music Journal* 36 (July
1978): 22+.

A review of the première of the opera in Stockholm. "... the whole opera teems
with musical fantasy, probably without its like in the modern repertoire.... To
characterize the variety of the musical styles ... in a few words would be
hopeless; let it suffice to say that perhaps the only contemporary idioms which

Ligeti does not use are firstly the cheap quotations technique and secondly the
dry thematic texture of Hindemith & Sons." See: W54a.

B409.   Heindrichs, Heinz-Albert. "'Urbs 71'--das Festival zwischen Rhein
und Ruhr." Melos 38 (1971): 422.

This festival including a performance of the Chamber Concerto by the
Continuum Ensemble of Dortmund directed by Werner Seiss. See: W46.

B410.   Helm, Everett. "All Out for Aleatory." New York Times, Nov. 5, 1961,
sec. 2, p. 11.

The 1961 Donaueschingen Festival of Contemporary Music featured the world
première of Atmosphères. "Practically nothing happens in the course of its nine
minutes except that one titillating sound gives way to another in a completely
static ambient." See: W27a.

B411.   -------. "Anniversary Year." Musical America 81 (Dec. 1961): 23.

This is another review of the 1961 Donaueschingen Music Festival featuring the
première of Atmosphères. "It seems clear that the most warmly-applauded
piece of the Festival (repeated by clamorous request) ... will not occupy an
important place in musical history." See: W27a.

B412.   -------. "Donaueschingen." Musical Times 102 (1961): 779.

Yet a third review of the première of Atmosphères. "Although Ligeti's music
makes no demands on the intellect, it does establish very definite moods and
stimulates direct kinetic responses." See: W27a.

B413.   -------. "I.S.C.M. Festival in Cologne." Music Review 21 (1960): 242-
43.

Reprinted from the New York Times, July 10, 1960, sec. 2, p. 9. A report on the
1960 festival which included the première of Apparitions. "Listening to György
Ligeti's Apparitions for orchestra was a little like watching the last house on the
planet Earth burn down." See: W26a.

B414.   Henahan, Donal. "2001--Ligeti Sued." New York Times, May 17,
1970, p. D25, D29.

A record review of Deutsche Grammophon (Heliodor) 2549-011 and 2549-003.
"[Ligeti] does indeed sound here like a Star Child who may discover the past
while rushing into the nebulous future." See: D4, D7, D17, D35, D59, D94.

B415.   -------. "Chamber: Ligeti Works." New York Times, April 15, 1980, p.
C8.

A review of a performance of the Six Bagatelles for Wind Quintet played by the
Chamber Music Society of Lincoln Center. "Ligeti is fairly certain to be
mentioned in history as a pathbreaker of the 1960's, but one would not like to
bet that any of his avant-garde works have a better chance of survival than these
little games for wind quintet." See: W15.

B416.   -------. "Concert: Dorian Quintet." *New York Times*, April 6, 1974, p. 17.

This concert included *Ten Pieces for Wind Quintet*. "A terse and often witty catalogue of woodwind effects, showed the Dorian virtuosos at their breathtaking best." *See:* W43.

B417.   -------. "Ligeti in 'Horizons' Opening." *New York Times*, May 22, 1986, p. C28.

This concert featured *Aventures et Nouvelles Aventures* ("The result on this occasion was that rarity in contemporary music, a fondly remembered work that in revival did not disappoint.") and *Scenes and Interludes from Le Grand Macabre* ("There were perhaps four or five minutes of evocative music, though nothing one would demand to hear again.") *See:* W33e, W34d, W36g, W55d, App. II, p. 173.

B418.   Herbort, Heinz Josef. "Antiszenische Abenteuer: György Ligetis *Nouvelles Aventures* in Hamburg uraufgeführt." *Stuttgarter Zeitung*, June 1, 1966.

The première is reviewed. "Und hier zeigt sich die ingeniös Phantasiekraft des autors." ["And here the ingenious imaginative power of the author shows itself."] *See:* W34a.

B419.   -------. "Falsche Verkehrtheit: Oper in Hamburg: Ligetis *Le Grand Macabre*. *Die Zeit*, Oct. 20, 1978, p. 56.

A look at the opera's second performance. "Gilbert Deflo setzt diese dauernd kippende surrealistisch-existentielle Welt um in eine ziemlich eindeutige Gauklerkomödie: die Dompteuse als Hausdrachen voll unbefriedigter erotischer wie sado-masochistischer Gelüste; das Harlekinduo als Ministerpaar, das sich zum Kasperletheater ebenso(wenig) eignet wie zur Politfarce; der Tod als der Zelebrans einer schwarzen Messe, gefolgt von einer Ministrantenschar der Clowns; und selbst die Geheimpolizei kann in Harmlosigkeit getaucht werden, als gälte es, eine Revue, eine Disco-Show oder eine Maskerade zu bestükken [sic]. Das hat allen Anspielungen (außer den obszönen) aus dem Wege, verliert sich in billigen Klamauk und erspart uns keine Peinlichkeit. Hier ist sogar die Verkehrtheit falsch." ["Gilbert Deflo transforms this permanently off-balance surrealistic-existential world into a rather unmistakable clown show: the animal trainer is an insatiable sado-masochistic shrew; two harlequins are ministers just as (un)suitable for a Punch and Judy show as for a political farce; Death is the celebrant of a black mass, followed by a troop of clown-acolytes; and even the secret police can be harmlessly dunked, as would befit the armament of a revue, a disco show or a masquerade. Nothing remains of Ligeti's ambiguities. All allusions are pushed aside (except the obscenities), are lost in cheap noise, and we are spared no embarrassment. Here even the absurdity is artificial."] *See:* W54b.

B420.   -------. "Wer hat Angst vor dem Operntod? Eine Uraufführung, auf die dreizehn Jahre gewartet werden mußte." *Die Zeit* no. 17 (April 21, 1978), p. 48.

A review of the Stockholm première of *Le Grand Macabre*, which also includes a brief survey of Ligeti's career and musical style. "Ein Stück also, das wie in kurz geschnittenen Filmstreifen funktioniert--springend, aber doch mit Zusammenhalt." ["A work, therefore, which functions as in short film strips--jumping, but yet with coherence."] *See:* W54a.

B421. Hiemenz, Jack. "Juilliard: Rochberg, Ligeti." *High Fidelity/Musical America* 25 (March 1975): MA28.

A review of the U.S. première of the *Double Concerto* performed by flutist Nadine Asin, oboist George Paradise, Julliard student players directed by Richard Dufallo. "Even in this student performance its craftsmanship was impressive...." *See*: W48.

B422. Hinke, Roman. "Wirklichkeit als Hypothese: Das Komponistenporträt György Ligeti." *Der Tagesspiegel*, Sept. 28, 1988.

A review of a series of four concerts devoted to Ligeti's works. These concerts took place during the 1988 Berliner Festwochen. "... wurde in durchweg hochrangigen Interpretationen an einem Ligeti-Puzzle gearbeitet, das der faszinierenden Aura des 'denkenden Musikmachers' zur Ehre gereichte." ["... uniformly first-rate interpretations worked on a 'Ligeti puzzle' that did credit to the fascinating aura of the 'thinking musician."] *See*: App. II, p. 174.

B423. Hitchcock, H. Wiley. "New York." *Musical Quarterly* 51 (1965): 537-38.

A performance of *Poème symphonique* was conducted by Lukas Foss. "If it began by being [funny] it ended as an oddly engaging if quirky experience. One suddenly realized that in contrast to a tendency in listening to the conventional symphony orchestra to dehumanize the performers, in the face of Ligeti's metronomes one humanized the instruments." *See*: W32c.

B424. Hohlweg, Rudolf. "Henzes Medusa -- Ligetis Requiem." *Süddeutsche Zeitung*, Nov. 18, 1969.

A record review of Wergo 60045 (*Requiem*) *See*: D59.

B425. -------. "In Avignon wimmelt es von Jugend." *Melos* 37 (1970): 420.

A review of a performance of *Aventures et Nouvelles Aventures* by Gertie Charlent, Marie-Thérèse Cahn and William Pearson under the direction of Diego Masson. "... psychologische Einengung, Rückzug auf Oper mit stammelnden, stimmlosen, ja stummen Sängern, Verlust der einschüchternden Sade-Genet-Dimension. Munterkeit statt Schrecken. Donizetti in der Taubstummen-Anstalt." ["... psychological confinement, a retreat to opera with stammering and voiceless singers, a loss of the intimidated Sade-Genet dimension. Liveliness instead of terror. Donizetti in the deaf-and-mute asylum."] *See*: W33, W34, W36.

B426. -------. "Mikrobenklänge: Ligetis neues Orchesterstück beim Holland-Festival." *Süddeutsche Zeitung*, June 27, 1975.

The first European performance of *San Francisco Polyphony*, by the Dutch Radio Philharmonic Orchestra under Hans Zender. "Die Aufführung des ... Meisterwerks ... ließ spüren, wie hoch Ligeti die Forderungen an die Musiker gestellt hat." ["The performance of the ... masterpiece ... gave a sense of what great demands Ligeti makes on the musicians."] *See*: W51.

B427. Hommel, Friedrich. "Ligeti-Uraufführung in Köln: Selbstporträt." *Orchester* 25, no. 1 (1977): 36.

A review of the first performance of *Monument-Selbstporträt-Bewegung*. The review is based on an article which appeared in *Frankfurter Allgemeine Zeitung*, June 9, 1976, p. 27. "Die rein physischen, manuell-technischen Anforderungen sind enorm und sicher auch als bewußte Herausforderung der in Sachen neuester Musik ja ohnehin hochtrainierten Kontarskys gedacht." ["The purely physical, technical requirements are enormous, and surely also meant as a conscious challenge to the Kontarskys who are highly trained in new music."] *See:* W52a.

B428.   Honolka, Kurt. "Anti-Opern von Ligeti und Killmayer." *Musica* 21 (1967): 15-16.

A staged performance of *Aventures et Nouvelles Aventures* took place in Stuttgart. An English summary appeared in: *Opera* 18 (Jan. 1967): 62. "Mit ungeheurem Aufwand an Nuancen wird produziert, was elektronische Tonerzeugung einfacher bewirkt. Den Interpreten ... werden schier unlösbar Artikulationsaufgaben gestellt." ["Effects are produced at enormous expense, which could be achieved more easily by electronic means. The interpreters ... are faced with nearly unsolvable tasks of articulation."] *See:* W33b, W34b, W36b.

B429.   -------. "Eine Story müsste geschehen--Ligeti Uraufführung in Stuttgart." *Opernwelt* 18, no. 4 (1977): 42-43.

This article is based on: "Inspirationen auf dem Lokus: Wolfgang Höper in einem musik-losen Stück des Ungarn." *Stuttgarter Nachrichten*, Feb. 28, 1977. A review of the première of *Rondeau.* "Daß die 23 Minuten nicht als Theaterewigkeit, sondern manchmal als Kurzweiligkeit empfunden wurden, ist sicher mehr das Verdienst des exzellenten, im schnoddrigen Unterspielen werknahen dennoch augenblinzelnde Komödiantik nicht versagenden Mimen Wolfgang Höper." ["That the 23 minutes did not seem an eternity, but were at times even entertaining is surely more to the credit of the excellent mime Wolfgang Höper, who underplayed insolently, yet did not spurn tongue-in-cheek buffoonery."] *See:* W53a.

B430.   -------. "Ligetis *Aventures*, jüngste Version: experimentelles Musiktheater in der Stuttgarter Staatsoper." *Opernwelt* 13 (Dec. 1972): 22.

A staged performance which took place on Oct. 26, 1972 was produced by Ernst Poettgen, with soloists Gertie Charlent and Elke Estlinbaum, conducted by Bernard Kontarsky. The baritone soloist is not named. Part of the review appeared in English in "Stuttgart." *Opera* 24 (1973): 30-31. "Die vom Komponisten mit penibelster Präzision notierte Umsetzung von Emotionen wird zugunsten szenischer Strukturen eingeebnet." ["The shifting emotions, notated with such meticulous precision by the composer, were evened out in favor of scenic structures."] *See:* W33, W34, W36f.

B431.   Hopkins, G.W. "Record Guide." *Tempo* no. 93 (Summer 1970): 31-32.

A substantial review of two discs: Heliodor Wergo 2548003, and Heliodor Wergo 2549011. "Ligeti knows how to play on the very nerve of aural fascination without any reference to extra-acoustical associations." *See:* D4, D7, D17, D35, D59, D94.

B432.   Hughes, Allen. "Music: Boulez Lecture." *New York Times*, May 5, 1974, p. 75, col. 4-5.

Pierre Boulez lectured at a New York Philharmonic concert. He said that Ligeti's music reminded him of "insects in the south of France at noon."

B433.   Hume, Paul. "Rewarding Youth Concert." *Washington Post*, July 18, 1972, sec. B, p. 7, col. 1-3.

A review of a performance of *Atmosphères* by the Wolf Trap Academy Orchestra under Maurice Peress. "Peress is as good at helping an audience with a piece of new music as he is at getting a youthful orchestra way inside it." *See*: W27.

B434.   Hyatt, Willard. "Los Angeles." *Music Journal* 30 (June 1972): 41.

The American première of *Melodien* by the Los Angeles Philharmonic under Zubin Mehta. "... form and structure in the work seem to be missing." *See*: W47c.

B435.   Jack, Adrian. "Avantgarde." *Music and Musicians* 23 (Oct. 1974): 58-59.

This concert featured the Barry Tuckwell Wind Quintet playing *Ten Pieces for Wind Quintet*, and the London Sinfonietta playing *Clocks and Clouds*. Ligeti was present and spoke prior to the performance. "The concert confirmed that his music has a far narrower range than he himself would claim, a fact allied in his case to meticulous concern with craftsmanship, and to the widespread respect and confidence this inspires in the musical public." *See*: W43, W50c, App. II, p. 170.

B436.   --------. "Boulez proms." *Music and Musicians* 22 (Oct. 1973): 63-64.

A review of the *Chamber Concerto* performed by the London Sinfonietta under Elgar Howarth. "Its deft calculation is perhaps too evident to draw the listener beyond amused curiosity and complacent admiration. Its four movements are like demonstrations in the virtuosic craft of building up textures and motions." *See*: W46.

B437.   Jöckle, Rudolf. "Um Mitternacht soll die Welt untergehen: Ligetis *Grand Macabre* ermuntert das Musiktheater: Deutsche Erstaufführung in Hamburg." *Frankfurter Neue Presse*, Oct. 17, 1978.

The Hamburg performance of the opera is described. "Faszinierend war das musikalische Niveau dieser Erstaufführung. Die Leitung hatte -- wie in Stockholm -- der Engländer Elgar Howarth, der die ganze Vielfältigkeit der Partitur zusammen mit dem Philharmonischen Staatsorchester prägnant und mit mitreißendem Schwung verdeutlichte.... Viel Beifall, der sich durch heftige Buhs gegen Ligeti immer wieder steigerte." ['The musical level of this performance was fascinating. It was conducted, as in Stockholm, by the Englishman Elgar Howarth, who, together with the Philharmonic State Orchestra elucidated the very diverse score precisely and with thrilling energy.... Much applause, which was augmented by vigorous boos directed at Ligeti."] *See*: W54b.

B438.   --------. "Das komische Ende einer Welt, György Ligetis lang erwartete Oper *Le Grand Macabre* in Stockholm." *Musica* 32 (1978): 348-49.

A review based on similar ones which appeared in *Badische Zeitung*, April 15, 1978, and *HiFi Stereophonie* 17 (1978): 694-95. "Das musikalische Füllhorn erschöpft sich in den beiden langen akten (rund 135 Minuten Musik) nicht. Derbe, ordinäre, schrill-drastische Töne werden angeschlagen, wie man sie Ligeti kaum zugetraut hätte.... Ligetis Opernfiguren sind Marionetten einer von den Dogmen des absurden Theaters vampiristisch ausgesogenen Phantasie. In die dergestalt leblosen Hüllen wird autonome Musik hineingepumpt: So bekommen die Figuren das zweite Leben bizarrer Monster. Eine komplette Frankenstein-

Operation ist damit gelungen.... Oper, als Kunst-Stück wieder einmal gerettet. Bedarf es solcher Rettungen?" ["The musical cornucopia does not exhaust itself in the two long acts (about 135 minutes of music). One would scarcely think Ligeti capable of such coarse, vulgar, drastically shrill sounds.... Ligeti's opera characters are marionettes in a fantasy whose blood has been sucked as if by a vampire, by the dogmas of absurd theater. Into the resulting lifeless shells, independent music is pumped. The characters thus receive the second life of bizarre monsters, and a complete Frankenstein operation is completed.... Opera-as-art has once again been rescued. Does it need such a rescue?"] *See*: W54a.

B439.   Kaiser, Joachim. *"Le Grand Macabre*--am Libretto gestorben Ligetis Oper in Hamburg." *Musica* 33 (1979): 50-52.

This review was reprinted from "Der große Makabre geht im Zirkus unter." *Süddeutsche Zeitung*, Oct. 17, 1978. "Man sieht Zirkusvolk und lacht nicht über dessen Aktionen (das Publikum saß bleiern die vier Akte ab, danach bejubelte es die Ausführenden), sondern man grinst höchst belustigt darüber, daß solch ein Unfug komisch sein soll." ["One sees circus people, and one does not laugh at their actions (the audience sat leaden through the four acts, then afterward applauded the performers), but rather one grins, greatly amused that such shenanigans should be thought funny."] *See*: W54b.

B440.   -------. "Rondeau ohne tiefere Bedeutung." *Süddeutscher Zeitung*, March 2, 1977.

The première of *Rondeau* is reviewed. "Ein winziger Spaß.... Sie demonstrierten, daß der 53jährige nach wie vor zu den kühnen und originellen Köpfen des modernen Musiktheaters gehört." ["A tiny joke.... It demonstrated that the 53-year-old still as before is one of the bold and original minds in modern musical theater."] *See*: W53a.

B441.   -------. "Sinnfälligkeit und Oratorium: Ligeti, Weeks und Holloway im 1. musica-viva-Konzert." *Süddeutsche Zeitung*, Dec. 5, 1983, p. 28.

A review of the performance of *Scenes and Interludes From Le Grand Macabre*, at the Munich Musica Viva festival. *See*: W55c.

B442.   -------. "Verwirrung unter Fachleuten: Ligeti in Stuttgart--Festtage in Donaueschingen." *Der Monat* 18, no. 219 (Dec. 1966): 49-54.

A review of the Stuttgart staging of *Aventures et Nouvelles Aventures* is included in a discussion of the role that specialists play in the fine arts. The review section is a revised version of "Opern-Affekte ohne Opern-Vorwand." *Süddeutsche Zeitung*. Oct. 21, 1966, p. 26. "Als ... an die durchaus bunte und brillante Realisation gingen, merkte man bald, wieviel da unmöglich ist.... So .. liegt ein höchst präzis vorgegebenes Ausdrucksschema und ein doch noch zu vages Bild-Assoziationsschema vor. Auf der Opernbühne kann das noch nicht konvergieren." ["As [the performers] tackled this thoroughly colorful and brilliant realization, the impossibilities were immediately noticeable.... So we have a pretext of a highly precise system of expression and yet an all too vague system of image-association. These cannot converge on the operatic stage."] *See*: W33b, W34b, W36b.

B443.   Karallus, Manfred. "Schallplatte des Monats." *Neue Zeitschrift für Musik* 144, no. 10 (1983): 38.

A record review of Caprice CAP 1209. "... die Entwicklung von Ligetis Schaffen seit jenen Jahren sichtbar werden läßt: von den diskret ineinander-schießenden Mikropolyphonien der Werke der sechziger Jahre, von *Atmosphères* bis

Ramifications etwa, zum aufgebrochenen und geweiteten, mitunter sogar wieder entfernt tonalen Idiom der Siebziger." ["... the development of Ligeti's work since those years is seen: from the discrete, flowing micropolyphonic figures of the sixties (from *Atmosphères* to *Ramifications*), to the opened and broadened, occasionally even, distant, tonal idiom of the seventies."] *See:* D20, D32, D51.

B444. Kaufmann, Harald. "György Ligetis szenische Abenteuer." *Neues Forum* 13 (1966): 773-74.

This pantomime version of *Aventures et Nouvelles Aventures*, was performed in Stuttgart. Ligeti had nothing to do with this production and issued a statement to that effect. "Ebenso ist freilich festzustellen, daß für den Kenner des Originallibrettos ... die Stuttgarter Fassung manche empfindliche Unzulänglichkeiten zeigte, die -- ohne zusatzliche Kosten -- korrigierbar gewesen wären." ["It is certainly apparent that for those familiar with the original libretto ... the Stuttgart version displayed some serious shortcomings, which would have been correctable without any additional expense."] *See:* W33b, W34b, W36b.

B445. Kaupert, A. "Hamburg: Slapsticks mit Musik." *Die Bühne* no. 242 (Nov. 1978): 20.

The German première of *Le Grand Macabre* is reviewed here. "Die hitzigen Bravo- und Buh rufe des Publikums als Epilog einer zirzensisch bunten Opernshow konnten es mit des Komponisten Autohupen-Ouvertüre durchaus aufnehmen." ["The audience's passionate bravos and boos served as an epilog to a circusy opera show, as good as the composer's autohorn overture."] *See:* W54b.

B446. Kazmaier, Martin. "Aus dem Opern-Mausoleum des Palais Garnier: György Ligetis *Le Grand Macabre* nun auch in Paris." *Stuttgarter Zeitung*, April 3, 1981.

The controversial Paris production is the subject of this review. "Was beim Umgang mit toten Kunsterheben üblich ist, mußte György Ligeti bei lebendem Leibe erfahren: Mesguich und sein dramaturgischer Mitarbeiter haben das Libretto umstruktuiert. Ganz totschweigen ließ sich der eingestandenermaßen mit Mesguichs Interpretation unzufriedene Komponist nicht." ["What is usual in association with deceased artists, György Ligeti had to suffer in a living body: Mesguich and his dramaturgical associates reconstructed the libretto. The composer did not keep totally silent about his admitted dissatisfaction with Mesguich's interpretation."] *See:* W54d.

B447. Kerner, Leighton. "Clarinets and Walking Sticks." *Village Voice*, June 24, 1986, p. 73.

A review of the New York Philharmonic series, "Horizons 86" which included performances of *Aventures et Nouvelles Aventures* and *Scenes and Interludes from Le Grand Macabre*. "... what we got of *Macabre* was a tantalizing mix of pathos and diabolical farce.... As for the twin *Aventures* ... the new staging succeeded both as humor and as a depiction of spiritual rope-ends." *See:* W33e, W34d, W36g, W55d, App. II, p. 173.

B448. Kessler, Sinah. "Der Weltuntergang als Hornberger Schießen." *Frankfurter Allgemeine Zeitung*, May 28, 1979, p. 21.

A report on the Italian première of *Le Grand Macabre* in Bologna. "Ligeti sagte in einigen Interviews: 'Ohne auch nur im mindesten die bisherigen Aufführungen von Stockholm, Hamburg und Saarbrücken abwerten zu wollen: hier in Bologna aber ist tatsächlich alles so gelungen, wie ich es mir immer vorgestellt habe'." ["Ligeti said in several interviews, 'Not to undervalue in the least the previous performances in Stockholm, Hamburg and Saarbrücken, but here in Bologna everything is really well done as I have always imagined it'."] *See*: W54c.

B449. Kirchberg, Klaus. "Schallplatten." *Musica* 40 (1986): 481.

A review of Wergo WER 60100. *See*: D33, D53, D46, D91.

B450. Klein, Rudolf. "Musiktheater Nürnberg gastierte mit Ligetis *Le Grand Macabre*." *Österreichische Musikzeitschrift* 37 (1982): 38-39.

A performance in Graz of the Nuremberg production is the subject of this review. "Immer wieder versucht [Ligeti] in Vorträgen und Schriften auf seine Verwurzelung in der Tradition hinzuweisen. Als ob es von Breughel und Bosch einen Weg zu den geschmacklosen und primitiven Cartoons unserer Tage gäbe! So ist man also im Grunde geschichtslos und rückhaltlos den apokalyptischen Reitern des "Grand Macabre" ausgesetzt, die da heißen: Häßlichkeit, Dummheit, Gemeinheit." ["[Ligeti] always seeks in his lectures and writings to point out his close attachment with tradition. As if there were a direct connection from Breughel and Bosch to the tasteless and primitive cartoons of today! So one is therefore basically historyless and openly abandoned to the apocalyptic riddles of the "Grand Macabre", which means: ugliness, stupidity, vulgarity."] *See*: W54g.

B451. -------. "Neue Werke--junge Künstler." *Österreichische Musikzeitschrift* 37 (1982): 49.

The all-Ligeti concert in the "Wege in unsere Zeit" concert series (*See*: App. II, p. 171) inspired this evaluation of Ligeti's static style. "Das solcherart mangelne Formerlibnis führt trotz intensiver Bedachtnahme auf Abwechslung schnell zur Ermüdung, zumal keine Verbindung zwischen Hörerlebnis und Emotion hergestellt werden kann, die nur einigermaßen der Kapazität eigentlicher Musik enspräche." ["Such lack of formal event leads, despite intensive attention to variation, quickly to fatigue, especially since no connection between the listener's experience and emotion can be established, which only roughly corresponds to the capacity of real music."]

B452. Knessl, Lothar. "Anrainer kommen mit Novitäten nach Wien." *Melos* 34 (1967): 308-10.

This staging of *Aventures et Nouvelles Aventures* was directed by Rolf Scharre and performed by the Württemberg State Opera. The works were performed in Vienna as part of the 1967 Wiener Festwochen. "[Ligetis Szenarium] ist derart gespickt mit theatralisch mehrgleisig verlaufenden Fenessen, daß es in der vom Komponisten gewünschten Komplexität wahrscheinlich nur filmisch wird verwirklicht werden können. Darum mußte sich Stuttgart zu einer vereinfachten ... Version entschließen." ["[Ligeti's libretto] is so larded with theatrical trickery that to realize it in the complexity desired by the composer would probably require the cinema. So Stuttgart needed to decide on a simplified version."] *See*: W33b, W34b, W36b.

B453. -------. "Neue Musik im Wiener Museum des 20. Jahrhunderts." *Melos* 30 (1963): 351-53.

This concert in Vienna featured *Aventures*, performed by Charlent, Cahn, and Pearson with die Reihe Ensemble directed by Friedrich Cerha. "Man erlebt bei Ligeti's *Aventures* einen geglückten Ansatz zum absurden Musiktheater." ["In Ligeti's *Aventures* one experiences a successful expansion into absurd musical theater."] *See*: W33.

B454.   Knussen, Oliver. "Recordings: Scenes and Interludes from *Le Grand Macabre.*" *Tempo* no. 136 (1981): 27-29.

A record review of Wergo WER 60085. "The bulk of the music in the opera is here, shorn of lengthy repetitions.... A very good live performance under Ligeti's chosen conductor." *See*: W55, D59.

B455.   Koch, Gerhard R. "Das Emanzipierte Streichquartett." *Neue Musikzeitung* 19, no. 1 (1970): p. 18.

This article includes a review of the première of the *String Quartet No. 2.* "Neu sind weniger die Mittel als ihre Konstellationen, die dialektische Verschlungenheit avanciertester Passagen mit im Grunde traditionellen Modellen." ["The methods are not as new as the configurations, the dialectic intricacy of advanced passages with basically traditional models."] *See*: W42a.

B456.   -------. "Für Klaviere." *Musica* 30 (1976): 325.

The première of *Monument-Selbstportrait-Bewegung* was performed by Alfons and Aloys Kontarsky. "... hochreflektierte Kompositionen, denen im Mischungsverhältnis neuartiger und gleichsam resümierender Züge fast der Charakter eines Spätwerkes erwächst." ["... highly reflective compositions in which the mixture of novel and summarizing tendencies almost results in the character of a late work."] *See*: W52a.

B457.   -------. "Große Szene in Darmstadt: György Ligetis *Aventures I und II* bei den Ferienkursen für Neue Musik." *Frankfurter Allgemeine Zeitung*, Aug. 30, 1966, p. 16.

This performance by soloists Charlent, Cahn and Pearson took place at the 1966 Darmstadt Festival. "Daß die beiden Stücke weniger überzeugend wirken als Ligetis bisher rein instrumentale Kompositionen, mag mit Problemen zusammenhängen, die die neuere Oper insgesamt zu belasten scheinen. Gedacht ist hier vor allem an eine eindeutige Umsetzung von Affekt-Werten in musikalischen Ausdruck." ["That the two pieces are less convincing than Ligeti's previous, purely instrumental compositions may relate to problems which appear to burden new opera in general. Especially difficult is a clear transposition of affect values into musical expression."] *See*: W33, W34, W36.

B458.   -------. "Heinz Holligers *Siebengesang.*" *Musica* 23 (1969): 32-34.

Includes a review of a performance of the *Requiem* featuring Liliana Poli, Barbro Ericson, and the Bavarian Radio Choir conducted by Michael Gielen. "Es beschwört eine Monumentalität mit umgekehrten Vorzeichen." ["It evokes monumentality with completely opposite premises."] *See*: W35.

B459.   -------. "Heller Horror." *Opernwelt* 12, no. 5 (May 1971): 36-37.

A review of the television production of *Aventures et Nouvelles Aventures* staged by Klaus Lindemann. "Die Überfülle der Situationen, Bilder und Gags in Ligetis Libretto, aber auch die zahlreichen überraschungseffekte der Komposition lassen sich fast in Analogie zur filmischen Schnitt- und Montagetechnik sehen, zumal Ligeti selber aus seinem Faible für bestimmte Filme, vor allem des grotesken Genres, kein Hehl gemacht hat." ["The abundance of situations, images, and gags in Ligeti's libretto, but also the numerous surprising effects in the music appear nearly analogous to cinematic cutting and montage techniques. Indeed, Ligeti himself makes no secret of his fondness for certain films, above all those of the grotesque genres."] *See*: W36e.

B460.   --------. "Ligetis *Aventures*, Madernas *Von A bis Z.*" *Musica* 24 (1970): 269-70.

Based on an article which appeared in the *Stuttgarter Zeitung*, Feb. 27, 1970. The Darmstadt production of *Aventures et Nouvelles Aventures* was directed by Harro Dicks. "... hält Dicks an das Inventar der Opern-Regie mit ihren Gesten, Allüren und Affekten und inszenierte fast so etwas wie eine Handlung." ["... Dicks stuck to the inventory of opera direction with its gestures, mannerisms and emotions and staged it almost like a story."] *See*: W33c, W34c, W36d.

B461.   Koch, Heinz W. "Gehupt wie gesungen: Ligetis *Le Grand Macabre* in Freiburg." *Stuttgarter Zeitung*, March 9, 1984.

A review. "... eine überaus gründliche, aufs sorgsamste aufgeschlüsselte, hellhörig geschärfte Ligeti-Wiedergabe...." ["... an extremely thorough Ligeti performance, carefully developed and keenly sharpened...."] *See*: W54h.

B462.   --------. "Der plaudernde Avantgardist: eine Opernaufführung, ein Sonderkonzert und eine Diskussion: György Ligeti in Freiburg." *Badische Zeitung*, May 30-31, 1984.

This concert featured *Ramifications*, five songs, *Monument-Selbstportrait-Bewegung*, *Poème symphonique*, and selections from *Le Grand Macabre*. Ligeti spoke and Eberhard Kloke conducted. "Das Philharmonische Orchester, seine Solisten, das 'Macabre'-Finalquintett - sie alle waren außerordentlich konzentriert, mit aller Sensibilität und Genauigkeit am Werk." ["The Philharmonic, the soloists, the 'Macabre' finale-quintet, they were all extraordinarily focused, with all sensitivity and precision in performance."] *See*: W44, W52, W32, W55.

B463.   --------. "Schrecken ohne Worte: Experimente von György Ligeti und Bruno Maderna in Darmstadt." *Der Tagesspiegel*, Feb. 25, 1970.

This performance included a staging of *Aventures et Nouvelles Aventures*. "Hände schweben von oben herunter, eine Galerie von Augen senkt sich, Höhepunkt der Bizarrerie, auf die Akteure, Ende der Kommunikation, Ende des Aneinandervorbeiredens, Erkenntnis der absoluten Sinnlosigkeit, Isolation, Verstummen, Beckett auf der Musikbühne." ["Hands float down from above; as the high point of strangeness a gallery of eyes settle on the actors. End of communication, end of talking at cross purposes, realization of absolute absurdity, isolation, silence. Beckett on the musical stage."] *See*: W33c, W34c, W36d.

B464.   --------. "Vampir aus dem Grabe; Ligetis "Großer Makabrer" in Freiburg." *Opernwelt* 25 (1984): 42-43.

This is a review of the Freiburg production of *Le Grand Macabre*. "Kloke zeigt in diesem 'Grand Macabre' daß er auch bei komplizierten musikalischen Sachverhalten den Durchblick hat. Vor allem: Man 'erkennt' was Ligeti 'macht'." ["Kloke shows in this 'Grand Macabre' that he also understands complex musical situations. Above all, one hears what Ligeti does."] *See*: W54h.

B465.   Koch-Martin, Nicolas. "Amsterdam." *Rassegna Musicale Curci* 26, no. 2 (1973): 43-44.

This concert included a performance of *Aventures et Nouvelles Aventures*. "'E' questo l'annunciato 'collage'? E dove è rimasta la musica di "Aventures" di Ligeti, tanto vantanta oltre il Reno? Soffocata dalla trasposizione scenica ..." ["Is this the announced 'collage'? And what happened to the music of Ligeti's

Aventures so highly praised across the Rhine? Suffocated by the scenic transposition."] *See*: W33, W34, W36.

B466.   Koegler, Horst. "Gipfeltreffen der europäischen Musik: Konzert zum sechzigsten Geburtstag von György Ligeti. *Stuttgarter Zeitung*, May 20, 1983.

This was a concert celebrating Ligeti's 60th birthday. The program included the *Horn Trio* (Saschko Gawriloff, violin, Hermann Baumann, horn, and Eckhard Besch, piano), *Ramifications* and the *Chamber Concerto* (Pierre Boulez, Stuttgart Radio Symphony), *Magyar Etüdök* (Clytus Gottwald, Schola Cantorum Stuttgart), *Passacaglia ungherese* and *Hungarian Rock* (Elisabeth Chojnacka, harpsichord). Mauricio Kagel also directed his own *Intermezzo*. "Was Ligetis Musik so attraktiv macht, ist einmal, daß sie kein Dogma predigt, und daß sie zum andern sich beim ersten Hören ausreichend faßlich gibt...." ["What makes Ligeti's music so attractive is first, that it doesn't preach any dogma, and also it is sufficiently accessible on the first hearing...."] *See*: W59, W44, W46f, W62a, W56, W57, App. II, p. 171.

B467.   -------. "Ein Ire vom Balkan: Ligeti *Aventures* wieder im Repertoire des Kammertheaters." *Stuttgarter Zeitung* Feb. 28, 1978.

This staged production was conducted by Bernard Kontarsky. "Den drei beteiligten Sängermimikern, Gertie Charlent, Elke Estlinbaum und Klaus Hirte mit ihrer komödiantischen Verve, Kehlkopfakrobatik und Lippenvirtuosität, gebührt nach dieser *Tour de force* der Titel der Württembergischen Kammer-Phantasten." ["After this *tour de force* the three singer-mimes (Gertie Charlent, Elke Estlinbaum and Klaus Hirte) with their comedic verve, vocal acrobatics and virtuosity deserve the title of 'Württemberg Chamber Visionaries'." *See*: W33, W34, W36f.

B468.   Kölmel, Dieter. "Breughel-Land ist Menschenland: *Der große Makabre* von György Ligeti in Hamburg erstaufgeführt: Regisseur Gilbert Deflo verlegt die Handlung in einen Zirkus." *Stuttgarter Nachrichten*, Oct. 17, 1978.

The Hamburg production *Le Grand Macabre* featured circus scenery. "Clowns in allen Variationen sind die Akteure in diesem großen Dressurakt, anhand dessen Ligeti den Menschen, dem Publikum einen Spiegel vorhalten will: Schaut her, das seid Ihr!" ["The actors in this great circus act are clowns in all variations, by means of which Ligeti would hold up a mirror to the public: look here, this is you!"] *See*: W54b.

B469.   -------. "Das Jüngste Gericht fand nur in den Köpfen statt: David Freeman inszeniert in Freiburg György Ligetis Anti-Anti-Oper *Le Grand Macabre*." *Stuttgarter Nachrichten*, March 5, 1984.

The Freiburg production of the opera inspired this statement: "... die bislang überzeugendste und geschlossenste Wiedergabe dieses Werks...." ["... so far the most convincing, consistent production of this work...."] *See*: W54h.

B470.   Kolodin, Irving. "Music to my ears." *The Saturday Review* 54 (Nov. 13, 1971): 24.

Cellist Siegfried Palm performed the *Concerto for Violoncello* accompanied by members of the New York Philharmonic under Michael Gielen. "... none of [the instrumentalists] have much to do between 8:59 and 9:14, except play a tremolo here, a sustained tone there, a pizzicato now and then.... Ligeti's Concerto isn't long, but it is dull." *See*: W38.

B471.   Kotschenreuther, Hellmut. "Ausdrucksloser Ausdruck: György Ligetis *Violoncello-Konzert* in Berlin Uraufgeführt." *Stuttgarter Zeitung*, April 25, 1967.

The première of the *Concerto for Violoncello* was performed as part of a series of concerts entitled "Musik der Gegenwart." "... demonstrierte zweierlei: einmal die Originalität des Talents, das man Ligeti keinesfalls absprechen kann; zum anderen aber auch die Gefahr, daß seine Ausdrucksmittel zur Manier, ja zur Masche verkommen Könnten." ["... demonstrates two things: first, Ligeti's originality of talent, which no one can deny; but also the danger that his means of expression may deteriorate into mannerism or mere trickery."] *See*: W38a.

B472.   -------. "Musik der Gegenwart." *Musica* 23 (1969): 360-61.

This concert featured a performance of *Ramifications*. The review includes this quote from the composer: "... ein Beispiel dekadenter Kunst." ["... an example of decadent art."] *See*: W44.

B473.   Kraft, Leo. "Current Chronicle: Lenox, Massachusetts." *Musical Quarterly* 58 (1972): 132-35.

The Music Theater Project was a new element in the 1970 Festival of Contemporary Music at Tanglewood. *Aventures et Nouvelles Aventures* was staged. *See*: W33, W34, W36.

B474.   Kramer, Gerhard. "Musikfest 'Österreich -- heute.'" *Das Orchester* 35 (1987): 159-60.

This festival included performances of *String Quartet No. 1*, *Studies for Piano* (book 1), and the *Piano Concerto*. "Erster, wenngleich trügerischer Eindruck: Auch in der Musik Ligetis ist der Postmodernismus voll ausgebrochen." ["A first, though deceptive impression: postmodernism has even broken out in Ligeti's music."] *See*: W19, W63, W64.

B475.   -------. "Reden über Neue Musik: 'Komponistenwerkstatt György Ligeti' im Konzerthaus." *Die Presse* (Vienna), Jan. 17, 1983.

San Francisco Polyphony was performed by Gerd Albrecht and the Austrian Radio Symphony. Ligeti introduced the piece and remarked on the style and structure. "... es war im höchsten Grad verdienstlich, ein Werk wie Ligetis *San Francisco Polyphony* einmal wie auf dem Seziertisch vorgeführt zu bekommen." ["... it was highly profitable to see a work like Ligetis *San Francisco Polyphony* presented on the operating table, as it were."] *See*: W51.

B476.   -------. "Wien: konservative Front geschlagen." *Melos* 37 (1970): 304.

The première of the three-movement version of the *Chamber Concerto* was performed by the Reihe Ensemble directed by Friedrich Cerha. "Tatsächlich zeigt das Resultat von Ligetis Bemühungen die Risiken des Verfahrens sehr deutlich auf. Es ist unüberhörbar, wie eminent tonale Wirkungen ein deutlich hervortretender Einzelton (oder gar deren mehrere) gerade inmitten mehr oder weniger amorpher Strukturen hervorzurufen vermag." ["The result of Ligeti's efforts with the risks of this technique are quite clear. It is unmistakable that an eminently tonal effect can be produced by a clearly emerging single tone (or even several tones) in the middle of a more or less amorphous structure."] *See*: W46a.

B477.   Kroó, György. "Music of Our Age '84." *New Hungarian Quarterly* 26
(summer 1985): 214-17.

This Budapest festival included the Hungarian première of *Drei Phantasien*,
performed by the BBC Singers. "Its background lacks the kind of formal
metatheses, stylizations, and philosophies that one felt behind the *Requiem* and
Grand Macabre. Here the choice of text implies a personal and emotional
prompting: a sense of life's evening closing in." *See*: W61.

B478.   Lang, Hermann. "Klang an sich: Ligetis *Requiem* in Köln."
Stuttgarter Zeitung, Jan 24, 1967.

This was the first performance of the work in Germany, with soloists Liliana Poli
and Barbro Ericson, and the conductor Andrzej Markowski. "Das
Faszinierendste des ganzen Werkes ist sein Abschluß: im Lacrimosa verspinnen
sich die Stimmen der beiden Solistinnen mit denen eines kleinen
Instrumentalensembles zu einem zarten, lyrisch vergehenden Ausklang." ["The
most fascinating part of the work is its ending: in the Lacrimosa the two solo
voices blend with a small instrumental ensemble into a tender lyrically fading
final sound."] *See*: W35b.

B479.   Lesch, Helmut. "Betrunkener Sensenmann verschläft die
Katastrophe." *Abendzeitung*, October 17, 1978.

This item deals with the Hamburg production of *Le Grand Macabre*. "... eine
Bagatelle im notleidenden Spielplan unserer überfüllten Opernhäuser." ["... a
much-needed bagatelle for the overstocked repertoire of our opera houses."]
See: W54b.

B480.   Lesle, Lutz. "8 1/2-Konzert im Hamburger Opera Stabile: Neues von
György Ligeti. *Üben und Musizieren* 3, no. 2 (1986): 191-92.

In this concert, Piano etudes 2-6 were performed by Volker Banfield. Nos. 4 and
5 received their first performance here. "Das Publikum im randvollen Studio
feierte den Komponisten und seinen kongenialen Interpreten enthusiastisch."
["The audience in the packed studio applauded the composer and his congenial
interpreter enthusiastically."] *See*: W63c.

B481.   -------. "Huldigungen für György Ligeti in Hamburg." *Orchester* 32
(1984): 433-34.

This lecture-concert was devoted to Ligeti, and included a performance of the
Horn Trio. *See*: W59.

B482.   -------. "Ligeti im 'neuen Werk'." *Melos/Neue Zeitschrift für Musik* 4
(1978): 118.

This concert of keyboard works included *Musica ricercata* played by Eckart
Besch, *Monument-Selbstportrait-Bewegung* played by Besch and Hans-Jürgen
Hofer, *Continuum* played by Carol Tainton, and *Two Etudes for Organ* and
Volumina played by Heinz Wunderlichs. "Ich will nicht zurückgehen, nicht in
Nostalgie, nicht in Tonalität. Ich will versuchen, den Experimenten-Gestus etwas
abzubauen. Ich habe die Nase voll vom großgeschriebenen Experiment." ["I will
not go back, not to nostalgia, not to tonality. I will try to cut out experimental
gestures. I am fed up with exaggerated experiments."] *See*: W14, W52, W41,
W40, W45, W31, App. II, p. 170.

B483. -------. "Ligeti-Retrospektive bei den Sommerlichen Musiktagen in Hitzacker." *Orchester* 35 (1987): 1045-1048.

This festival included performances of the three harpsichord pieces (Elisabeth Chojnacka), the six *Etudes for Piano* (Volker Banfield), and a lecture on Ligeti by Constantin Floros. "Im Gegensatz zu den Serialisten, die sich ... von der 'Diktatur des Einfalls' losbinden wollten und dabei um so tiefer in die Unfreiheit gerieten, habe Ligeti mit Macht das 'Primat der Erfindung' hochgehalten." [Contrary to the serialists who ... would be freed from the 'dictatorship of ideas' and thereby fall deeper into bondage, Ligeti has vigorously upheld the primacy of invention."] *See*: W41, W56, W57, W63, App. II, p. 173.

B484. Lewinski, Wolf-Eberhard von. "Jubiläum eines Musikfestivals." *Musica* 15 (1961): 674-76.

The 1961 Donaueschingen Music Festival included the première of *Atmosphères*. "Die beiden Grundtendenzen der neuesten Musik, Klang als formales Element und Form als klingende Entfaltung bestimmter Keimzellen-Gedanken ohne vorher fixierte äußere Gestalt, kamen in Donaueschingen deutlich zutage und fanden in Ligetis *Atmosphères* ... den überzeugendsten Ausdruck." ["The two basic tendencies of the newest music -- sound as a formal element, and form as the audible development of certain germ-ideas without pre-determined outer shape -- came clearly to view in Donaueschingen and found most convincing expression in Ligeti's *Atmosphères*."] *See*: W27a.

B485. -------. "Neue Werke von Ligeti und Penderecki." *Musica* 22 (1968): 9-10.

A review of the Donaueschingen festival which mentions the première of *Lontano*. "... gestalterisch erstaunlich eindringlich zum Klang geführt." ["... the sound is handled with remarkable creative force."] *See*: W39a.

B486. -------. "Singende Wachsfiguren und Stumme Opernsänger in Darmstadt." *Melos* 37 (1970): 150-51.

This review is based on one which appeared in the *Süddeutsche Zeitung*, March 3, 1970. It examines the staging of *Aventures et Nouvelles Aventures* by Harro Dicks. "Hier kam eine Identifikation mit der Komposition legitim zur Geltung, weil eine Grundsituation des Menschen suggestiv gedeutet war. Aber die anderen Passagen richteten sich doch gegen die Absicht des Komponisten, degradierten die Musik zur Illustration." ["Here, a legitimate identification with the composition was seen because the basic situation of humanity was suggestively interpreted. But other passages oppose the intentions of the composer and reduce the music to illustration."] *See*: W33c, W34c, W36d.

B487. "Ligetis Abenteuer und neue Abenteuer im 'Neuen Werk'." *Melos* 33 (1966): 241-42.

This Hamburg Radio broadcast featured *Aventures et Nouvelles Aventures* (it was the première performance of *Nouvelles Aventures*). This review includes Ligeti's program notes for the occasion: "Die musikalisch-phonetisch-dramatischen Stücke *Aventures et Nouvelles Aventures* stellen insofern ein neue Kunstgattung dar, als in ihnen Text, Musik und ein imaginäres Bühnengeschehen vollständig ineinander aufgehen und eine gemeinsame kompositorische Struktur bilden. Es gibt hier keinen meinenden und bedeutungstragenden Text, der dann durch Musik 'vertont' wäre; dagegen gibt es einen musikalisch-phonetischen 'Text', der weder zu einer bestimmten menschlichen Sprache gehört, noch durch Transformation oder Verfremdung einer Sprache entstanden ist." ["The musical-phonetic-dramatic pieces *Aventures et Nouvelles Aventures* represent a new genre of art; in it, text, music, and imaginary stage action completely merge together and form a collective compositional structure. There is no meaningful text that is set to music. Rather there is a musical-phonetic 'text', which doesn't belong to any human language, nor is it derived through transformation or alienation of a language."] *See*: W33, W34a.

B488.   Limmert, Erich. "Hannover: Albrechts Sonderkonzert neuer Musik." *Neue Zeitschrift für Musik* 133 (1972): 729-30.

This concert included a performance by the Lower Saxony State Orchestra of *Melodien*. "Auf dem feingetönten, durchsichtig bleibenden Klanggrund entfalten sich die Melodien nicht etwa im romantischen Sinne, sondern sie bilden einen kontrapunktisch gewirkten Teppich, aus dem sich bei genauem Hinhören die Melodieinstrumente als Farbkomplexe, darüber hinaus aber auch deutlich linear, und zwar in rhythmischer Profilierung, abheben." ["Over the delicate, transparent background the melodies do not develop in a romantic sense, but rather they form a contrapuntally woven tapestry out of which (with careful attention) the melody instruments stand out as a complex of colors, but also in clearly linear and even rhythmic profile."] *See*: W47.

B489.   -------. "Killmayers 1. Sinfonie in Hannover uraufgeführt." *Melos* 38 (1971): 203-4.

The concert also included *Lontano* performed by the State Orchestra of Lower Saxony directed by George Alexander Albrecht. "Bei einer so atmosphärisch sich verflüchtigenden Klangebene ist in der Wiedergabe ein mehr impressionistisch verfeinerter als gefühlsbestimmt romantischer Gesamtklang ratsam." ["When performing such atmospheric, volatile sound-planes, a more impressionistically refined sound, rather than a romantic one is advisable."] *See*: W39.

B490.   Löhlein, Heinz-Harald. "Musik und Vorlesungen im slowakischen Smolenice." *Melos* 36 (1969): 270.

This music festival featured a performance of *Poème symphonique* directed by Ladislav Kupkovič, and a lecture by Ligeti on his *Requiem*. "Die vier Sätze des *Requiems* vergleicht er mit dem brutalen chirurgischen Eingriff in eine herrliche Seide: Der Stoff wird behutsam geglättet und gestreichelt (Introitus), zerknittert, Fäden herausgezogen (Kyrie), ganz zerstört und wie ein Spinnennetz zerrissen (Dies Irae), schließlich tastend das Kaputte neu komponiert (Lacrimosa)." ["He compared the four movements of the *Requiem* to brutal surgery with a splendid silk: the material is carefully smoothed and stroked (Introit), crumpled, unraveled (Kyrie), completely destroyed and torn like a cobweb (Dies Irae), and finally the pieces are tentatively rejoined (Lacrimosa)."] *See*: W32b, W35.

B491.   Lohmüller, Helmut. "Münchner Musica Viva erinnert an die Pioniere der neuen Musik." *Melos* 28 (1961): 123-24.

This was an early performance of *Apparitions*. "Bei weitem schlechter erging es György Ligeti. Das Publikum belustigte sich bereits während der Aufführung ... und empfing den Komponisten am Schluß mit einem kräftigen Pfeifkonzert. Ligeti quittierte den unfreundlichen Empfang lachelnd -- wohl im Bewußtsein, daß die Problematik seiner *Apparitions* auch durch Beifall nicht überdeckt werden kann." ["Things went far worse for György Ligeti. The public was amused during the performance ... and greeted the composer at the end with loud cat-calls. Ligeti took the unfriendly reception with a smile, knowing that the problematic nature of his *Apparitions* cannot be concealed by applause."] *See*: W26.

B492.   Loppert, Max. "Germany: Ligeti in Hamburg." *Opera* 30 (1979): 63-64.

> The second performance of *Le Grand Macabre*, produced by Gilbert Deflo is reviewed here. "Breughelland and its inhabitants became that easiest and most pusillanimous of lets-find-a-metaphor-for-the-human-condition settings, the Circus.... Rumour has it that the composer has expressed serious disappointment with the show. If this is so, who can blame him?" *See*: W54b.

B493.   -------. "Ligeti Performance in Queen Elizabeth Hall." *The Financial Times*, May 21, 1982, p. 21.

> Translated into German in: *Neue Zeitschrift für Musik* 143, no. 10 (1982): 66. This concert included performances by the London Sinfonietta of *Melodien, Ten Pieces for Wind Quintet*, the *Concerto for Violoncello* (Christopher van Kampen, soloist), and *Aventures et Nouvelles Aventures* (Pamela Smith, Linda Hirst, Simon Grant, vocalists; James Holland, percussion), under the direction of Elgar Howarth. "In Ligeti's compositions--this makes him a great rarity among the producers of truly modern music--the listener perceives an artist of the highest skill who is at the same time a whole human being." *See*: W47, W43, W38, W33, W34.

B494.   Lück, Hartmut. "Nicht nur Revolutionär: 'Bremer Podium für neue Kammermusik' mit dem Komponisten György Ligeti." *Bremer Nachrichten*, Sept. 28, 1983.

> This workshop and concert featured *Artikulation*, String Quartets nos. 1 and 2, and the *Horn Trio*. Performers were the Arditti Quartet, and the Ligeti Trio. "In den so gefüllt, juchzenden, Beifall klatschenden und pfeifenden Saal blickend, erklärte der Komponist spontan, wenn er das geahnt hätte, wäre er nicht im Anzug, sondern in Jeans erschienen...." ["Seeing the packed, cheering, clapping and whistling hall, the composer explained spontaneously that if he had expected this he would have appeared in jeans rather than a suit...."] *See*: W25, W19, W42, W59.

B495.   Ludwig, Heinz, and Giovanna Kessler. "Zweimal Ligeti: *Le Grand Macabre* in Saarbrücken ... und in Bologna." *Opernwelt* 20, no. 7 (1979): 27-29.

> These two reviews are of the Saarbrücken and Bologna productions respectively. The second is based on an article which appeared in *Frankfurter Allgemeine Zeitung* (*See*: B448). Saarbrücken: "Mit Akribie, Geschick und Können hatten Matthias Kuntzsch, der Dirigent der Aufführung, Christof Bitter als Inszenator und der Bühnenbildner Walter Jahrreiss den Beweis angetreten, daß Ligetis heterogene Collagen die künstlerischen Möglichkeiten einer Provinzbühne nicht überschreiten." ["With extreme precision, skill and ability, Matthias Kuntzsch the conductor, Christof Bitter the director, and the set designer Walter Jahrreiss offered proof that Ligeti's heterogeneous collage doesn't exceed the artistic possibilities of a provincial stage."] *See*: W54f, W54c.

B496.   Mahlke, Sybill. "Piet-vom-Faß und Othello: 'Musik der Gegenwart' im SFB-Sendesaal." *Der Tagesspiegel*, Dec. 23, 1978.

> An abridged concert performance of *Le Grand Macabre* was given by members of the Hamburg Production. "Eine doppelbödige Musik, die ahnungslose Opernhaftigkeit des Liebespaares ... in der Instrumentierung denunziert, eine Oper und gleichzeitig ein Werk über Oper...." ["a false-bottomed music which denounces the naive operatics of the lovers ... in the orchestra. An opera and at the same time a work about opera...."] *See*: W55a.

B497. Mangs, Runar. "Skräkens projektioner på oändlighetens vägg."
Dagens Nyheter, March 17, 1965.

A brief review of the first performance of the Requiem. "Med all sin enorma
uttryckskraft är 'Requiem' begrepps- (men inte teori-!) musik, en oerhörd
sammanfattning, ett rop från allt levande." ["With all its enormous expressive
force 'Requiem' is conceptual (but not theoretical!) music; a tremendous
recapitulation; a shout from all living things."] See: W35a.

B498. Mann, Carl-Heinz. "Ein Ende am Fliegenfänger: Opera stabile,
Ligetis Aventures szenische erstaufgeführt." Hamburger
Abendblatt, Oct. 1, 1976.

This performance featured soloists Klaus Hirte, Elke Estlinbaum and Gertie
Charlent, and was conducted by Bernard Kontarsky. "Wie Insekten kleben die
drei im Schlußbild an dem leise knackenden Plastikband, das an einen alten
Fliegenfänger erinnert." ["In the final scene, the three are stuck like insects to
the softly crackling plastic ribbon which is reminiscent of old-fashioned
flypaper."] See: W33, W36f.

B499. Mann, William. "Le Grand Macabre: English National Opera at the
London Coliseum." Opera 34 (1983): 207-11.

This was the British première of the opera, produced by the English National
Opera. "While the serious implications of Le Grand Macabre will readily be
appreciated and argued, I hope nobody will forget to notice what a spry comic
opera Ligeti has written, something most difficult to achieve at the present time."
See: W54e.

B500. -------. "Holland Festival." The Times, June 27, 1975, p. 7.

This festival featured a performance by the Radio Philharmonic Orchestra of San
Francisco Polyphony. "The more sparse the texture, the more cogent the
playing sounded; in the more grandiose passages some seemingly important
details were not clearly audible." See: W51.

B501. -------. "Ligeti's Requiem: Festival Hall." The Times, Nov. 11, 1971, p.
12.

This performance by the BBC Symphony and Chorus with Liliana Poli and Anna
Malewicz-Madey, soloists, was conducted by Michael Gielen. "In this
persuasive, devoted performance ... the compulsive impress of the Requiem was
such that I would gladly have foregone Beethoven's ninth symphony after the
interval." See: W35c.

B502. -------. "London Sinfonietta: Queen Elizabeth Hall." The Times, Jan.
14, 1971, p. 10.

This performance of the Chamber Concerto was conducted by David Atherton.
"Two of its four movements (the 1st and 3rd) at once impress as Ligeti at his
most eloquent." See: W46c.

B503. -------. "Lontano: Free Trade Hall, Manchester." The Times, Jan. 28,
1972, p. 12.

This performance was conducted by James Loughran. "The feeling of the piece
came across, if not all its specific flavours, and left no doubt of the conductor's
enthusiasm. If only the Hallé could play it as an encore after every concert for,
say, six months!" See: W39.

B504.   -------. "LSO/Ligeti: Queen Elizabeth Hall." *The Times*, May 9, 1974, p. 23.

A short review of the Ligeti concert/lecture sponsored by the English Bach Festival. "Ligeti on Tuesday confirmed his status as the most sympathetic among progressive composers today."

B505.   -------. "Sweden: Ligeti's Success." *Opera* 29 (1978): 678-80.

This was the world première of *Le Grand Macabre*. "It is eventful music, and an eventful, surprisingly coherent evenings musical theatre: the last scene seems least purposefully designed, struggling to achieve its conclusion, just as the second scene appears the most effective. Other productions will doubtless alter that verdict: it is rumoured that Ligeti is revising the score for the forthcoming Hamburg premier. I hope it will be staged in Britain: worthwhile modern comic operas are rare birds, and *Le Grand Macabre* is certainly worthwhile for a country that loves the Marx Brothers and the Goons." *See:* W54a.

B506.   Marsh, Robert C. "Yun Opera, Ligeti Mass." *High Fidelity/Musical America* 20 (June 1970), sec. 2, p. 25.

This performance by the Northwestern University Symphony of *Requiem* was conducted by Bernard Rubenstein. The soloists are not named. "The effect of the interaction of many individual melodic lines produces a deep, constantly changing texture of sustained sonorities that seems at once a development of polyphonic writing and a bridge between concert music and product of the electronic studio." *See:* W35.

B507.   Mason, John. "Arditti String Quartet: Ligeti." *The Strad*, 96 (July, 1985): 170.

Both string quartets were performed in Vienna. "... the Quartet revealed a level of stylistic assurance and interpretative insight which rendered unnecessary many of Ligeti's words." *See:* W19, W42.

B508.   Matzner, Joachim. "Berlin: Tonsetzer mit Qualitäten." *Das Orchester* 17 (1969): 270.

This review of the première of *Ramifications* is based on one which appeared in *Die Welt*, April 28, 1969. "Es erscheint eine ganz neue Art von 'unsicherer Harmonik, als ob die Harmonien verdorben wären." [It seems to be a whole new kind of unsteady harmony, as if the harmony had gone bad."] *See:* W44.

B509.   -------. "Keine Angst vor großen Makabren: In Stockholm wurde Ligetis erste Oper uraufgeführt." *Süddeutsche Zeitung*, April 15, 1978, p. 16.

A review of the première of *Le Grand Macabre*. "Daß *Le Grand Macabre* ... nicht unbedingt die Gewichtigkeit besitzt, die manche vom Ligeti des *Requiems*, der *Aventures* und der *Nouvelles Aventures* vielleicht erwartet haben, dürfte in der Natur der textlichen Sache liegen." [The reason that *Le Grand Macabre* ... does not completely reach the momentousness which some perhaps expected from the Ligeti of the *Requiem* and *Aventures et Nouvelles Aventures*, may lie in the nature of the text."] *See:* W54a.

B510.   Mayer, Gerhard. "Angst vor Spinnen: György Ligeti im Rahmen des Konzerthaus-Zyklus 'Wege in unsere Zeit'." *Die Wochenpresse*, Dec. 9, 1981.

This concert consisted of the *String Quartet No. 2* (Arditti Quartet), *Melodien* and the *Chamber Concerto* (die Reihe Ensemble, Friedrich Cerha, conductor). Ligeti also spoke. "'Die Angst vor Spinnen, die ich habe', und die sich in Ligetis spinnwebigen Klanggespinsten niederschlägt, kam beim Streichquartett ebenso zur Geltung wie beim abschließenden 'Kammerkonzert für 13 Instrumente' von 1969/70, einem Stück, 'das fast bis zur Grenze des Möglichen geht'...." ["'The fear of spiders, which I have' and which is struck down in Ligeti's weblike sonorities, became important in the string quartet and likewise in the definitive *Chamber Concerto* of 1969/70, a piece 'which goes almost to the limits of the possible'...."] *See*: W42, W47, W46e, App. II, p. 171.

B511.   McMullen, R. "New Music About Other Music." *High Fidelity/Musical America* 18 (June 1968): MA28.

This performance of *Aventures et Nouvelles Aventures* was given by Charlent, Cahn, Pearson, and Cerha conducting die Reihe Ensemble. "But all this ... was incidental to the main business, which was to comment irreverently on the ludicrous difficulty of being actually, not just potentially, operatic." *See*: W33, W34, W36.

B512.   Meyers, Klaus. "Von Telemann zur Avantgarde." *Musica* 34 (1980): 307-8.

Includes a record review of Christophorus SCK 70350. "Werner Jacob, erfahrener Interpret neuer Musik, beherrscht die enorme Klangpalette seiner Orgel in virtuoser Weise." ["Werner Jacob, expert interpreter of new music, masters the enormous sound palette of his organ in a virtuosic manner."] *See*: D81, D100.

B513.   Monson, Karen. "Ligeti's Cello Concerto Via the New Muse." *High Fidelity/Musical America* 23 (March 1973): MA20.

The West Coast première of this work was conducted by Leonard Rosenman, with soloist Joel Krosnick. "The supporting New Musers ... captured the changing textures of the Concerto's first movement but stumbled on the etude-like stretches of the second section." *See*: W38.

B514.   -------. "Ligeti's *Melodien* in L.A. Shows New Phase." *High Fidelity/Musical America* 22 (July 1972): MA25.

A review of the American première by the Los Angeles Philharmonic conducted by Zubin Mehta. "... problems arose in Mehta's failure to give the form sufficient definition.... The composer, who was in the audience for the occasion, declined ... invitations to join Mehta for an onstage bow...." *See*: W47.

B515.   Morgan, Robert P. "At Last the Avant-garde Remembers the Organ (Recording)." *High Fidelity/Musical America* 19 (April 1969): 92.

A review of Deutsche Grammophon 137003 (*Study for Organ No. 1*). "This is what one might call 'wallpaper music', music concerned almost exclusively with texture and pattern.... one can start almost anywhere without affecting the overall design." *See*: W40, D78.

B516.   --------. "Gerd Zacher: Music for Solo Organ." In *Records in Review: 1970 Edition*, 492-94. New York: Scribners, 1970.

> A review of Deutsche Grammophon 137003 (*Study for Organ No. 1*). "... the registration is constantly changing, usually in a gradual way so that one color seems to merge into the next. This requires the performer to 'play' on the registration buttons as much as he does on the keyboard, and thus demands an entirely new technique.... the performances by Gerd Zacher are impressive both for their virtuosity and their musicality." *See*: W40, D78.

B517.   --------. "Ligeti." *High Fidelity/Musical America* 30 (May 1980): 75-76.

> Reprinted in *Records in Review: 1981 Edition*, 182-84. Great Barrington, Mass.: Wyeth Press, 1981. A review of Decca Headline HEAD 12. "... there *is* complex new music being written that is well within the reach of concert audiences. The performances ... are, despite one or two minor lapses, faithful in both detail and spirit. Ligeti himself supplies very informative liner notes." *See*: W47, W48, W46, D11, D22, D44.

B518.   Moss, Lawrence K. "Last Year at Marienhöhe." *Perspectives of New Music* 3, no. 2 (1965): 171.

> This festival featured a performance of *Aventures*. "... showed his familiar elegance where timbre is concerned and a weakness ... in handling pitches." *See*: W33.

B519.   Näslund, Eric. "Stockholm Opera." *Opera Canada* 19, no. 4 (1978): 39.

> One of the most negative reviews of the première of *Le Grand Macabre*. "Produced in another field of the arts, it would be laughed off as an infantile, meaningless mess built on the premise that words like 'ass' always get laughs when sung by an opera singer." *See*: W54a.

B520.   Neukirchen, Alfons. "Von Jux Überschüttet." *Rheinische Post*, Oct. 17, 1978.

> A review of the Hamburg production of *Le Grand Macabre*. "Gewiß ist es György Ligeti gelungen, mit neuen Mitteln dramatische Musik nicht als Wortillustration, als bloßen Kommentar des Geschehens zu schreiben, sondern Geschehnisse und Gestalten durch Musik erst eigentlich zu erschaffen. Aber diese bewundernswerte Leistung wird an einem Objekt erprobt, das mehr modischen Schick als Gehalt hat. Der bedeutende Musiker Ligeti hat sein Talent für das Musiktheater demonstriert. Mehr als eine Hoffnung konnte er aber bei diesem nichtnutzigen Jux nicht wecken." ["György Ligeti has certainly been successful--not in writing modern dramatic music as text illustration or simple commentary on the action, but rather in creating real events and forms through music. This marvelous accomplishment was tried out, unfortunately, on an object that has more style than content. The remarkable musician Ligeti has demonstrated his talent for music theater, but he couldn't awake more than a hope with this good-for-nothing joke."] *See*: W54b.

B521.   "New Works." *Music Journal* 22 (Feb. 1964): 55.

> The New York Philharmonic avant-garde series included a performance of *Atmosphères* conducted by Leonard Bernstein. "The composer's aim in this music is simply 'the revivification of the sonorous aspect of musical form', and in this he has totally succeeded." *See*: W27b.

B522.   Nordwall, Trygve. "Ligetis Bläserquintett." *Musica* 23 (1969): 250-51.

A performance by the Stockholm Philharmonic Wind Quintet of *Ten Pieces for Wind Quintet.* "Seine Musik ist kompromißlos und baut immer auf den speziellen Voraussetzungen der verwendeten Instrumente auf." ["His music is uncompromising and always builds on the special requirements of the instruments."] *See:* W43.

B523.   Northcott, Bayan. "Radio." *Music and Musicians* 19 (March 1971): 68.

A performance of the *Requiem.* "... if one is going to isolate the [atmospheric] aspect from all the others that normally comprise fully composed music, is it necessary for the resulting pieces to be so remorselessly long?" *See:* W35.

B524.   -------. "Recordings." *Tempo* no. 119 (Dec. 1976): 32-33.

A review of Deutsche Grammophon 2530 392, and Decca Head 12. Mr. Northcott remarks aptly on both the style of the music, and on the quality of the recordings. *See:* D11, D22, D44, D38, D75, D78, D95.

B525.   Norton-Welsh, Christopher. "Graz." *Opera* 22 (1971): 34-35.

This was the first performance of *Aventures et Nouvelles Aventures* using the composer's own scenario. "His setting was a pedestrian crossing and the first event was that the soprano and alto help a blind man across the road to fall into the orchestra pit. The further events depended greatly on the efforts of three mimes and a large number of extras.... Many of these [events] were in fact very effective and amusing but, not surprisingly, few survived the exact repeat of the work after the interval." *See:* W33, W34, W36a.

B526.   -------. "Graz." *Opera* 33 (1982): 405.

A performance of *Le Grand Macabre* by the Musiktheater Nürnberg, directed by Götz Fischer, and conducted by Wolfgang Gayler. "... stressed the jokiness and puerile elements of libretto and score so that it was hard to detect the 'worthwhile modern comic opera' review by William Mann in *Opera*, July 1978, pp 678-80." *See:* W54g, B505.

B527.   Oakes, Meredith. "Brilliantly daft." *The Independent*, Oct. 31, 1989.

This review of the London "Ligeti by Ligeti" festival focuses on the *Nonsense Madrigals.* "If the *Madrigals* show Ligeti jumping the narrowest and most elegant technical hurdles that he can devise for himself, they are also brilliantly alive, full of contrapuntal wit and imaginative paradox. They are very funny." *See:* W65, App. II, p. 174.

B528.   Oehlschlägel, Reinhard. "Aktionen von heute und Morgen." *Opernwelt* no. 3 (1969): 40.

This concert of new music featured Ligeti's "lecture" entitled "Die Zukunft der Musik" (The Future of Music). *See:* W29.

B529.   -------. "Experimente auf Bühnen und Mattscheiben." *Neue Musikzeitung* 20, no. 2 (1971): p. 5.

This review includes a paragraph on the film version of *Aventures et Nouvelles Aventures* directed by Klaus Lindemann and broadcast on Zweite Deutsche

Fernsehen. "Ein schöner Nonsens-Film." ["A beautiful nonsense-film."] *See:* W36e.

B530.   -------. "Ein zwanzigstimmiges Monument: Erfolgreiche Erstaufführung von György Ligetis *Requiem* in Köln." *Frankfurter Allgemeine Zeitung*, Jan. 27, 1967, p. 9.

This was the German première of the work. "In ... dem *Requiem*, kommt es auf Textverständlichkeit nicht primär an, obschon sie keineswegs konsequent gemieden wird. Trotzdem kann jede Stelle als folgrichtige Komposition der betreffenden Textstelle aufgefaßt werden." ["In ... the *Requiem*, understandability of the text is not the primary concern, although it is in no way avoided. Nonetheless, each passage can be understood as a logical setting of the text at hand."] *See:* W35b.

B531.   Orga, Ates. "Boulez." *Music and Musicians* 22 (April 1974): 56+.

This concert by the BBC Symphony Orchestra with Pierre Boulez conducting featured *Ramifications*. "This is a fascinating exploration in pitch diffraction, but nevertheless it could be argued that a lot of Ligeti's effects are rapidly becoming exhausted of their initial potential." *See:* W44.

B532.   Oswald, Peter. "'Ich bin froh, daß ich heute nicht weiß, wo Gott wohnt': György Ligeti beim Musikprotokoll des 'Steirischen Herbsts'." *Neue Zeitschrift für Musik* 145, no. 12 (Dec. 1984): 32-33.

A report of this festival which was devoted exclusively to the music of Ligeti. A symposium on the theme, "György Ligeti: Personal style, Avant-garde, Popularity" was held simultaneously. Performers included the Austrian Radio Symphony Orchestra, piano duo Uriarte-Mrongovius, the Reihe Ensemble directed by Friedrich Cerha, the Vienna Wind Ensemble, Elisabeth Chojnacka, Heinrich Schiff, the Arditti Quartet, and Zsigmond Szathmáry. Ligeti himself made extensive comments regarding his music and his development through the 1970s. "Bedauerlich war die Tatsache, daß durch den Ausfall des Chorkonzerts Ligeti's neueste Schaffensphase unterbelichtet blieb." ["Unfortunately, the paucity of choral performances prevented exposure to Ligeti's newest creative phase."] *See:* App. II, p. 172.

B533.   -------. "Ligeti--Personale und -Symposion in Graz." *Österreichische Musikzeitschrift* 39 (1984): 596-98.

A report of the 1984 "Styrian Autumn" Festival, which featured performances of a number of Ligeti's works and a lecture on serial music by the composer. There was also a symposium entitled 'György Ligeti, Personal Style--Avantgardism--Popularity.' Presentations were made by Monika Lichtenfeld, Martin Zenck and Rudolf Frisius. *See:* App. II, p. 172.

B534.   Owen, Barbara. "Martha Folts." *American Organist* 7 (April 1969): 7.

A performance of *Volumina* in Boston. Although the review is positive, the author argues that such works should not be referred to as "music." *See:* W31.

B535.   Paap, Wouter. "Avantgardistisch Muziektheater: Ligeti en Maderna bij de Nederlandse Opera." *Mens en Melodie* 28 (1973): 152-54.

A performance of *Aventures et Nouvelles Aventures*. The author feels that the works are better suited to a small concert hall and that the inventive subtleties are lost in the theater. *See:* W33, W34, W36.

B536. -------. "Het 'Kammerkonzert' van György Ligeti." *Mens en Melodie* 26 (1971): 183-85.

The first performance of the *Chamber Concerto* in the Netherlands (Dutch Radio Chamber Orchestra; Paul Hupperts, conductor) is reviewed. "Slechts na vele repetities leert men leven med deze schijnbaar zwevende, onbestamde muziek, die tenslotte toch haar eigen contour en suggestie verkrijgt. Beide elementen werden tijdens deze uitvoeringen tot een boeiende synthese gebracht." ["Only after many repetitions does one learn to live with this seemingly floating, undefined music, which in the end assumes its own contour and suggestion. In this performance both elements were brought to a fascinating synthesis."] *See:* W46.

B537. -------. "Muziek van Klank en Kleur." *Mens en Melodie* 18 (1963): 1-3.

This discussion of *Atmosphères* mentions a performance by the Utrecht Municipal Orchestra directed by Paul Hupperts. The author wonders if the mysterious sound world in *Atmosphères* will become important to music. *See:* W27.

B538. Page, Tim. "György Ligeti." *New York Times*, Nov. 14, 1986, p. C34.

A review of the Merkin Hall concert given on the occasion of Ligeti's winning the Grawemeyer Award for his *Etudes for piano*. "Within the works one finds, cheek by jowl, pretty bows to Chopin and Debussy, the fierce energy and density of Mr. Nancarrow's studies for player piano, some of the richly contrapuntal stasis of Mr. Reich's work and a little of the sheer giddiness of Chabrier. Yet the synthesis is Mr. Ligeti's own." *See:* W63.

B539. Parsons, Michael. "Avant-garde Operas?" *Musical Times* 109 (1968): 452.

A performance by the Focus Opera Group, of *Aventures et Nouvelles Aventures* directed by Michael Graubart. "... it seemed an impoverishment of conventional vocal music which has all this and verbal meaning as well." *See:* W33, W34, W36c.

B540. Pernick, Ben. "An Important Modern." *Fanfare*, July-Aug. 1978, p. 48-49.

A review of Bis LP 53. "Ligeti's music, always interesting and admirable, grows with repeated listening. Adventurous listeners should try this album." *See:* D19, D23, D61, D72.

B541. -------. "Ligeti." *Fanfare*, Sept.-Oct. 1978, p. 70.

A review of Wergo WER 60076. As the BIS [LP 53] and Wergo discs are equal in every technical aspect, the buyer's choice must be decided by the couplings. Here the BIS set wins, for the *String Quartet No. 1* from 1953-54 and *Continuum* (1968 piece) are of greater musical interest and value than Wergo's *Two Etudes* and *Glissandi*." *See:* D19, D23, D30, D61, D72, D79, D84.

B542. Peterson, Hans-Gunnar. "Världsmusikfest med stilkonflikt." Svenska Dagbladet, Nov. 17, 1983.

A review of the 1983 ISCM festival in Århus, Denmark. "György Ligetis bidrag ... gav den starkaste upplevelsen av relationen mellan tradition, samtid och framtid i musiken." ["György Ligeti's participation ... gave the strongest impression on the relation between tradition, contemporary and future in music."]

B543.   Pettitt, Stephen. "Orchestral, Choral." *Musical Times* 122 (1981): 401.

A review of the first English performance of scenes and interludes from *Le Grand Macabre* performed by the BBC Symphony Orchestra led by Elgar Howarth. "Ligeti's writing is not as facile as such a plot might have us believe.... If, like me, you were able to swallow the naivety of the tale, it made for an exhilaratingly uproarious evening." *See*: W55.

B544.   Pinard-Legry, Jean-Luc. "*Le Grand Macabre* à l'Opéra." *Quinzaine Litteraire*, May 1-15, 1981, p. 27.

A review of the Paris production of *Le Grand Macabre*. "On le sait, la conception que Daniel Mesguich a réussi à imposer n'a pas ètè du goût de Ligeti qui a même quitté la salle le soir de la première sous prétexte d'une défaillance technique. Moment cocasse qui n'était pas prévu au programme, mais qui dit bien qu'aujourd'hiu les metteurs en scène font la loi sur les scènes lyriques." ["We know that the conception Daniel Mesguich was able to impose wasn't to Ligeti's taste; he even left the room on the pretext of a technical failure. This was an absurd moment that wasn't in the program but which shows well that today the directors control the artistic context."] *See*: W54d.

B545.   Pitt, Charles. "Paris." *Opera* 30 (1979): 594.

A performance of *Aventures et Nouvelles Aventures* by Marie Thérèse Cahn, Gabriella Ravazzi, and François LeRoux, produced by Brigitte Jaques. "... two old ladies and an old man, all fairly gaga, looking through a photo album and emitting sounds obviously recalling their earlier life while three silent youngsters - perhaps geriatric nurses - look on from above...." *See*: W33, W34, W36.

B546.   -------. "Paris: 'Showbiz' Opera." *Opera* 32 (1981): 694-96.

A review of the highly controversial Paris production of *Le Grand Macabre*. "One's final impression was that Daniel Mesguich, with a complete command of every facet of showbiz and by completely relegating boredom, had convinced the Parisian public that they like modern opera. That in itself was no mean achievement but I wonder if the music has really been allowed to speak for itself?" *See*: W54d.

B547.   Polaczek, Dietmar. "Der Jüngste Tag mißlang, die Oper blieb am Leben: György Ligetis *Le Grand Macabre* in Stockholm uraufgeführt." *Frankfurter Allgemeine Zeitung*, April 15, 1978, p. 25.

The first performance of this opera is reviewed. "Das Vergnügen an diesem Stück ist zweifach: es bietet intellektuellenwie sinnlichen Reiz, ist mit einegem dramatischen Geschick gebaut und läßt wohl einen sehr großen Spielraum für die Möglichkeiten szenischer Darstellung...." ["The pleasure in this piece is twofold: it offers intellectual as well as sensual charm. It is structured with a single dramatic destiny, yet provides a wide latitude for the possibilities of scenic representation."] *See*: W54a.

B548.   -------. "Neues von Heute und von Gestern in Graz." *Opernwelt* no. 12 (Dec. 1970): 40-41.

This review of a production of *Aventures et Nouvelles Aventures* by Hans Neugebauer, includes a discussion of the term "premier performance" in relation to new stagings of vocal works. "[Neugebauer] hat das Originalszenarium stark zurechtgestutzt, in einer etwas surrealen straßenszenerie und die Handlung trivialisiert, vielleicht allzu vordergründig, zu witzig aufgefaßt." ["[Neugebauer]

trimmed the original staging drastically, to a rather surreal street scene ... and
trivialized the action, interpreting it perhaps too superficially, too jokingly, too
wittily."] *See:* W33, W34, W36a.

B549.   -------. "Reife Fruchte und saure Trauben beim Musikprotokolle in
Graz." *Melos* 41 (1974): 38-42.

The première of *Clocks and Clouds* by the Austrian Radio Symphony and
Chorus, conducted by Friedrich Cerha. Refers to Ligeti's friendship with Cerha
and with Harald Kaufmann. *See:* W50a.

B550.   -------. "Der Weltuntergang im Zirkus: Ligetis Oper *Le Grand
Macabre* in der Hamburgischen Staatsoper." *Frankfurter
Allgemeine Zeitung*, Oct. 17, 1978.

The Hamburg production is reviewed. "Trotz allem war es ein beeindruckender
Erfolg. Trotz einigen Buh-Rufern, die vielleicht beweisen wollten, daß die positive
Resonanz auf eine Uraufführung im fernen Stockholm noch lange kein Grund ist,
auf die eigene Urteilsbildung zu verzichten, selbst auf die Gefahr hin, daß der
Vergleich zwischen hamburgischen und Stockholmer Kunstverstand zu
ungunsten der Hanseaten ausgeht. Und trotz einer Inszenierung, die manche
Vorzüge eines Werks mehr verdeckte als vorzeigte. Und trotz der
dramaturgischen und sprachlichen Fragwurdigkeiten einer Oper, die von der
musikalischen Substanz mehr als wettgemacht werden." ["In spite of everything
it was an impressive success. In spite of some booers, who perhaps wanted to
demonstrate that the success of a première in distant Stockholm is no reason to
give up forming one's own opinion (even at the risk that the comparison
between Hamburg's and Stockholm's artistic discernment would be to the
Hanseatics' disadvantage). And despite a staging which hid some merits of a
work more than it displayed them. And despite the dramaturgical and linguistic
questionability of an opera which more than compensates in musical
substance."] *See:* W54b.

B551.   Porter, Andrew. "Musical Events: Orchestral Adventures." *New
Yorker*, Feb. 5, 1990, p. 113-15.

The New York première of the *Piano Concerto* was performed by Anthony di
Bonaventura with the St. Louis Symphony conducted by Leonard Slatkin. "... I
wanted to admire and enjoy it but at first hearing found it somewhat unattractive
and schematic. A second hearing might have clarified things. *See:* W64.

B552.   -------. "Musical Events: Prize-giving." *New Yorker*, June 8, 1987, 85-
86.

This report on the Grawemeyer Award includes a description of the *Six Studies*
and a review of a performance of the work which took place in Louisville. The
pianist was Volker Banfield. "I thought him capable, but too literal and too
nearly monochrome to make the most of the music .... In the Trio, Saschko
Gawriloff, violin, and Robin Graham, horn, joined Mr. Banfield. Their
performance was plainer, less masterly, less captivating ...." *See:* W63, W59c.

B553.   -------. "Musical Events: The Silver Answer Rang." *New Yorker*,
March 4, 1985, 101-3.

A performance in Carnegie Hall by the Chamber Orchestra of Europe was
conducted by Claudio Abbado. The program included *Ramifications*. "Today, it
seems more a careful experiment of the past, carried out by a subtle and
scrupulous creator, than a lasting work of art." *See:* W44.

B554.   -------. "Musical Events: Transmutation." *New Yorker*, Oct. 15, 1985, 160.

A League ISCM concert which featured the American première of the *Horn Trio* was performed by William Purvis (horn), Rolf Schulte (violin), and Alan Feinberg (piano). "... a disquieting and beautiful piece." *See*: W59b.

B555.   -------. "Musical Events: What? When? How?" *New Yorker*, Feb. 14, 1983, 85-86+.

A review of the London première of *Le Grand Macabre*. Includes a summary of Ligeti's career going back to the 1960 Cologne ISCM festival where *Apparitions* was first performed. "*Le Grand Macabre*, despite some clumsy episodes in the libretto, is both entertaining and serious. The music is never clumsy. In an age when many new works flounder, some in their endeavor to startle and shock, some in their 'neo-Romantic' determination not to, it gathers up two decades of musical discoveries, captures and reshapes them surely for the lyrical theatre, and takes new strides down the path Monteverdi began and Mozart, Rossini, and (despite Ligeti's disclaimer) Berg continued." *See*: W54e.

B556.   Potter, Keith. "York." *Music and Musicians* 22 (Sept. 1973): 72+.

This performance of the *Chamber Concerto* was given by Friedrich Cerha conducting die Reihe. "One of the most remarkable things about Ligeti is his ability to take a simple idea - very often an idea about motion - and make it the basis of a whole work which can become bewilderingly, but never confusingly or needlessly, complex." *See*: W46.

B557.   Rapoport, Paul. "Ligeti." *Fanfare*, Nov.-Dec. 1979, p. 97.

A review of Wergo 60079. "But when Ligeti writes (in the fourth movement) "presto furioso, brutale, tumultoso," the Arditti quartet really lets you have it. Their demonic fury and other extremes of approach may not be subtle, but they aren't meant to be. They work, and that's that." *See*: W19, W42, D73, D77.

B558.   Redvall, Eva. "Stockholm." *Opera News* 43 (July 1978): 34-35.

English translation of a review which appeared in *Schweizerische Musikzeitung* 118, no. 3 (1978): 162-64. Reviews the world première of *Le Grand Macabre*. "With Ligeti's flare for comedy combined with his love for the decadent, his opera could have become what the title indicates. But it seems he and especially Meschke were afraid of being regarded as highbrow and instead resorted to fun and frolic." *See*: W54a.

B559.   Restagno, Enzo. "Da Graz." *Nuova Revista Musicale Italiana* 7 (1973): 463-64.

A review of the "Styrian Autumn" festival which featured the première of *Clocks and Clouds*. *See*: W50a.

B560.   Rexroth, Dieter. "Die Bewährungsprobe bestanden: György Ligetis Anti-Oper *Le Grand Macabre* nun in Hamburg." *Frankfurter Rundschau*, Oct. 20, 1978.

The Hamburg production of this opera is reviewed. "Ohne Frage ist *Le Grand Macabre* in der überarbeiteten Form trotz des absurden Charakters um einiges runder, ausgeschliffener, in ihren ganz verschiedenen musiksprachlichen Qualitäten und Facetten aber auch viel prägnanter geworden.... Unbedingter Pluspunkt dieser Hamburger Einstudierung ist das Außerordentlich hohe musikalische Niveau. Das betrifft nicht nur die Sänger, sondern vor allem das

Philharmonische Staatsorchester...." ["Despite the absurd characters, *Le Grand Macabre* has unquestionably become, in its reworked form, somewhat plainer and clearer, but also more precise in its contrasting musical qualities and facets.... An absolute asset of this Hamburg production is the extraordinarily high musical level. This is not only meant for the vocalists, but above all for the Philharmonic State Orchestra."] *See:* W54b.

B561.   Rhein, John von. "Records. Ligeti." *Chicago Tribune*, July 29, 1984, sec. 13, p. 14.

A review of Deutsche Grammophon DG 410 651-1. "The DG performances are good and benefit from the clean analytical scrutiny accorded them by Boulez as well as by the crisp analog engineering." Reprinted as "A Retrospective of Seminal Ligeti." *Ovation* 5 (Oct. 1984): 57. *See:* D9, D13, D58.

B562.   Rochelt, Hans. "Wien: Kulinarisches und provozierendes bei den Festwochen." *Neue Zeitschrift für Musik* 134 (1973): 592-94.

A brief review of a Ligeti concert which featured *Lux aeterna*, *Melodien*, the *Concerto for Violoncello*, the *Double Concerto*, and *Atmosphères*. *See:* W37, W47, W38, W48, W27, App. II, p. 170.

B563.   -------. "Wien: von Verdi zu Ligeti." *Neue Zeitschrift für Musik* 131 (1970): 350-52.

This concert included the *Chamber Concerto* performed by die Reihe under Friedrich Cerha. *See:* W46.

B564.   -------. "Wien: Alban Bergs *Lulu* erstmals in der Staatsoper." *Neue Zeitschrift für Musik* 130 (1969): 68-70.

A performance of the *Concerto for Violoncello* given by Siegfried Palm, with die Reihe and Friedrich Cerha. *See:* W38.

B565.   Rockwell, John. "Ligeti and Stockhausen have Premiers of Operas." *New York Times*, March 29, 1981, p. 60.

This is a review of the Paris production of *Le Grand Macabre*. "The Ligeti in Paris was something of a triumph for the beleaguered regime of Bernard Lefort. Ironically, the only person who seemed unhappy was Mr. Ligeti himself.... The fashionable first-night Paris public found all of this, as well as a devil figure, triple manifestations by identically dressed extras of the principal characters and cameo appearances by the Marx Brothers, Spiderman, and the heros and heroines from all your favorite operas, plus much, much more, to be vastly amusing." *See:* W54d.

B566.   Roelcke, Eckhard. "Verspäteter Hommage für György Ligeti in Hamburg: ein Schwärmer." *Die Zeit*, March 2, 1984, p. 52.

This is a report of a lecture-concert in which Ligeti discussed his own works using examples. "Ich habe nicht den Hang, mich hinter meinen Werken zu verbergen, mich zu maskieren. Ich bemühe mich, zufrichtig zu komponieren, nicht darauf zu sehen, welchen Effekt die Musik hat. Ich will nicht gefallen, sondern das tun, was ich empfinde. Es gibt in meinen Werken demnach direkte Emotionalität." ["I am not inclined to hide behind my works, to disguise myself. I try to compose sincerely, not trying to see what effect the music has. I don't want to please, but rather do what I feel. Consequently there is direct emotionality in my works."] *See:* App. II, p. 172.

B567.   Roschitz, Karlheinz. "Nachtstudio im Theater an der Wien."
         Österreichische Musikzeitschrift 22 (1967): 421-22.

A review of the Stuttgart staging of *Aventures et Nouvelles Aventures* performed
in Vienna. "Die Inszenierung Rolf Scharres, die für jede musikalische Floskel
eine theatralische Aktion erfindet, entspricht zwar nicht unbedingt Ligetis
Konzept von der Autonomie der Musik, amüsiert aber und läßt oft staunen."
["Rolf Scharre's staging, which finds a theatrical action for each musical flourish,
certainly does not correspond to Ligeti's concept of the autonomy of the music,
but it amuses and often astounds."] *See:* W33b, W34b, W36b.

B568.   Rostand, Claude. "Donaueschingen ist immer noch eine Reise wert."
         Melos 28 (1961): 405-410.

A review of the world première of *Atmosphères*. "... ist dieses Werk eine der
spektakulären Attraktionen des Musikfestes.... Man glaubt, nicht ein normales
Orchester zu hören, sondern aus Lautsprechern kommende konkrete und
elektronische Klänge." ["... this work is one of the spectacular attractions of the
music festival.... One believes one is hearing "concrete" and electronic sounds
from a loudspeaker instead of a real orchestra."] *See:* W27a.

B569.   Ruppel, K.H. "Im Zeichen des Klanges." *Süddeutsche Zeitung*, Dec.
         5, 1960, "Feuilleton" section, p. 6.

A performance of *Apparitions* appeared in the "Musica Viva" concert series.
Bruno Maderna conducted the South German Radio Orchestra. "Möge Ligeti,
der ein kluger und selbständiger, gegen den seriellen Akademismus
aufbegehrender Mann ist, nicht zum Begründer des musikalischen "Ennuismus",
Jahrgang 1960." ["Ligeti is one of the more intelligent and independent
opponents of serial academism. May he not become the founder of the 1960
school of musical 'ennui-ism.'"] *See:* W26.

B570.   -------. "Klangstrukturen und Klangflächen." *Süddeutsche Zeitung*.
         March 27, 1962.

The première of *Fragment* is reviewed. "... ich vorläufig nichts anderes als eine
Art Selbstparodie auf die *Apparitions* zu sehen vermag." ["For now, I can only
view it as a kind of self parody of *Apparitions*."] *See:* W28a.

B571.   -------. "Ein Stück wunderschöner Musik: Uraufführung von György
         Ligetis *Melodien* unter Hans Gierster in Nürnberg." *Süddeutsche
         Zeitung*, Dec. 13, 1971.

The first performance of this work is reviewed. "Sucht man nach einem
Vergleich aus einer früheren Epoche der modernen Musik, so würde ich am
ehesten 'Nuages' nennen, das erste der drei 'Nocturnes' von Debussy." ["If one
looks for a comparison with earlier epochs of modern music, I would name
'Nuages,' the first of the 3 'Nocturnes' by Debussy."] *See:* W47a.

B572.   Sabbe, Herman. "De Dood (Van de Opera) gaat niet door ..." *Mens
         en Melodie* 34 (1979): 55-58.

A review of the Hamburg production of *Le Grand Macabre*. *See:* W54b.

B573.   -------. "Ligeti: Bartók Geminiaturiseerd." *Mens en Melodie* 33
         (1978): 59-60.

A review of an all-Ligeti concert which was presented as part of the 1977
Flanders Festival. The *String Quartet No. 2* (Arditti Quartet), *Ten Pieces for Wind*

Quintet (Belgian Wind Quintet), and *Monument-Selbstportrait-Bewegung* (Canino-Ballista) were performed. The quartet inspired comparison with Bartók. *See*: W42, W43, W52, App. II, p. 170.

B574.   Sadie, Stanley. "Avant garde, but is it progress?" *Times*, March 12, 1968, p. 13.

A review of a program given by the Focus Opera Group, including *Aventures et Nouvelles Aventures*. "The effect was sometimes funny, sometimes alarming, sometimes (no doubt deliberately) boring. Michael Graubart directed none too assured a performance." *See*: W33, W34, W36c.

B575.   Salzman, Eric. "New Music from Heliodor Wergo." Stereo Review 25, no. 4 (Oct. 1970): 104.

A review of Heliodor 2549 011 and 2549 003. "For better or worse, the [Requiem] as a whole is something quite different from what the fragments in the film [2001] suggest it is." *See*: W35, D4, D7, D17, D35, D59, D94.

B576.   Sandner, Wolfgang. "Ende der Welt -- mit Ladehemmung: György Ligetis Oper *Le Grand Macabre* in Hamburg erstaufgeführt." *Musik + Medizin* 4, no. 11 (1978): 51-54.

Theoretically, there are two styles in which this work could be produced. The first is a bare, empty stage in which the performers and the music would represent this grotesque story to greater effect. The other possibility is a wild, absurd scene, a surrealistic entertainment. Hamburg avoids both extremes, and the result is a "half-hearted melange." Deborah Browne's performance as Mescalina is singled out for occasionally bringing the stage to life. *See*: W54b.

B577.   -------. "Graz: Musikprotokoll beim 'Steirer Herbst' 1973." *Neue Zeitschrift für Musik* 134 (1973): 800-802.

The première of *Clocks and Clouds* was performed by the Austrian Radio Symphony Orchestra and Choir under Friedrich Cerha. The performance also included the *Double Concerto* with Karlheinz Zöller (flute) and Maurice Bourgue (oboe). "Ein Werk von eindringlicher Monotonie und fast sanfter Expressivität...." ["A work of emphatic monotony and almost gentle expressiveness...."] *See*: W48, W50a.

B578.   Schalz-Laurenze, Ute. "Bergedorf: Klagelandschaft." *Frankfurter Allgemeine Zeitung*, Aug. 19, 1982, p. 17.

Reprinted in *Neue Zeitschrift für Musik* 143, no. 10 (1982): 65-66. This review of the première of the *Horn Trio* also reviews Ligeti's previous work and describes each movement of the new work. "Gut zwanzig Jahre nach *Atmosphères* spielen die Kategorien Intervall, Rhythmus und Dynamik wieder die strukturgebende Rolle." ["A good twenty years after *Atmosphères* the categories of interval, rhythm and dynamics again play a structural role."] *See*: W59a.

B579.   Schibli, Sigfried. "Wie ein verrücktes Uhrwerk: Werke von György Ligeti in Frankfurt." *Frankfurter Allgemeine Zeitung*, May 9, 1986.

This concert consisted of the *Six Bagatelles for Wind Quintet*, the *Concerto for Violoncello* (Kai Scheffler, cello), and *Aventures et Nouvelles Aventures* (Gabriele Auenmüller, sop., Linda Hirst, mez., Jürgen Hartfiel, bar.), performed by the Ensemble Modern directed by Zoltan Pesko. "Jedenfalls machte die Wiedergabe unter Pesko einen geschlossenen Eindruck und bildete den glanzvollen Abschluß des Ligeti-Konzerts." ["In any case the performance under Pesko was

uniformly impressive, and formed a magnificent ending for the Ligeti concert."]
See: W15, W38, W33, W34, W36, App. II, p. 173.

B580.   Schiffer, Brigitte. "Begeisterung für die zweite Wiener Schule und Boulez in London." *Melos* 36 (1969): 385.

The Camden Festival included a performance of the *Concerto for Violoncello* (Göran Holmstrand, cello, Musica Nova Ensemble directed by Siegfried Naumann), *Volumina* (Karl-Erik Welin), and *Ten Pieces for Wind Quintet* (Stockholm Philharmonic Wind Quintet). See: W38, W31, W43.

B581.   Schleicher, Fritz. "Die Farce zur Apokalypse: György Ligetis Oper *Le Grand Macabre* in Nürnberg." *Das Orchester* 28 (1980): 309-10.

A review of the Nuremberg production, reprinted from *Nürnberger Nachrichten*, Feb. 4, 1980. "Eine realistisch-surrealistische Farce in Becketts Endzeit-Dimension, zwischen Banalität und Transzendenz ...." ["A realistic-surrealistic farce in Beckett's "Endtime dimension" between banality and transcendence."] See: W54g.

B582.   Schmidt-Garre, Helmut. "München: Musica-Viva--immer interessant." *Neue Zeitschrift für Musik* 132 (1971): 257.

This concert included a performance of *Lontano*. "Musik ist hier reduziert oder vorgetrieben auf eine Stunde Null, in einen brodelnden Urzustand versetzt, musikalischer Urschlamm, in dem noch alles möglich oder bereits alles erstorben ist." ["Music is reduced or driven for a time to nothing: set into a bubbling primitive state, the primeval slime of music in which all possibilities fade away."] See: W39.

B583.   -------. "Vier Komponisten in eigener Sache." *Neue Zeitschrift für Musik* 125 (1964): 68.

A concert by die Reihe with Friedrich Cerha which included *Atmosphères*. "Dieses vor zwei Jahren in Donaueschingen mit größtem Erfolg uraufgeführte Stück fand jetzt, zwei Jahre danach, nur eine vergleichsweise laue Aufnahme, vermutlich weil seine Aggressivität von der noch größeren Cerhas zuvor übertrumpft worden war." ["This piece, first performed two years ago in Donaueschingen with great success, received only a lukewarm reception here, presumably because its aggressiveness was overshadowed by that of Cerha."] See: W27.

B584.   Schneider, Marcel. "Ligeti's *Le Grand Macabre* in Paris." *Österreichische Musikzeitschrift* 36 (1981): 339-40.

The Paris production of the opera is reviewed. "Das Publikum schien nicht allzu genau zu wissen, was es davon halten sollte. Es hatte wohl den Eindruck eines anziehenden Werkes, dessen Attraktivität aber von der schwierigen Vielschichtigkeit des 20. Jahrhunderts zu begreifen ist." ["The audience did not seem to know exactly what to make of [the music]. It had the impression of a charming work, but one whose attractiveness is to be understood in terms of the intricate stratification of the 20th century."] See: W54d.

B585.   Schreiber, Wolfgang. "Musikalische Intelligenz: Ligeti. Eine Studiomatinee im Bayerischen Rundfunk." *Süddeutsche Zeitung*, May 13, 1981.

This article reports on a Munich Musica Viva concert which consisted of both wind quintets (Syrinx Quintet), both string quartets (Arditti Quartet), and *Passacaglia ungherese* and *Hungarian Rock* (Elisabeth Chojnacka). Ligeti also spoke. "Und Ligeti als Kommentator? Ein Riese an Geist und Witz, auch gestischer Beweglichkeit, spontaner Formulierungslust, kommunikativer Sinnlichkeit. Man war hingerissen." ["And Ligeti as commentator? A giant in spirit and wit, as well as gesticular agility, a fondness for spontaneous formulations, communicative sensuality. It was fascinating."] *See*: W15d, W19d, W42c, W43c, W56c, W57c, App. II, p. 171.

B586. -------. "Der Tod fährt Rollstuhl: Das Freiburger Theater wagt Ligetis *Le Grand Macabre*." *Süddeutsche Zeitung*, March 10, 1984, p. 16.

A review of the production of this opera in Freiburg. "In Freiburg bemühte man sich, des Guten nicht zuviel zu tun, auch in puncto vulgärer Bürgerschreck-Öbszönität. Die Aufführung steigerte sich in dieser Hinsicht im Laufe des Brillanz und Faszination des Einfachen." ["In Freiburg every effort was made not to overdo a good thing, even in regard to bourgeois-shocking obscenities. The performance improved in this respect in the course of the third scene and in the fourth achieved the brilliance and fascination of simplicity."] *See*: W54h.

B587. Schröder, Walter. "Riesenjubel über Sex-Oper." *Bild* (Hamburg), Oct. 17, 1978, p. 4.

The German première of *Le Grand Macabre* in Hamburg is the subject of this review. "Dreimal setzen die Gegner zum Buhsturm an. Die einen, weil ihnen wie Kaiser Wilhelm 'die ganze moderne Richtung nicht paßt'. Die anderen, weil Ligeti für sie ein Verräter an der Moderne ist. Dann siegte der Beifall. Er dauerte (gestoppt) 25 Minuten und 37 Sekunden." ["Three times the opponents began to boo. Some because they, like Kaiser Wilhelm 'are not suited to the whole modern orientation'. The others because for them Ligeti is a traitor to modernism. Then applause won out. It lasted (timed) 25 minutes and 37 seconds."] *See*: W54b.

B588. Schweizer, Klaus. "Schallplatten." *Neue Zeitschrift für Musik* 148, no. 1 (Jan. 1987): 56-57.

A review of Wergo WER 60100. *See*: D21, D33, D46, D53, D91.

B589. Schwinger, Wolfram. "25. Holland-Festival." *Stuttgarter Zeitung*, June 29, 1972.

Reprinted in *Musica* 26 (1972): 449-50. This festival included a performance of *Melodien* played by the Concertgebouw Orchestra under Michael Gielen. "Da die Bläser sowieso solistisch besetzt sind, hat Gielen nun somit insgesamt eine Erhellung der Partitur erreicht, die man ... kaum für möglich gehalten hätte. Ligeti selbst, eigentlich fast nie mit Aufführungen seiner Werke zufrieden, nannte Gielens Interpretation hell entzuckt 'authentisch'." ["As the winds are set more or less soloistically, Gielen used only one player on each string part and thus achieved a total illumination of the score which one ... would hardly have thought possible. Ligeti himself, who in fact is almost never satisfied with performances of his works, was clearly delighted and termed Gielen's interpretation 'authentic'."] *See*: W47d.

B590. -------. "Festwochenkonzerte mit Penderecki, Henze und Ligeti." *Musica* 24 (1970): 560-62.

Reprinted in part in *Stuttgarter Zeitung*, Oct. 5, 1970. The first performance of the *Chamber Concerto* was given by Friedrich Cerha and die Reihe. "Das Kammerkonzert ist ein Kompendium all dessen, was Ligeti an musikalischen Vorstellungen und Kompioniertechniken bisher ausgebreitet hat." ["The *Chamber Concerto* is a compendium of all that, which Ligeti has used to expand musical presentation and compositional techniques."] *See*: W46b.

B591.   -------. "Ganz absichtlos: 'Beispiele (4)' im Stuttgarter Kammertheater mit Stücken von John Cage und Ligeti." *Stuttgarter Zeitung*, Oct. 28, 1972.

This performance of *Aventures* (without *Nouvelles Aventures*) was performed by Gertie Charlent, Elke Estlinbaum and Klaus Hirte conducted by Ernst Poettgen. "... sie kriegt mehr die grotske Seite dieser kleinen phonetische, dämonische Dimensionen." ["... they catch more of the grotesque side and less of the grave, diabolical dimensions of this phonetic, imaginary adventure."] *See*: W33.

B592.   -------. "Ligeti und Messiaen." *Stuttgarter Zeitung*, July 19, 1969.

Reprinted in part in *Musica* 23 (1969): 479-80. This performance of *Requiem* was given as part of the Stuttgarter Kirchenmusiktage 1969. Michael Gielen directed the South German Radio Orchestra and Choir with soloists Liliana Poli and Barbro Ericson. "... Ligetis *Requiem* [ist] ein nahezu einsmes Meisterwerk, eine der wesentlichsten Kompositionen wohl nicht nur dieses Jahrzehnts." ["Ligeti's *Requiem* [is] an almost solitary masterpiece, one of the most essential compositions, and not only of this decade."] *See*: W35.

B593.   -------. "Ligetis neues Doppelkonzert." *Stuttgarter Zeitung*, Sept. 20, 1972.

Reprinted in part in *Musica* 26 (1972): 572-73. The première of the *Double Concerto* is reviewed. "Die Uraufführyug hat Christoph von Dohnányi vorzüglich einstudiert, sensibel und präzis wachte er über dem zunächst leicht bewölkten, dann aber doch heiteren Klanggeschehen, und auch die Solisten ließen sich's nicht verdrießen, ihre eher undankbaren schwierigen Stimmen mit höchster Perfektion und tonlicher intensität zu blasen." ["Christoph von Dohnányi rehearsed the première excellently. With sensitivity and precision, he watched over music which was one moment lightly overcast and the next clear and bright. The soloists also did not allow themselves to be vexed, but played their difficult and thankless parts with the highest perfection and intensity of tone."] *See*: W48a.

B594.   -------. Ligetis neues Streichquartett." *Stuttgarter Zeitung*, Dec. 16, 1969.

Reprinted in part in *Musica* 24 (1970): 154-55. The première of *String Quartet No. 2* is reviewed. "... ein Streichquartett von dem ich das sichere Gefühl habe, daß es - nehmen wir Bartók aus -das wichtigste und bedeutendste Quartett seit Alban Bergs *Lyrischer Suite* ist.... Die LaSalle-Leute haben jede Nuance pointiert, manchmal schienen sie mit Geisterhänden zu musizieren. Ligeti wurde in ihrem Kreise aufs herzlichste gefeiert." ["... a string quartet which I feel sure (Bartók aside) is the most important and remarkable work since Alban Berg's *Lyric Suite*.... The LaSalle people caught every nuance, sometimes appearing to play with ghostly hands. In their circle, Ligeti was most affectionately celebrated."] *See*: W42a.

B595.   -------. "Neues von Ligeti und Penderecki." *Musica* 26 (1972): 149-50.

This review of the première of *Melodien* was reprinted from the *Stuttgarter Zeitung*. "... sicher werden sich noch weit diffizilere Qualitäten des Stücks hörend entdecken lassen, wenn ein mit neuester Musik erfahreneres Orchester und ein rhythmische flexibler und klanglich sensibler Dirigent aus dieser so feingliedrigen und farbigen, aber eben doch höchst schwierigen Partitur noch mehr herausholen werden." ["... surely an orchestra more experienced with new music would be able to bring out the more difficult qualities of the piece, and a director who is more rhythmically flexible and sensitive to tone would draw even more out of this finely proportioned and colored but yet most difficult score."] *See:* W47a.

B596. -------. "Tage zeitgenössischer Music." *Musica* 26 (1972): 358-60.

This performance by Bruno Maderna and the Stuttgart Radio Symphony of *Melodien* took place in Mannheim. "Maderna und die Stuttgarter Musiker gaben dem ungemein reizvoll gewobenen, sehr klangschönen und von Minute zu Minute ausdrucksvoller werdenden Stück noch eine delikatere Staffelung von Vorder- und Hintergrund, deutlichem oder undeutichem Hervorschimmern jener titelgebenden Melodien, die sich in Rhythmik und Tempo vielschichtig überlagern und somit jenen Schwebezustand herstellen, der für Ligeti's Stil so charakteristisch ist." ["Maderna and the Stuttgart musicians gave the piece, woven with uncommon charm and growing more expressive each minute, a still more delicate gradation of foreground and background. The 'melodies' of the title glistened forth now clearly, now unclearly, overlapping many layers of rhythm and tempo and so producing a suspended condition ... which is so characteristic of Ligeti's style."] *See:* W47.

B597. Seckerson, Edward. "Sound Odyssey on a Higher Plane." *The Sunday Correspondent*, Oct. 29, 1989.

This is a review of the Oct. 23 Concert in the "Ligeti by Ligeti" festival in London. "Two minutes into the second concert of the South Bank's retrospective, there were smiles all round for a composer who knows exactly when not to take himself too seriously." *See:* App. II, p. 174.

B598. Seebohm, Andrea. "Der Tod im Breughelland: Uraufführung von Ligetis *Le Grand Macabre*." *Kurier* (Vienna), April 14, 1978.

A review of the Stockholm production. "Ein deftiges, pralles, buntes Welttheater also, halb Zirkusspektakel, halb Schmierenvorstellung, mit platten Dialogen und simplen Reimen.... Unpsychologisch, verblüffend, total überdreht - ein Comic strip." ["A sturdy, well-rounded, colorful world theater; half circus spectacle, half traveling show, with flat dialog and simple rhymes.... Unpsychological, bewildering, completely stripped - a comic strip."] *See:* W54a.

B599. Spingel, Hans Otto. "Sprachlose Sprache." *Opernwelt* 11, no. 4 (April 1970): 37-38.

This performance of *Aventures et Nouvelles Aventures* took place in Darmstadt. "Eine Handlung gibt es also nicht, kann deshalb auch nicht erzählt werden. Die Musik ist ein ingeniös verzahntes Bündel von Clustern, utopischen Klängen und Geräuschen, die sich zur präzisen Fieberkurve zusammenfügen, zum Elektrokardiogramm des Menschen heute in der heutigen Sozietät." ["There is no story then, so none is told. The music is an ingeniously interlocking bundle of clusters, utopian tones and noises brought together to a precise temperature curve, to an electrocardiogram of modern man in modern society."] *See:* W33c, W34c, W36d.

B600. -------. "Wenn der Kieselstein weiteste Kreise zieht: die Freie Akademie und die Staatsoper ehrten den ungarischen Komponisten György Ligeti." *Die Welt*, Jan. 23, 1984.

A report of a performance in honor of Ligeti's 60th birthday of *Continuum, Hungarian Rock, Passacaglia ungherese* (Elisabeth Chojnacka), and the *Horn Trio* (Hermann Baumann, Saschko Gawriloff, and Eckhard Besch). "... wurde einer der bedeutendsten Komponisten der Gegenwart geehrt." ["... one of the most significant of contemporary composers was honored."] *See:* W41, W56, W57, W59.

B601.   Stadlen, Peter. "The I.S.C.M. Festival at Cologne." *Musical Times*
101 (1960): 484-486.

A review of the première of *Apparitions*. "Pitch has become a positive liability."
See: W26a.

B602.   Steinke, Wolfgang. "Das 34. Weltmusikfest der IGNM." *Neue
Zeitschrift für Musik* 121 (1960): 257.

A review of the première of *Apparitions*. "... muß auf einen Namen hingewiesen
werden, den es zu merken gilt, nicht nur weil er mit geradezu frenetischem
Beifall akklamiert wurde, sondern auch, weil hier unversehens eine
kompositorische Begabung von Rang hervortrat, die nur durch äußere Umstande
bisher verborgen blieb." ["... mention must be made of a name which is worth
noting not only because it was acclaimed with frenetic applause, but also
because here, unexpectedly, a great compositional talent was revealed which
had only remained hidden through exceptional circumstances."] *See:* W26a.

B603.   Stephens, Kevin. "Rennes: Contemporary Opera Feast." *Opera* 31
(1980): 286.

This review mentions a performance of *Aventures et Nouvelles Aventures*
produced by the Stuttgart Opera. "... backed up by an extremely lively, circus-
style stage presentation." *See:* W33, W34, W36.

B604.   Stevens, David. "Paris." Opera News 46 (Aug. 1981): 34.

The Paris production of *Le Grand Macabre* was the subject of much
controversy. "A series of interpolated opera scenes were mimed in the
background (Madama Butterfly, Lulu). The passionate young couple who
wandered through the devastated landscape, looking for a quiet place to make
love, became parodies of baroque opera characters. The Death figure tried
unsuccessfully to overthrow the conductor's control of the musical proceedings.
At the end, a scale model of the Palais Garnier was set on fire. The original
libretto does contain multiple parodistic opera references, but it is a long jump
to a staging that seems to say, 'Opera is dead--long live opera!'" *See:* W54d.

B605.   Stöckl, Rudolf. "Fragen an die Oper: Vier 'szenische Monologe' im
'Theater am Hexenturm' in Coburg." *Opernwelt* 25, no. 3 (March
1984): 53.

Rondeau was performed here by Helmut Thiele. *See:* W53.

B606.   -------. "Renaissance der Melodie? Eine Ligeti-Uraufführung zum
Dürerjahr." *Der Tagesspiegel,* Dec. 17, 1971.

A review of the première of *Melodien*. "Obwohl rhythmische Impulse eine
untergeordnete Rolle spielen, man beinähe von stehenden Klängen sprechen
möchte, atmet diese Musik." ["Although rhythmic impulse plays a subordinate
role (one might almost speak of stationary sounds), this music breathes."] *See:*
W47a.

B607.   -------. "Verschobener Weltuntergang: Ligeti's *Le Grand Macabre* in
Nürnberg." *Neue Zeitschrift für Musik* 142 (1980): 138.

The Nuremberg production of this opera is reviewed. "Einige
Mißfallenskundgebungen aus den Publikum galten dem anwesenden
Komponisten; für Sänger und Orchester gab es einhelligen Beifall." ["Some
expressions of disapproval from the public were directed at the composer who

was present. For the singers and the orchestra there was unanimous applause."] *See:* W54g.

B608. Stuckenschmidt, H.H. "Nachwuchssorgen auch in Donaueschingen." *Melos* 34 (1967): 456-62.

Mentions the première of *Lontano*. "Die geflissentliche Substanzlosigkeit suggeriert das Bild eines Schmetterlings, von dem der Flügelstaub übriggeblieben ist." ["The deliberate lack of substance suggests the image of a butterfly with only the dust of its wings remaining."] *See:* W39a.

B609. Sutcliffe, James Helme. "Hamburg Opera." *Opera Canada* 20, no 2 (1979): 37.

The Hamburg production of *Le Grand Macabre* is the subject of this report. "But it was the work itself, falsely labelled an 'anti-opera' (can there be such a thing?) which finally fascinated, beguiled and--a marvel on the contemporary music scene--amused." *See:* W54b.

B610. Sutcliffe, Tom. "A Dream of the Macabre." *The Guardian*, April 14, 1978, Arts section, p. 10.

This is a review of the Stockholm production of *Le Grand Macabre*. "Ligeti's first opera, though not specially macabre or great was filled with such strong, expressive, refreshingly imaginative music, and was written with such wit and also intellectual honesty, that if anybody is going to succeed in resurrecting the art of the opera now, Ligeti looks the man." *See:* W54a.

B611. Taylor, Timothy D. "Ligeti." *American Record Guide*, July-Aug. 1988, p. 33.

A review of Bis 53 (compact disc). "György Ligeti's music glistens, shimmers, sparkles. In this music he's primarily concerned with sound, not techniques or procedures." *See:* D19, D23, D61, D72.

B612. Thomas, Ernst. "Klang gegen Struktur? problematische Aspekte auf den Musiktagen 1961." *Neue Zeitschrift für Musik* 122 (1961): 524.

Includes a review of the première of *Atmosphères*. "Er glaubt an eine neue musikalische Form, in der es 'keine Ereignisse, sondern nur Zustände, keine Konturen und Gestalten, sondern nur den unbevölkerten, imaginären musikalischen Raum' gibt." ["He believes in a new musical form in which there are 'no events, but only states, no contours or shapes, only uninhabited imaginary musical space."] *See:* W27a.

B613. Thomson, Joan. "New York." *Opera News*, April 16, 1977, p. 36.

Reprinted in *Opera* 28 (1977): 448-49. This performance of *Aventures et Nouvelles Aventures* was directed by Ian Strasfogel with soloists Richard Barrett, Susan Kay Peterson and Phyllis Hunter, accompanied by members of Speculum Musicae led by David Gilbert. "... three strangers meeting in a room from which they cannot escape." *See:* W33, W34, W36.

B614. Tircuit, Henwell. "A Festival of Ligeti at Stanford." *San Francisco Chronicle*, May 15, 1972, p. 40.

An all-Ligeti lecture concert included *Artikulation, Poème symphonique, Lux aeterna*, and *Ten Pieces for Wind Quintet*. "Ligeti--a shy, very nervous man-- seemed to be having a wonderfully good time. So did the rest of us." *See:* W25, W32, W37, W43, App. II, p. 170.

B615.   -------. "Unusual Program with a Dedication." *San Francisco Chronicle*, Jan. 17, 1977, p. 40.

A performance of *Monument-Selbstportrait-Bewegung* was presented by Alfons and Aloys Kontarsky. "Its three movements, relatively docile in use of dissonance, came closer to classical sonata than anything Ligeti has yet given us." *See*: W52.

B616.   Tomzig, Sabine. "Imaginäres Musiktheater: Ligeti-Uraufführung im NDR." *Hamburger Abendblatt*, May 27, 1966.

The première of *Nouvelles Aventures* is reviewed. Ligeti had planned to give a lecture on imaginary music theater, but was suddenly taken ill. "... der Affektgehalt dieser imaginären 'Oper' prägt sich in der Wirkung weit geringer aus, als der fünfzeilige Untertitel verspricht." ["... the emotional content of this imaginary 'opera' proved to be more modest in practice than the five-line subtitle promised."] *See*: W34a.

B617.   -------. "In Hamburg gehört: Wieder Klaviermusik von Ligeti." *Hamburger Abendblatt*, Nov. 4, 1985.

The première of *Piano Etudes*, (nos. 1-5) was played by Volker Banfield, as part of a concert series called "8 1/2." "Er spielte die Etüden mit unheimlicher Klarheit, bisweilen aggressiv losdonnernd. Vor allem wirkten sie nicht nur rhythmisch kompliziert, sondern auch geschmeidig brillant und emotionell hochgesteigert." ["He played the etudes with uncanny clarity, at times thundering aggressively. Their effect was not primarily only rhythmically complex, but also smoothly brilliant and emotionally intense."] *See*: W63, W63c.

B618.   -------. "Schwere Musik--griffig erklärt." *Hamburger Abendblatt*, Feb. 15, 1984.

A brief review of a lecture concert given by Ligeti and including a broad cross-section of examples from his works. "'Ich komponiere für niemand, aber meine Musik ist für alle da.'" ["'I do not compose for anyone in particular, but my music is there for everyone.'"] *See*: App. II, p. 172.

B619.   -------. "Tumulte beim Katastrophenspiel: Staatsoper, Ligetis *Grand Macabre*," *Hamburger Abendblatt*, Jan. 21, 1980, p. 9.

A review of a revival of the Hamburg production. "... gab es jedenfalls lautstarke Zwischenrufe, die auf das irrwitzig Groteske dieser Folge von Comic strips über den Tod mit Empörung (Aufhören! Auf nach Pakistan!) reagierten.... am schluß verblüffend starken Beifall." ["There was intense heckling, an indignant reaction to the crazily witty grotesqueness of the series of comic strips on death.... at the end amazingly vigorous applause."] *See*: W54, W54b.

B620.   -------. "Weltpremiere in Bergedorf: Ligeti wird gefühlvoll." *Hamburger Abendblatt*, Aug. 9, 1982.

Reprinted in *Das Orchester* 30 (1982): 836-37. This is a review of the première of the *Horn Trio*. "Mit rhythmishcer Lockerheit und differenzierter Tongebung spürten sie den anspielungsreichen Gestaltungsmomenten ... nach." ["With rhythmic looseness and distinctive tone they felt the allusive organizational elements."] *See*: W59a.

B621.   ------. "Weltuntergang im Zirkuszelt." *Orchester* 27 (Jan. 1979): 22-23.

This review of the Hamburg production of *Le Grand Macabre* is based on one which appeared in *Hamburger Abendblatt*, Oct. 16, 1978, p. 11. Includes excerpts from other critics. "Die Hoffnungen wurden weit übertroffen. Dirigent Elgar Howarth, Regisseur Gilbert Deflo und sein Bühnenbildner Eckehard Grübler sind mit beispielhafter Konsequenz neue Wege gegangen. Vor allem: Das Hamburger Solistenensemble war phänomenal." ["Hopes were far surpassed. Conductor Elgar Howarth, director Gilbert Deflo and his set designer Eckehard Grübler have gone new ways with exemplary results. Above all: the Hamburg ensemble was phenomenal."] *See*: W54b.

B622.   ------. "Zwölf Autohupen blasen zum Weltuntergang: Ligeti-Oper *Le Grand Macabre* in Stockholm uraufgeführt." *Hamburger Abendblatt*, April 14, 1978.

This was the first performance of the opera. "Kein Zweifel: Das ist ein ganz neuer Ligeti, der plötzlich Spaß an einer Art Pop und Lust am phänomenal komischen Spektakel hat." ["No doubt: this is a completely new Ligeti who suddenly enjoys a pop style and delights in a phenomenally comic spectacle."] *See*: W54a.

B623.   Trilling, Ossia. "Der Skandal blieb aus: Ligetis *Le Grand Macabre* in London erstaufgeführt." *Opernwelt* 24, no. 2 (Feb. 1983): 30.

A review of the London production. "Der Tatort mag wohl auf englischen Boden verlegt worden sein, aber der große Makaber hat unter diesen Umständen an Gefährlichkeit verloren, seine Drohungen sind kaum ernst zu nehmen." ["The setting may work on an English stage, but the Grand Macabre loses gravity under these circumstances. His threats can hardly be taken seriously."] *See*: W54e.

B624.   Trumpff, G.A. "Darmstadt: Zweimal zwischen Furcht und Hoffnung." *Neue Zeitschrift für Musik* 131 (1970): 174.

This was a staging by Harro Dicks of *Aventures et Nouvelles Aventures*. "Harro Dicks verlegte die Handlung in ein Wachsfigurenkabinett, das von einer schnatternden Reisegesellschaft besichtigt wird." ["Harro Dicks set the action in a waxworks which is being viewed by a party of chattering tourists."] *See*: W33c, W34c, W36d.

B625.   ------. "György Ligetis Zweites Quartett." *Neue Zeitschrift für Musik* 131 (1970): 62.

Reprinted in *Das Orchester* 18 (1970): 119. A review of the première performance by the LaSalle Quartet in the Southwest German Radio. "... errang dem absolut teuflischen Werk, wie der Komponist einem Stockholmer Freund geschrieben hatte, vor einem kennerischen Publikum im Beisein des Autors einen triumphalen Erfolg." ["... [the quartet] achieved a triumphant success in the presence of the composer and a knowledgeable public with this 'absolutely devilish' work, as Ligeti has described it to a friend in Stockholm."] *See*: W42a.

B626.   Tucker, Marilyn. "Adventurous Experiment in Theater and Music." *San Francisco Chronicle*, Sept. 16, 1983, p. 65.

The Berkeley Stage's second annual Theater Festival of New Music featured a performance of *Aventures et Nouvelles Aventures* with Ligeti's scenario. "Under Robert Macdougall's direction, the effect is rich, emotionally charged and somewhat schizophrenic." *See*: W33, W34, W36.

B627.   Umbach, Klaus. "Comic-Oper mit Gotteswort und Minus-Frau." *Der Spiegel*, April 17, 1978, p. 237-39.

This review of the première of *Le Grand Macabre* includes a brief interview with the composer. "Der Zweiakter ... erwies sich als Spektakel voll griffiger Musik und nacktem Leben." ["The two-act opera ... proved to be a spectacle full of gripping music and naked life."] *See*: W54a.

B628.   Urmetzer, Reinhold. "Lebt wohl so lang in Heiterkeit: Ligetis *Grand Macabre* in Saarbrücken." *Stuttgarter Zeitung*, June 19, 1979.

A review. "Das Tragische und das Komische sollten zusammenkommen, Musik und Inszenierung verdeutlichten...." ["Music and staging clarified the merging of the tragic and the comic...."] *See*: W54f.

B629.   Vermeulen, Ernst. "Holland Festival 1967." *Sonorum Speculum* no. 32 (autumn 1967): 29-30.

This festival included a performance by the Hague Philharmonic Orchestra of the *Requiem*, with the Ghent Oratorio Society, under Bruno Maderna. "Although the technical vocal difficulties are not so towering, as in *Aventures*, this requiem demands almost the utmost." *See*: W33.

B630.   Vogel, Johann Peter. "Die Kontarskys." *Musica* 35 (1981): 397.

A review Deutsche Grammophon DG-2531-102 (*Monument-Selbstportrait-Bewegung*). "... wer die ... Werke ... hört, merkt schnell, mit welch atemberaubender Souveränität die technischen Schwierigkeiten bewältigt werden, vor allem aber, mit welcher Intelligenz ... Ligetis organische Formen aufgedeckt und begreiflich gemacht werden." ["Upon hearing the works, one quickly notes with what breathtaking mastery the technical difficulties are overcome, but above all, with what intelligence Ligeti's organic form is uncovered and made clear."] *See*: W52, D45.

B631.   Vogt, Harry. "Schallplatten: Aus verschiedenen Richtungen." *Musica* 38 (1984): 578-80.

A review of Deutsche Grammophon DGG 410 651-1. "Gewiß machen diese Neueinspielungen nicht die älteren Aufnahmen unter Maderna, Cerha oder Bour überflüssig; doch ist es erfreulich zu registrieren, daß wichtige zeitgenössische Werke gelegentlich durch kompetente Alternativinterpretationen neu beleuchtet werden." ["Certainly these new performances do not render superfluous the older recordings under Maderna, Cerha or Bour; yet it is gratifying to note that important contemporary works are occasionally re-illuminated through competent alternative interpretations."] *See*: W33, W34, W44, W46, D9, D13, D58.

B632.   Wagner, Rainer. "Hupkonzert und Klangkollision: Ligetis *Le Grand Macabre* in Hamburg erstaufgeführt." *Hannoversche Allgemeine Zeitung*, Oct. 17, 1978.

The first German performance of the opera is reviewed. "Kein Zweifel, die Oper hat ein neues Repertoire-Stück ..." ["Without a doubt, opera has a new repertoire piece..."] *See*: W54b.

B633.   Walsh, Stephen. "Last Week's Broadcast Music." *The Listener* 91 (1974): 643.

The English Bach Festival included an all-Ligeti concert. "Ligeti, in fact, has established his credentials, and persuaded us to listen fascinatedly to his investigations into the interior nature of sound. He has yet to establish his ability to excite and move the heart." *See*: App. II, p. 170.

B634. ------. "Out of the Ordinary--New Recordings of Works by Boito, Puccini, Verdi, Liszt, Mahler, Ligeti, and Balassa." *New Hungarian Quarterly* 25 (autumn 1984): 195-98.

Includes a review of Deutsche Grammophon 410 651-1. "... presents a cross-section of the music he wrote during the sixties.... beautifully played and sung." *See*: W33, W34, W44, W46, D9, D13, D58.

B635. Warnaby, John. "Ligeti's *Piano Concerto*." *Tempo* no. 163 (Dec. 1987): 47-49.

The UK première of this work was featured in the 1987 Almeida Festival. "The conclusions to be drawn from Ligeti's *Piano Concerto* are that his renewed involvement with keyboard music has helped him to create a flexibility of style that had previously been restricted to his vocal writing. The technical possibilities of the piano have been used to forge a link between the rhythmic and textual aspects of his creative imagination, and as a result, the rigid distinction between the main features of his musical personality has been substantially abolished." *See*: App. II, p. 173.

B636. Warnecke, Kläre. "Wenn das Horn weint: Ligeti-Trio mit großem Erfolg uraufgeführt." *Die Welt*, Aug. 9, 1982.

A review of the première of the *Horn Trio*. "Ein Trio, das von Brahms ... zwar klanglich meilenweit entfernt ist, aber an Kraft und Originalität sehr gut mit ihm aufnehmen kann." ["A trio which is miles removed from Brahms in sound, yet is a match for him in power and originality."] *See*: W59a.

B637. Webber, Nicholas. "Organ." *Music and Musicians* 22 (July 1974): 56.

Timothy Raymond performed *Continuum* and *Two Etudes for Organ*. The review amounts to a scathing critique of Ligeti's keyboard writing. "However much the registrations are varied during this process, the resultant sound can only be a shabby grey." *See*: W41, W40, W45.

B638. White, John Michael. "Marking Time." *The Independent*, Nov. 1, 1989.

A performance of *Poème Symphonique* took place at the London "Ligeti by Ligeti" festival. "Rarely have I witnessed harder listening or more tense involvement as the metronomes, neatly arranged across the platform like a television advertisement for long-life batteries, slowly wound down. *See*: W32e, App. II, p. 174.

B639. Whittall, Arnold. "Dutilleux; Ligeti." *Gramophone* 63 (Sept. 1985): 365.

A record review of Erato/Conifer STU71546. "[the 1st string quartet] displays an ebullient inventiveness...." *See*: W19, D74.

B640. ------. "Ligeti." *Gramophone* 61 (June 1983): 56.

A record review of Deutsche Grammophon 2543 818. "The music may not be Ligeti's finest, but the performances are first-rate." *See*: D38, D75, D78, D95.

B641.   Wiesmann, Sigrid. "Stockholm." *Oper und Konzert* 16, no. 6 (1978): 29.

A review of the première of *Le Grand Macabre.* "Eine Oper, die wieder auf die Kunstform Oper hoffen läßt." ["An opera which offers hope for opera as an artistic form."] *See:* W54a.

B642.   Wilkening, Martin. "Drei Tage mit György Ligeti: Festwochen-Zyklus zum 60. Geburtstag des Komponisten beendet." *Der Tagesspiegel,* Sept. 27, 1983.

This Berliner Festwochen featured *Hungarian Rock, Passacaglia ungherese, Continuum* (Elisabeth Chojnacka), *Six Bagatelles, Ten Pieces for Wind Quintet, Chamber Concerto, Melodien* (Elgar Howarth and the London Sinfonietta), the *Concerto for Violoncello* (Wolfgang Boettcher, cello), *Aventures et Nouvelles Aventures* (Penelope Walmsley-Clark, Linda Hirst, and Simon Grant), and the complete works for organ (Peter Schwarz). "Ligeti schätzt die Musiker, für die er schreibt, und dies drückt sich gerade in dem aus, was er den Instrumentalisten an Virtuosität abverlangt--diese ist aber stets aus der Vertrautheit mit den spezifischen Möglichkeiten des Instruments heraus erdacht." ["Ligeti respects the musicians for whom he writes, and this is shown precisely in the virtuosic demands he makes of the instrumentalists--but these are always devised out of a familiarity with the specific possibilities of the instruments."] *See:* W56, W57, W41, W15, W43, W46, W47, W38, W33, W34, W36, W31, W40, W45, App. II, p. 172.

B643.   Worbs, Hans-Christoph. "Neue Orgelwerke." *Musica* 22 (1968): 17.

An organ performance by Gerd Zacher featured the première of *Etude no. 1* (Harmonies). "... eine einzige Absage an den konventionellen Örgelstil." ["... a unique break with conventional organ style."] *See:* W40.

B644.   Żielinski, Tadeusz A. "Ligeti i Mâche." *Ruch Muzyczny* 29, no. 24 (1985): 7-8.

The Warsaw Autumn Festival of 1985 featured performances of a great number of Ligeti's works. "... Ligeti jest w istocie romantykiem wcale nie tak "zimnym," jak mozna bylo sadzic na poczatku choc -- niewatpliwie dyskretnym i powsciagliwym w swych gleboko przezywanych uczuciach -- intelektualista." ["... Ligeti is not after all such a "cold" romantic, but he is undoubtedly discreet, reserved in his deeply experienced feelings -- an intellectual."]

VI. Miscellaneous

This section contains writings and miscellaneous items which may be of interest, but which do not fit into other categories. These items include program notes, newspaper articles, bibliographies, articles in reference works, and writings in which Ligeti's music is a peripheral issue.

B645. *All Clouds are Clocks*. A film documentary produced by the BBC. It is available in the U.S. in 1/2 inch VHS video format through Films Incorporated, 5547 N. Ravenswood Ave., Chicago, IL 60640-1199.

B646. "Atmosphères." *Philadelphia Orchestra Program Notes*, Dec. 10, 1965, p. 24+.

Notes to accompany a performance by the Philadelphia Orchestra conducted by Seiji Ozawa. *See*: W27.

B647. Barić, Srdan. "Quo Vadis Musica?" *Zvuk* no. 75-76 (1967): 45-51.

In Serbo-Croatian. This report on the 1966 Darmstadt Summer Course includes a report on Ligeti's involvement as lecturer (Webern, his own Requiem) and composer (*Aventures et Nouvelles Aventures*). *See*: W33, W34, W35.

B648. Barry, Malcolm. "Hungarian Music in London." *Music and Musicians* 24 (Feb. 1976): 8+.

Announces an upcoming performance of Hungarian music including the British première of *San Francisco Polyphony*, and discusses the style of that work. "Ligeti wrote of the work, 'it is dry and sometimes harsh ... there is a disorder (which I like in everyday life too)'." *See*: W51.

B649. Boldemann, Marcus. "En makaber urpremiär på Kungliga Operan." *Dagens Nyheter*, March 18, 1978.

This 2-page spread announces the forthcoming première of *Le Grand Macabre*. Includes five photos. *See*: W54a.

B650. Brincker, Jens. "György Ligetisom gæsteforelæser." *Dansk Musiktidsskrift*. 40 (1965): 41-42.

A report on lectures given by the composer on February 10 and 11, 1965. Ligeti discussed the role of a modern composer.

B651. Burde, Wolfgang. "Wie aus der Ferne: Komponisten in Berlin zu Gäst --Penderecki und Ligeti." *Der Tagesspiegel*, Nov. 22, 1970.

Introduces Ligeti's work and also discusses his feelings about Berlin.

B652. Cadieu, Martine. "Evénement à l'opéra: *Le Grand Macabre*." *Panorama Musiques*, no. 40 (1981): 38-39.

A short summary of the opera to publicize the Paris production. *See*: W54d.

B653.   "Chamber Concerto." *Los Angeles Philharmonic Program Notes*, Feb. 13, 1986, p. UCLA-23.

   Notes, provided by IRCAM, to accompany a performance by the Ensemble InterContemporain conducted by Pierre Boulez. *See:* W46.

B654.   Christensen, Louis. "Ligeti Literature." *Numus West* No. 2 (1972): 21-22.

   A review of *Det omöjligas konst, Ligeti-dokument,* and *György Ligeti: eine Monographie* by Ove Nordwall, *Ligeti, Artikulation: an Aural Score* by Rainer Wehinger, and "Über neue Wege im Kompositionsunterricht" by Ligeti which appeared in *Three Aspects of New Music. See:* B110, B119, B121, B126.

B655.   Christoff, Dimiter. "Le Compositeur dans le monde contemporaine." *The Canada Music Book* 11-12 (1975-76): 259-79.

   This article explores the psychological aspects of modern composition, and includes quotes from many great 20th century composers. Ligeti mentions the use of socks in modern composition.

B656.   "Concerto for Cello and Orchestra." *Los Angeles Philharmonic Program Notes*, Oct. 18-21, 1984, p. LAPO-23.

   Notes to accompany performances by soloist Lynn Harrell with the Los Angeles Philharmonic under Garcia Navarro. *See:* W38.

B657.   Cone, Edward T. "One Hundred Metronomes." *The American Scholar* 46 (1977): 443-57.

   Reprinted in: *Australian Journal of Music Education* No. 26 (1980): 19-24. The author use *Poème symphonique* to illustrate an argument concerning the nature of art. He concludes that his time could be better spent than in listening to 100 metronomes. *See:* W32.

B658.   Derrien, Jean-Pierre. "Ligeti-Tage im Centre Acanthes." *Neue Zeitschrift für Musik* 140 (1979): 601-2.

   Translated from the French by Hanns Heismann. A brief description of a conference dedicated to the work of Ligeti, and held in Aix-en-Provence, July 19-Aug. 6, 1979. *See:* App. II, p. 171.

B659.   Dorian, Frederick. "*Lontano* for large orchestra." *Pittsburgh Symphony Orchestra Program Notes*, April 26, 28, 1974, p. 1007-11.

   Notes to accompany a performance by William Steinberg and the Pittsburgh Symphony Orchestra. *See:* W39.

B660.   Edberg, Ulla-Britt. "Järngänget 1: Intervju med Kerstin Meyer, hovsångerska, sent på kvällen den 2 maj 1978." *Nutida Musik* 22 (1978-79): 16-23.

   An interview with Kerstin Meyer on the occasion of the world première of *Le Grand Macabre* in which she sang the part of Spermando. She tells how she came to appreciate Ligeti's music. *See:* W54a.

B661.   Emmerson, Simon. "Ligeti in London." *Music and Musicians* 25
        (May 1977): 12+.

        Announces an upcoming concert devoted exclusively to the music of Ligeti. The
        performance included both string quartets, both wind quintets, and the British
        première of *Monument-Selbstportrait-Bewegung*. Ligeti's career is briefly
        summarized. *See*: W15c, W19c, W42b, W43b, W52b, App. II, p. 170.

B662.   Fabian, Imre. "Die Bühnen- und Kostümbilderin Aliute Meczies."
        Opernwelt 19, no. 6 (1978): 8-9.

        A presentation of the work of Aliute Meczies which focuses on her work in
        designing the sets for *Le Grand Macabre*. *See*: W54a.

B663.   Ford, Christopher. "[untitled article]." *The Guardian*, May 7, 1974,
        Arts section, p. 12.

        A report of an interview with the composer on the occasion of the English Bach
        Festival Ligeti Concert in London. Ligeti's career and work is summarized
        including descriptions of his flight from Hungary and the "2001" affair. *See*: App.
        II, p. 170.

B664.   Gammons, Donald T. "György Ligeti, *Atmosphères*." *Boston
        Symphony Orchestra Program Notes*, Nov. 13, 14, 24, 1970, p.
        425-26.

        Notes to accompany performances by the BSO under Seiji Ozawa and Joseph
        Silverstein (on the 24th). *See*: W27.

B665.   "*Le Grand Macabre*." *Staatsoper*, Sept. 25, 1978, p. 3-6.

        Program notes for the Hamburg production of the opera. *See*: W54b.

B666.   Griffiths, Paul. "Bright, magical--and serious." *Times*, May 19, 1982,
        p. 8.

        This overview of Ligeti's influences and views appeared for the occasion of an all
        Ligeti concert in London. "There are quite a number of different Ligetis, all
        different though touched with a family likeness.... There are .. Ligetis of wild,
        crazy humour and delicate, precise, efficient chamber music." *See*: App. II, p.
        171.

B667.   "György Ligeti: Kammerkonzert för 13 Spelare." *Nutida Musik* 17,
        no. 3 (1973-74): 35.

        General program notes focusing on harmony and rhythm. *See*: W46.

B668.   *György Ligeti: Werkverzeichnis*. Mainz: Schott, 1977. 20 p.

        Catalog of works published by Universal, Peters and Schott, including first
        performances. A short biography and survey of works in English and German by
        Imre Fabian is included.

B669.   Hanschke, Gerhard. "György Ligeti erhielt in Lübeck 'pour le
        mérite'." *Orchester* 23 (Dec. 1975): 784.

        A report of the presentation of this honor to the composer.

B670.   Helm, Everett. "Art is lies ..." *High Fidelity/Musical America* 18 (Nov. 1968): MA34.

A report on the International Seminar on Contemporary Operatic Creation, held in Bregenz, Austria. Ligeti is quoted as saying: "I separate everyday life and art. I prefer unnatural art. Art is not truth, it is lies...."

B671.   Henahan, Donal. "Searching--Still--for a Weathervane Composer." *New York Times*, June 1, 1986, p. H23.

This critique of the state of music was inspired by the "Horizons 86" Ligeti concert given in New York. *See:* App. II, p. 173.

B672.   Hermann, Ingrid. "Ligeti-Bibliographie." *Musik und Bildung*. 15, no. 5 (1983): 24-25.

B673.   Hersh, Howard. "San Francisco Polyphony." *San Francisco Symphony Orchestra Program*, Jan. 8, 1975, p. 10-12.

Notes to accompany the first performance of this work. *See:* W51a.

B674.   Holmes, Robert. "Apparitions." *Detroit Symphony Orchestra Program Notes*, Jan. 28, 1971, p. 421, 423.

Notes to accompany a performance by the Detroit Symphony. *See:* W26.

B675.   Karkoschka, Erhard. "Eine Hörpartitur elektronischer Musik." *Melos* 38 (1971): 468-75.

A discussion of the possibilities inherent in the visual representation of music, with special reference to Rainer Wehinger's listening score to *Artikulation*. Also refers to *Continuum. See:* W25, B126.

B676.   Kaufmann, Harald. "Szenen zu 'absurder' Music: Anmerkungen zu György Ligetis *Aventures*." *Opernwelt* 7, no. 9 (1966): 24-26.

Translated into Swedish as "Scener till 'absurd musik." *Nutida Musik* 12, no. 3 (1968-69): 2-5. A discussion of Ligeti's "libretto to *Aventures et Nouvelles Aventures*." *See:* W36.

B677.   Kesting, Marianne. "Musikalisierung des Theaters, Theatralisierung der Musik." *Melos* 36 (1969): 105-6.

Aventures et Nouvelles Aventures are mentioned within a discussion of musical theater. *See:* W33, W34, W36.

B678.   Kraus, Egon. "Bibliographie-Discographie: György Ligeti." *Musik und Bildung* 7 (1975): 524-25.

B679.   Leuchtmann, Horst. "Analyse als schöne Kunst verstanden: György Ligeti erläutert eine Komposition von Anton Webern." *Süddeutsche Zeitung*, Dec. 2, 1983.

A report of a lecture on the fifth of Webern's *Six Bagatelles for String Quartet* op. 9, given by Ligeti to commemorate the Webern centennial.

B680.   Lichtenfeld, Monika. "György Ligeti." In *Die Musik in Geschichte und Gegenwart*, edited by Friederich Blume, vol. 16, col. 1135-1138. Kassel: Bärenreiter, 1979.

B681.   --------. "György Ligeti." In *Riemann Musik-Lexikon*, edited by Carl Dahlhaus, Ergänzungsband Personenteil (L-Z), p. 57-58. Mainz, 1975.

B682.   --------. "Ligeti." In *Dictionary of Contemporary Music*, edited by J. Vinton. New York: Dutton, 1974.

B683.   Lievense, Willy. "De 60-jarige Ligeti en zijn anti-anti-opera "grand macabre." *Mens en Melodie* 38 (1983): 462-67.

This survey of the events celebrating Ligeti's 60th birth year focuses especially on *Le Grand Macabre* and the *Horn Trio*. Includes two sketches for costumes for *Le Grand Macabre*. See: W54, W59.

B684.   Lönn, Anders. "Tre texter." *Artes* 2, no. 3 (1976): 83-98.

Introduced by Ove Nordwall. Contains "Musikaliska minnen från barn- och ungdom" (Musical Memories from my childhood and youth), "Ungern 1945-1956" (Hungary 1945-1956), and an untitled survey of Ligeti's earlier works written for the first performance of *Lontano*. Also includes facsimiles of several sketches (also published as *György Ligeti: From Sketches and Unpublished Scores 1938-56 From the Collection of Ove Nordwall*). See: B94, B102.

B685.   Maycock, Robert. "Universal Range." *Classical Music*, Oct. 7, 1989, p. 29-32.

A brief introduction to Ligeti's works, written for the South Bank Centre's "Ligeti by Ligeti" festival. Reprinted as the introduction to the festival program. See: App. II, p. 174.

B686.   Mootz, William. "Grawemeyer Award Brings Composer and Donor Acclaim." *Louisville Courier Journal*, Nov. 11, 1986.

A report of activities in Louisville and New York surrounding the awarding of this prize.

B687.   "'Musica Viva' Ausstellung, Vortrag und Konzert." *Frankfurter Allgemeine Zeitung*, Nov. 18, 1963.

Mentions a lecture given by Ligeti on the topic, "New Forms of Notation in Avant Garde Music."

B688.   Nordwall, Ove. "György Ligeti." In *The New Grove Dictionary of Music and Musicians*, 6th ed., edited by Stanley Sadie, vol. 9, p. 853-56. London: Macmillan, 1980.

B689.   --------. "György Ligeti--Discografi mars 1978." *Musikrevy* 33, no. 3 (1978): 92-93.

A listing of 36 recordings with indications of whether or not the performances are recommended.

B690.   -------. "Ligetis Stora Makaber." *Musikern* no. 2 (Feb. 1978): 14-16.

A summary and brief discussion of *Le Grand Macabre* which appeared just before its world première. *See*: W54a.

B691.   -------. "Melodien." *Los Angeles Philharmonic Program Notes*, April 13-16, 1972, p. 29-30.

Notes to accompany the first U.S. performance by Zubin Mehta and the Los Angeles Philharmonic. *See*: W47b.

B692.   -------. "Musik Almanackan." *Musikern* no. 10 (Oct. 1967): 4.

This column briefly summarizes the musical activities surrounding Ligeti's visit to Stockholm during the summer of 1967.

B693.   *Passage du XXe siècle*. Paris: IRCAM & Arts et métiers graphiques, 1976.

A program book to accompany a series of concerts of 20th century music given in Paris in 1977. The concerts included performances of many of Ligeti's works from the mid 60s to the mid 70s. Includes a brief biography, discography and program notes by the composer and Monika Lichtenfeld. *See*: App. II, p. 170.

B694.   Plaistow, Stephen. "Ligeti's Recent Music." *Musical Times* 115 (1974): 379-81.

A survey and evaluation written on the occasion of the British première of *Clocks and Clouds*. *See*: W50c.

B695.   Poettgen, Ernst. "Abenteuer des Ausdrucks." *Stuttgarter Zeitung*, Oct. 25, 1972.

The director of a stage version of *Aventures* introduces the work and explains that in this version the singers and instrumentalists will be completely visible at all times so as not to obscure the composer's intentions. *See*: W33.

B696.   Raeburn, Andrew. "György Ligeti, *Melodien* (1971)." *Boston Symphony Orchestra Program Notes*, Oct. 4-6, 1973, p. 75.

Notes which accompanied a concert performed by Seiji Ozawa and the Boston Symphony Orchestra. *See*: W47.

B697.   Rockwell, John. "Ligeti's Laurels Come at an Auspicious Time." *New York Times*, Nov. 11, 1986, p. C13.

This summary of Ligeti's career, his plans, and his influences was written on the occasion of his winning the Grawemeyer Award.

B698.   Rollin, Robert L. "Report: Proceedings of the Internationales Musikinstitut Darmstadt, July, 1976." *In Theory Only* 2 (Oct. 1976): 21-26.

A report of a lecture made by Ligeti at the 1976 Darmstadt Festival. Ligeti discussed his *Monument-Selbstportrait-Bewegung* which was also performed at the festival. *See*: W52.

B699.   Rourke, Sean. "Ligeti's Early Years in the West." *Musical Times* 130 (1989): 532-35.

This brief summary of Ligeti's work from 1956 to 1959 was written for the occasion of the South Bank Centre's "Ligeti by Ligeti" festival. *See*: App. II, p. 174.

B700.   Salmenhaara, Erkki. "György Ligeti *Artikulation, Aventures, Nouvelles Aventures*." Finnish Radio, March 29, 1966.

Program notes for a concert entitled "Musica nova." Text in Finnish and Swedish. *See*: W25, W33, W34.

B701.   -------. "György Ligeti-- rationaalinen mystikko." *Helsingin Sanomat*, Feb. 4, 1964.

B702.   -------. "György Ligeti *Sellokonsertto, Fragment*." Finnish Radio, April 8, 1970.

Program notes for a concert of the Finnish Radio Contemporary Music Ensemble. Text in Finnish and Swedish. *See*: W28, W38.

B703.   -------. "György Ligeti zum 50. Geburtstag." *Musiikki* 1 (1973): 3-9.

Text in Finnish with English summary. A brief homage on the occasion of the composers 50th birthday.

B704.   Sandner, Wolfgang. "Auf der Suche nach dem verlorenen Gegenstand: György Ligeti und seine Außenseiterstellung in der Neuen Musik--Von der Klangfläche zu einer neuen Dramatik." *Frankfurter Allgemeine Zeitung*, April 8, 1978, p. 25.

A discussion of Ligeti's style and philosophy, written for the occasion of the world première of *Le Grand Macabre*. It includes several quotes from the composer, commenting on the opera, and on "popular" music. *See*: W54a.

B705.   -------. "György Ligeti, der emotionale Skeptiker." *HiFi Stereophonie* 22 (1983): 498-99.

Words of praise for Ligeti on the occasion of his 60th birthday.

B706.   -------. "Ligeti als Gast in der Heimat: Reflexionen zu den diesjährigen Budapester Musikwochen." *Frankfurter Allgemeine Zeitung*, Nov. 20, 1979, p. 25.

A discussion of Ligeti's relationship to Hungary and with composer György Kurtág. It was written for the occasion of the Budapest Music Festival which featured both composers. *See*: App. II, p. 171.

B707.   Schubert, Giselher. "Werkidee und Kompositionstechnik zur seriellen Musik von Boulez, Stockhausen und Ligeti." In *Die Musik der Fünfziger Jahre: Versuch einer Revision*, edited by Carl Dahlhaus, 48-71. Veröffentlichungen des Instituts für Neue Musik und Musikerziehung, Bd. 26. Mainz: Schott, 1985.

The place of *Apparitions* in the musical development of the 50s is described on p. 69-71. *See*: W26.

B708.   Schwiezer, Gottfried. "Serielle Musik." *Musica* 18 (1964): 173.

A report of a lecture given by Ligeti on the topic of serial music.

B709.   Siegele, Ulrich. "Musik der Hoffnung." *Musik und Kirche* 39 (1969): 216-18.

A report of new music at the 1969 Stuttgart Church Music Festival. *Volumina*, *Lux aeterna*, *Harmonies*, and the *Requiem* are mentioned. *See*: W31, W35, W37, W40.

B710.   Steinberg, Michael. "György Ligeti *Atmosphères* for large orchestra without percussion." *San Francisco Symphony Orchestra Program*, Jan. 9, 1980, p. 10-13.

Notes to accompany a performance. *See*: W27e.

B711.   -------. "György Ligeti, San Francisco Polyphony." *San Francisco Symphony Orchestra Program*, April 22, 1987, p. 20A-20B, 37-37A.

Notes to accompany a performance. *See*: W51b.

B712.   Sutcliffe, Tom. "A plight at the opera." *The Guardian*, April 19, 1978, Arts section, p. 10.

The author reflects on the state of contemporary art music and particularly opera. *Le Grand Macabre* is seen as an encouraging step in the right direction. *See*: W54.

B713.   Szersnovicz, Patrick. "Ligeti. Catalogue des oeuvres, discographie. Bibliographie sommaire." *Musique en jeu* 15 (Sept. 1974): 120-24.

B714.   Tenkku, Liisa. "Lapset ja *Atmosphères*." *Rondo* no. 1 (1965)

In Finnish, published in Helsinki. *See*: W27.

B715.   Tomzig, Sabine. "Endlich einmal Luft holen--Neues probieren: György Ligeti plant seine erste Oper." *Hamburger Abendblatt*, May 17, 1976.

Reports that Ligeti has given up nearly all other engagements to work on *Le Grand Macabre*. Also mentions the one-man theater piece *Rondeau*. *See*: W53, W54.

B716.   -------. "Gespräch mit György Ligeti: Der Schmerz des großen Komponisten." *Hamburger Abendblatt*, Aug. 4, 1982, p. 10.

Announces the forthcoming première of the *Horn Trio*. Also reports, with numerous quotes, an interview with the composer in which he speaks of his teaching in Hamburg, his plans, and his goals. *See*: W59a.

B717.   -------. "György Ligeti: der Berühmte den kaum einer kennt." *Hamburger Abendblatt*, July 15, 1975.

An announcement of Ligeti's induction into the *Ordens pour le mérite*. The article also describes Ligeti's work and lifestyle.

B718. -------. "Hamburg ein Zentrum für neue Kunst? Professor Ligeti entwickelt seine Pläne." *Hamburger Abendblatt*, Oct. 25, 1971.

Announces Ligeti's acceptance of a post in the Hamburg Music Academy, and summarizes the composer's career and current projects.

B719. -------. "Die Internationale Musikwelt schaut auf Hamburg: György Ligeti will die Opern-Demontage stoppen." *Hamburger Abendblatt*, Oct. 7, 1978.

Reports the forthcoming German première of *Le Grand Macabre*, describes the opera, and discusses changes that will be made from the Stockholm production. *See*: W54b.

B720. -------. "Keine Angst vor neuen und alten Noten: Gespräch mit dem Komponisten Prof. György Ligeti." *Hamburger Abendblatt*, Jan. 11, 1978.

Announces a concert of Ligeti's keyboard works, and mentions the forthcoming première of *Le Grand Macabre*. Includes some quotations taken during an interview with the composer. *See*: W54a.

B721. "Verkfoerteckning i urval 1946-1978." *Musikrevy* 33, no. 3 (1978): 91+.

A selected list of Ligeti's works.

B722. Vogt, Matthias Theodor. "Inseln voller Geräusche (Homage a Ligeti und Trojahn-Werkstatt in Hamburg)." *Neue Zeitschrift für Musik* 145, no. 3 (1984): 31-32.

Reports a concert commemorating Ligeti's 60th birthday. Also mentions works in progress: a piano concerto, and an opera based on "The Tempest." *See*: W64.

B723. "What's in a Name?" *Times*, Oct. 1, 1982, p. 10, col. 1.

A notice that the names of the characters Spermando and Clitoria had been changed to Amando and Miranda for the English National Opera production of *Le Grand Macabre*. *See*: W54e.

B724. White, John Michael. "Fears of a Clown." *The Independent*, Oct. 18, 1989.

This report of an interview with the composer was written for the occasion of the London "Ligeti by Ligeti" festival. "What interests me in the metronome piece is the extraordinary richness of the inner rhythms. On the outside you see all these metronomes and it's funny, maybe. But the impression doesn't interest me. It's the *musical idea* that matters. I'm not an evangelist, or a guru. I have no message. I just make art. *See*: App. II, p. 174.

B725. Wiesmann, Sigrid. "György Ligeti--ein Grenzgänger: Provokation und Leistung des ungarischen Komponisten." *Neue Zürcher Zeitung*, May 27, 1983, p. 35.

A description of Ligeti's life and work, published presumably to celebrate the composer's 60th birthday.

B726.   -------. "Ein Wiener zwischen Budapest und Hamburg: György Ligeti zum 60. Geburtstag." *Österreichische Musikzeitschrift* 38 (1983): 338.

A brief summary of Ligeti's life and work in commemoration of the composer's 60th birthday.

B727.   "Wohl und Wehe des seriellen Komponierens: György Ligeti sprach in der Musikhochschule." *Frankfurter Allgemeine Zeitung*, Feb. 6, 1964.

A report of a lecture given at the Staatliche Hochschule für Musik. Ligeti spoke on the history and problems of serialism, and also commented on his own style of composition.

B728.   Zenck, Martin. Entwurf einer Soziologie der musikalischen Rezeption." *Musikforschung* 33 (1980): 253-279.

The author describes his reaction to a performance of the *String Quartet No. 2*, especially in terms of his musical and sociological expectations. This discussion (p. 264-70) is part of a larger exposition of a system of understanding musical reception. *See*: W42.

B729.   Zosi, Giuliano. "A proposito di Ligeti." *Nuova Revista Musicale Italiana* 8 (1974): 234-38.

A report of a seminar held by Ligeti at the Accademia Musicale Chigiana in 1973. Refers to *Apparitions*, and *Atmosphères*. *See*: W26, W27.

5

Discography

Works are listed alphabetically. Recordings are listed chronologically under each work. The date given at the beginning of each entry is the recording date, or if that cannot be ascertained, the earliest issue date.

2 Capriccios for Piano

> see: Two Capriccios for Piano

2 Etudes for Organ

> see: Study for Organ No. 1
> Study for Organ No. 2

3 Pieces for Two Pianos

> see: Monument-Selbstportrait-Bewegung

10 Pieces for Wind Quintet

> see: Ten Pieces for Wind Quintet

Apparitions See: W26.

D1.   (196-?) Austrian Radio Symphony Orchestra, Milan Horvat, conductor.

Amadeo AVRS 6456.

Artikulation See: W25.

D2.   (1958) (3:45) All recordings are produced from the same master
       created in the Electronic Music Studio of the West German Radio,
       Cologne. The original 4 channels are mixed to two for stereo. and
       one for mono. recordings.

       Limelight LS 86048 (1968).
       Mercury SR2-9123 (1968).
       Philips 835 485-6, AY 835 485-6 (stereo.)
           A00366L/A835486Y (mono.)
       Trio PA1026
       Wergo WER 301.
                    60059 (197-).
                    60095 (1984). Notes by Ulrich Dibelius and the
                    composer.
                    60161-50 (compact disc) (1984/1988).

Atmosphères See: W27.

D3.   (1964) New York Philharmonic, Leonard Bernstein, conductor.
       Recorded Jan. 6, 1964.

       Columbia ML 6133 (1965).
                    MS-6733 (1965).
                    S 63420.
                    MS-6421.
                    MS-7176 (1968).

D4.   (1966) Southwest German Radio Orchestra, Ernest Bour, conductor.
       Recorded at the Southwest German Radio, Baden-Baden, May
       1966 (8:32).

       Electrola/Hör Zu Black Label SHZW 904.
       Heliodor 2549-003 (1970).
                    3313 003 (cassette) (1970).
       MGM Records 1-SE-13 (1968).
                    CS-6078.
       Wergo WER 305.
                    60022 (1971?).
                    60095 (1984). Notes by Harald Kaufmann, Ulrich
                    Dibelius and the composer.
                    60162-50 (compact disc) (1984/1988).

D5.   (1966) Yomiuri Nippon Symphony Orchestra, Seiji Ozawa, conductor.
       Recorded live on May 1, 2, and 4, 1966 at Tokyo's Nissei Theater.
       (8:02).

       Colosseum Schallplatten 3447253
       RCA SJV 1513.
       Varèse Sarabande VX 81060.
                    VCD-47253 (compact disc) (1986).

Aventures et Nouvelles Aventures See: W33, W34.

D6.   (196-) Gertie Charlent, Marie-Thérèse Cahn, William Pearson, die
        Reihe Ensemble, Friedrich Cerha, conductor. (24:20).

        Candide/Vox CE 31009 (1969). Liner notes by William B. Ober.
        Columbia OW 7577 (Japan).
        FSM 31009 Liner notes by William B. Ober.
        Musica Moderna MM 1106.
        Vox/Turnabout CT 4782 (cassette) (1973)
        Vox H-4401 (Japan).

D7.   (1966) Gertie Charlent, Marie-Thérèse Cahn, William Pearson,
        Darmstadt International Chamber Ensemble, Bruno Maderna,
        conductor. (22:47). Recorded at the International Music Institute
        Studio, Darmstadt, Aug. 1966.

        Heliodor 2549-003 (1970).
                3313 003 (cassette) (1970).
        Wergo 89-837. Liner notes: "Structures in the Structureless" by
        Harald Kaufmann.
                WER 60022 (1971?).
                        60095 (1984). Notes by the composer.
                        60 045-50 (compact disc) (1985).

D8.   (1970?) Gertie Charlent, Marie-Thérèse Cahn, William Pearson,
        Darmstadt International Chamber Ensemble, Bruno Maderna,
        conductor (*Aventures* only). (12:01).

        Electrola SHZW 904 BL.

D9.   (1983) Mary Thomas, sop.; Jane Manning contr.; William Pearson,
        bari.; Ensemble InterContemporain, Pierre Boulez, conductor.
        Recorded March 1981. (11:58, 11:22).

        Deutsche Grammophon 410 651-1 (1983). Notes by Monika
        Lichtenfeld.
                        423 244-2 (compact disc) (1988).
                        F 28G 50497 (compact disc) (Japan).

Bagatelles for Piano

        see: Three Bagatelles for Piano

Bagatelles for Wind Quintet

        see: Six Bagatelles for Wind Quintet

Capriccios for Piano

        see: Two Capriccios for Piano

Cello Concerto

see: Concerto for Violoncello

Chamber Concerto See: W46.

D10.   (197-) die Reihe Ensemble, Friedrich Cerha, conductor. (20:04).
Recorded at the Austrian Radio, Vienna.

Wergo WER 60059 (197-).
60095 (1984).
60162-50 (compact disc) (1984/1988).

D11.   (1975) London Sinfonietta, David Atherton, conductor. Recorded
October 1975, Kingsway Hall, London.

Decca Headline HEAD 12. (1976) Distributed by London Records.
SLA 6365 (Japan).

D12.   (1977?) Budapest Chamber Ensemble, András Mihály, conductor.

Hungaroton SLPX 11807.

D13.   (1982) Ensemble InterContemporain, Pierre Boulez, conductor.
(18:30). Recorded March 1982.

Deutsche Grammophon 410 651-1 (1983). Liner notes by Monika
Lichtenfeld.
423 244-2 (compact disc) (1988).
F 28G 50497 (compact disc) (Japan).

Clocks and Clouds See: W50.

D14.   (197-?) Austrian Radio Symphony Orchestra and Chorus, Friedrich
Cerha, conductor.

Austrian Radio 0120064.

D15.   (197-?) Austrian Radio Symphony Orchestra and Choir, Elgar
Howarth, conductor.

Austrian Radio 120857.

Concerto for Violoncello See: W38.

D16.   (1967) Siegfried Palm cello, Hesse Radio Symphony Orchestra,
Michael Gielen, conductor (12:35). Recorded at the Hesse Radio,
Frankfurt, Sept. 1967.

Electrola SHZW 904 BL.
Heliodor 2549004 (1970?).

Wergo WER 328.
60036.
60095 (1984). Program notes by the composer.
60163-50 (compact disc) (1988).

Continuum See: W41.

D17.   (1968) Antoinette Vischer, harpsichord. Recorded in Basel, Oct. 1968 (3:36).

Heliodor 2549 011 (1970).
3313 011 (cassette) (1970).
Wergo WER 305.
60045 (1969?).
60095 (1984).
60161-50 (compact disc) (1984/1988).

D18.   (1975?) Elisabeth Chojnacka, harpsichord (3:30).

Opus Musicum, OM 116--118 (*Die Neueste Musik und ihre neuesten Entwicklungen* (1975), notes by Eberhard Neumann & Christian Martin Schmidt).
Philips 6526 009.

D19.   (1976) Eva Nordwall, harpsichord (3:29). Recorded June 30-July 2, 1976 at Nacka Aula, Sweden.

Bis LP-53 (1976). Liner notes by Ove Nordwall.
53 (compact disc) (1987). Liner notes by Ove Nordwall.

D20.   (1981) Eva Nordwall, classical harpsichord. Recorded in the Music Museum, Stockholm, 1981.

Caprice CAP 1209 (1982/83).

D21.   (1983-84) Elisabeth Chojnacka, harpsichord (3:59). Recorded at Bavarian Radio, Munich, 1983-84.

Wergo WER 60100 (1986). Liner notes by Josef Häusler.
60100-50 (compact disc) (1986)

Coulée

see: Study for Organ No. 2

Doppelkonzert

see: Double Concerto

Double Concerto See: W48.

D22.   (1975) Aurele Nicolet, flute; Heinz Holliger, oboe; London Sinfonietta, David Atherton, conductor. Recorded June 1975 in Kingsway Hall, London.

Decca Headline HEAD 12. Distributed by London Records. Notes by the composer.
SLA 6365 (Japan).

D23.   (1975) Gunilla von Bahr, flute; Torleif Lännerholm, oboe; Swedish Radio Symphony Orchestra, Elgar Howarth, conductor. (12:40). Recorded Dec 19, 1975 at Circus, Stockholm.

Bis LP-53 (1976). Liner notes by Ove Nordwall.
53 (compact disc) (1987). Liner notes by Ove Nordwall.
Wergo WER 60076 (1976).
60095 (1984). Liner notes by Ove Nordwall.
60163-50 (compact disc) (1988).

Drei Phantasien nach Friedrich Hölderlin See: W61.

D24.   (198-) Pro Arte Chorus, Graz; Karl Ernst Hoffmann, conductor.

Austrian Radio ORF 120934.

Drei Stücke für Zwei Klaviere

see: Monument-Selbstportrait-Bewegung

Éjszaka; Reggel See: W20.

D25.   (1971?) Swedish Radio Choir, Eric Ericson, conductor.

EMI Electrola 1 C 153 29 916/9 (1971).
EMD 5506 (Voices for Today) (1972).

D26.   (198-) Moscow Youth & Student Choir

Melodiya S 10-09067/70

D27.   (1986) St. Olaf Choir; Kenneth Jennings, conductor. Recorded in 1986.

St. Olaf Records E-1637.

Etudes for Organ

see: Study for Organ No. 1
Study for Organ No. 2

Etudes for Piano. Book 1. *See*: W63.

D28.   (198-) Volker Banfield, piano.

Austrian Radio ORF 140007.

D29.   (1986) Volker Banfield, piano. Recorded at the North German Radio, 1986.

Wergo WER 60134 (1987).
60134-50 (compact disc) (1987).

Glissandi See: W23.

D30.   (1957) 1 channel tape produced in the Electronic Music Studio of the West German Radio, Cologne (7:30).

Wergo WER 60076 (1976).
60095 (1984).
60161-50 (compact disc) (1984/1988).

Harmonies

see: Study for Organ No. 1

Horn Trio

see: Trio for Violin, Horn, and Piano

Hungarian Rock See: W56.

D31.   (1979) Elisabeth Chojnacka, harpsichord. Recorded Jan. 1979 at the Cité universitaire à Paris, Salon Honnorat.

Erato STU 71266 (1980).

D32.   (1981) Eva Nordwall, harpsichord. Recorded in the Music Museum, Stockholm, 1981.

Caprice CAP 1209 (1982/83).

D33.   (1983-84) Elisabeth Chojnacka, harpsichord (5:00), recorded at the Bavarian Radio, Munich, 1983-84.

Wergo WER 60100 (1986). Liner notes by Josef Häusler.
60100-50 (compact disc) (1986).

Hungarian Studies

see: Magyar Etüdök

Invention for Piano See: W6.

D34.   (1985) Karl-Hermann Mrongovius, piano. Recorded at the Bavarian
Radio Munich, Aug. 1985.

Wergo WER 60131 (1987). Notes by Louise Duchesneau.
60131-50 (compact disc) (1987).

Kammerkonzert

see: Chamber Concerto

Lontano See: W39.

D35.   (1967) Southwest German Radio Orchestra, Ernest Bour, conductor.
Recorded live at the Southwest German Radio, Baden-Baden, Oct.
1967.

Heliodor 2549 011 (1970).
3313 011 (cassette) (1970).
MGM SE-4722 (2001: A Space Odyssey, v. 2) (6:32).
Warner Bros. HS 3449 (Soundtrack to "The Shining").
Warner-Pioneer (P 10894) (Japan).
Wergo WER 322.
60045 (1969?).
60095 (1984). Notes by the composer.
60163-50 (compact disc) (1988).

D36.   (196-?) Austrian Radio Symphony Orchestra, Carl Melles, conductor.

Austrian Radio ORF-1001.

Lux aeterna See: W37.

D37.   (1966) Schola Cantorum Stuttgart, Clytus Gottwald, conductor.
(9:29). Recorded at the Southwest Sound Studio, Stuttgart, 1966.

MGM Records 1-SE-13 (1968) 2001: A Space Odyssey.
CS 6078.
Wergo WER 60026 (1978?).
60095 (1984).
60162-50 (compact disc) (1984/1988).

D38.   (1968) Chorus of the North German Radio, Helmut Franz, conductor. (7:55). Recorded April 1968.

Deutsche Grammophon 104 991.
137 004 (1969).
2530 392 (1971).
2543 818 (1973).
419 475-1 (1987).
419 475-2 (compact disc) (1987).
423 244-2 (compact disc) (1988).
F 28G 22033 (compact disc) (Japan).
F 28G 50497 (compact disc) (Japan).
Opus Musicum OM 116--118 (1975), notes by Eberhard Neumann & Christian Martin Schmidt.
Schwann HL 00211.

D39.   (196-?) Swedish Radio Choir, Eric Ericson, conductor.

EMI 1 C 063 29 075.
1 C 153-29 716/9 (1971).
EMD-5506 (Voices for Today) (1972).

D40.   (1968?) Gregg Smith Singers, Gregg Smith, conductor.

CBS MS 7175.
MS 7176 (1968).
S 63420.

D41.   (19--) Berliner Capella, Peter Schwarz, conductor.

Marus 308539.

Magyar Etüdök See: W62.

D42.   (1984?) Schola Cantorum Stuttgart, Clytus Gottwald, conductor (5:50).

Wergo WER 60111 (1985).

Melodien See: W47.

D43.   (197-) Austrian Radio Symphony Orchestra, Elgar Howarth, conductor.

Austrian Radio ORF-120857.

D44.   (1975) London Sinfonietta, David Atherton, conductor. Recorded Oct. 1975.

Decca Headline HEAD 12. Distributed by London Records.

Métamorphoses nocturnes

see: String Quartet No. 1

Monument-Selbstportrait-Bewegung See: W52.

D45. (1979) Alfons & Aloys Kontarsky (ca. 17:00). Recorded June 13-15, 1979.

Deutsche Grammophon DG 2531 102 (1980). Notes by Monika Lichtenfeld in German, English and French.
MG 1274 (Japan).

D46. (1983-84) Bruno Canino and Antonio Ballista (16:06). Recorded at Bavarian Radio, Munich, 1983-84.

Wergo WER 60100 (1986). Notes by Josef Häusler.
60100-50 (compact disc) (1986).

D47. (1985) Karl-Hermann Mrongovius and Begoña Uriarte-Mrongovius. Recorded at the Bavarian Radio Munich, Aug. 1985.

Wergo WER 60131 (1987). Notes by Louise Duchesneau.
60131-50 (compact disc) (1987).

Morning

see: Éjszaka; Reggel

Musica ricercata See: W14.

D48. (1974) Liisa Pohjola, piano. Recorded Nov. 9, 1974, at Radio House, Stockholm.

Bis LP 18 (1975).
53 (compact disc) (1987). Liner notes by Ove Nordwall.

D49. (19--) Begoña Uriarte-Mrongovius and Karl-Hermann Mrongovius, piano (alternating).

Austrian Radio ORF-120857.

D50. (1985) Karl-Hermann Mrongovius, piano. Recorded at the Bavarian Radio Munich, Aug. 1985.

Wergo WER 60131 (1987). Notes by Louise Duchesneau.
60131-50 (compact disc) (1987).

Night; Morning

> see: Éjszaka; Reggel

Passacaglia ungherese See: W57.

D51.   (1981) Eva Nordwall. Recorded in the Music Museum, Stockholm
       1981.

      Caprice CAP 1209 (1982/83).

D52.   (198-?) Ekkehard Carbow (4:50).

      Thorofon Capella MTH 224 (1982?). Notes by Claude Ambroise.

D53.   (1983-84) Elisabeth Chojnacka, harpsichord (4:40). Recorded at the
       Bavarian Radio, Munich, 1983-84.

      Wergo WER 60100 (1986). Liner notes by Josef Häusler.
      60100-50 (compact disc) (1986).

Phantasien nach Friedrich Hölderlin

> see: Drei Phantasien nach Friedrich Hölderlin

Pieces for Wind Quintet

> see: Ten Pieces for Wind Quintet

Ramifications See: W44.

D54.   (1970; version for 12 soloists). Chamber Orchestra of the Saarland
       Radio, Antonio Janigro, conductor (7:36). Recorded at the
       Saarland Radio, Saarbrücken, Nov. 1970.

      Wergo WER 60059.
           60095 (1984).
           60162-50 (compact disc) (1984/1988).

D55.   (1970; version for string orchestra). Southwest German Radio
       Orchestra, Ernest Bour, conductor (7:53). Recorded at the
       Southwest German Radio, Baden-Baden, Dec. 1970.

      Wergo WER 60059.
           60095 (1984).
           60162-50 (compact disc) (1984/1988).

D56.   (1973). Concertgebouw Orchestra of Amsterdam; Bruno Maderna, conductor. Recorded at the 1973 Holland Festival.

Radio Nederland 6808.217/8 (1973).

D57.   (197-) Toulouse Chamber Orchestra, Louis Auriacombe, conductor.

EMI C 061 11316.

D58.   (1982; version for 12 soloists). Ensemble InterContemporain, Pierre Boulez, conductor. (8:41). Recorded March 1982.

Deutsche Grammophon 410 651-1 (1983). Liner notes in English, French and German by Monika Lichtenfeld.
                        423 244-2 (compact disc) (1988).
                        F 28G 50497 (compact disc) (Japan).

Reggel

see: Éjszaka; Reggel

Requiem See: W35.

D59.   (1968) Liliana Poli, sop., Barbro Ericson, mz., Bavarian Radio Chorus, Hesse Radio Symphony Orchestra, Michael Gielen, conductor (26:41). Recorded at the Hesse Radio, Frankfurt, Nov. 1968.

Cantate 658 229.
Heliodor 2549 011 (1970).
            3313 011 (cassette) (1970).
MGM S-4722 (2001: A Space Odyssey, v. 2) (5:20).
Wergo WER 60045 (1969?).
            60059 (1976).
            60095 (1984).
            60 045-50 (compact disc) (1985).

D60.   (196-?) Bavarian Radio Orchestra, Francis Travis, conductor.

MGM Records 1-SE-13 (1969) 2001: A Space Odyssey (Kyrie).
CS 6078.

San Francisco Polyphony See: W51.

D61.   (1975) Swedish Radio Symphony Orchestra, Elgar Howarth, conductor (10:25). Recorded Dec. 19, 1975 at Circus, Stockholm.

Bis LP-53 (1976). Liner notes by Ove Nordwall.
            53 (compact disc) (1987). Liner notes by Ove Nordwall.
Wergo WER 60076 (1976).
            60095 (1984).
            60163-50 (compact disc) (1988).

Scenes and Interludes from Le Grand Macabre See: W55.

D62.   (1979) Szenen und Zwischenspiele aus der Oper Le Grand Macabre.
Inga Nielsen, sop., Olive Fredricks, mz., Peter Haage, ten., Dieter
Weller, bar., Chorus and Orchestra of the Danish Radio, Elgar
Howarth, conductor (46:50). Recording of a live performance,
Jan. 19, 1979. Liner notes by the composer.

Wergo WER 60085 (1980).
   60085-50 (compact disc).

D63.   (1988) "Musique de notre temps." (22:12).

Ad'es 14.122.2 (1988).

Six Bagatelles for Wind Quintet See: W15.

D64.   (1969) Stockholm Philharmonic Wind Quintet. Recorded at Ekliden
School, Stockholm, Nov.-Dec. 1969. (11:50)

EMI E-061-34091 (1970).

D65.   (19--) Albert-Schweitzer-Quintett.

HM DMR 2013.

D66.   (19--) Albion Ensemble

Albion Ensemble FRS 1001.

D67.   (1980) Barry Tuckwell Wind Quintet. (10:14).

Nonesuch 78022-1 (1984).
   78022-4 (cassette) (1984).
EMI DAID 7612.

D68.   (1980) Stockholm Wind Quintet. Recorded May and Oct. 1980 at the
Royal Academy of Music, Stockholm. (11:20).

Caprice CAP 1150 (1981). Liner notes by Ove Nordwall.
EMI E-031-34047.

D69.   (1983?) Belgian Wind Quintet. (11:36).

Pavane ADW 7152 (1983).

D70.   (1984) Chalumeau Quintet. Recorded Nov. 2-4, 1984, at the Schloss
Wobbel, West Germany.

Ambitus 68802 (1985?).

D71.   (1985) Westwood Wind Quintet.

> Crystal Records S750 (1985).
> > CD750 (compact disc) (1985).

String Quartet No. 1 See: W19.

D72.   (1976) Voces Intimae Quartet (21:10). Recorded June 30-July 2, 1976 at Nacka Aula, Sweden.

> Bis LP-53 (1976). Liner notes by Ove Nordwall.
> > 53 (compact disc) (1987). Liner notes by Ove Nordwall.

D73.   (1978) Arditti Quartet (21:25). Recorded at the EMI Studios, London, May 1978.

> Wergo WER 60079 (1978). *See:* B331.
> > 60095 (1984).
> > 60079-50 (compact disc) (1984/1988).

D74.   (1982) Via Nova Quartet (22:40). Recorded Sept. 1982.

> Erato STU 71546 (1984). Notes by Harry Halbreich in French with English and German translations.

String Quartet No. 2 See: W42.

D75.   (1969) LaSalle Quartet (20:48). Recorded in Munich Dec. 1969.

> Deutsche Grammophon DG 2530 392.
> > 2543 002 (1971).
> > 2543 818 (1973).
> > 2561 040 (1971).
> > 2561 041.
> > 2720 025.
> > 3543 002.
> > 423 244-2 (compact disc) (1988).
> > F 28G 50497 (compact disc) (Japan).

D76.   (197-?) LaSalle Quartet.

> Schwann HL 00211 (4th mvt. only).

D77.   (1978) Arditti Quartet (21:06). Recorded at the EMI Studios, London, May 1978.

> Wergo WER 60079 (1978).
> > 60095 (1984).
> > 60079-50 (compact disc) (1984/1988).

Study for Organ No. 1 (Harmonies) See: W40.

D78.   (1969?) Gerd Zacher, organ. (7:00)

Candide CE 31009 (1969). Liner notes by William B. Ober.
Columbia OW 7577 (Japan).
Deutsche Grammophon DG 104 990.
137 003 (1969).
2530 392 (1971).
2543 818 (1973).
FSM 31009.
Vox/Turnabout CT 4782 (cassette) (1973)

D79.   (1971) Zsigmond Szathmáry, organ. Recorded July 6-7, 1971, at the
Schuke organ, Luther-Kirche, Hamburg-Wellingsbüttel. (6:40).

Da Camera Magna SM 93237 (1972?).
Wergo WER 60076 (1976).
60095 (1984).
60161-50 (compact disc) (1984/1988).

D80.   (197-?) P. Sweeney.

Brockagh BQR 822.

D81.   (197-) Werner Jacob, organ. Recorded at St. Sebald, Nuremberg.

Christophorus SCK 70 350 (Neue Klangmöglichkeiten der Orgel).

D82.   (1977) Peter Schumann, organ.

Cantate 658 229 (1977).

D83.   (1985-6) Hans-Ola Ericsson, organ. Recorded between March 1985
and April 1986.

Phono Suecia PS CD 31 (1987).

Study for Organ No. 2 (Coulée) See: W45.

D84.   (1971) Zsigmond Szathmáry, organ. Recorded July 6-7, 1971, at the
Schuke organ, Luther-Kirche, Hamburg-Wellingsbüttel. (3:18).
Da Camera Magna SM 93237 (1972?).
Wergo WER 60076 (1976).
60095 (1984).
60161-50 (compact disc) (1984/1988).

Ten Pieces for Wind Quintet See: W43.

D85.   (1969) Stockholm Philharmonic Wind Quintet. Recorded at the
        Ekliden School, Stockholm, Nov.-Dec. 1969. (15:22)

        EMI E 061 34091 (1970).

D86.   (1970) Southwest German Radio Wind Quintet (12:46).
        Recorded at the Southwest German Radio, Baden-Baden, Dec.
        1970.

        Wergo WER 60059 (197-).
                   60095 (1984).
                   60161-50 (compact disc) (1984/1988).

D87.   (1976) Vienna Wind Soloists (ca. 13:00). Recorded Oct. 1976 in the
        Sofiensaal, Vienna.

        London STS15419 (1977). Notes by D. Sutton (Treasury series).
        Ace of Diamonds, Decca SDD 523 (1977).

D88.   (1980) Stockholm Philharmonic Wind Quintet. Recorded May and
        Oct. 1980 at the Royal Academy of Music, Stockholm. (13:20).

        EMI 4 E 031 34047. Liner notes by Ove Nordwall.
        Caprice CAP 1150 (1980/81). Liner notes by Ove Nordwall.

Three Bagatelles for Piano See: W30.

D89.   (1961) Karl-Erik Welin, piano.

        Caprice CAP 1069 (1961).

D90.   (1969) Karl-Erik Welin, piano (2:00). Recorded between Apr. 21,
        1969 and Oct. 12, 1973.

        Caprice RIKS 69 (1975).

Three Pieces for Two Pianos

        see: Monument-Selbstportrait-Bewegung

Trio for Violin, Horn and Piano See: W59.

D91.   (1983-84) Saschko Gawriloff, violin, Hermann Baumann, horn, Eckart
        Besch, piano. Recorded at Bavarian Radio, Munich, 1983-84.
        (21:50).

        Wergo WER 60100 (1986). Liner notes by Josef Häusler.
                   60100-50 (compact disc) (1986).

D92.   (1988) Rolf Schulte, violin, William Purvis, horn, Alan Feinberg, piano.
        Recorded at Holy Trinity Episcopal Church, New York City, Oct. 6-
        7, 1988. (24:29).

        Bridge BCD 9012 (compact disc) (1988).

Trois Bagatelles

        see: Three Bagatelles for Piano

Two Capriccios for Piano See: W5.

D93.   (1985) Begoña Uriarte-Mrongovius, piano. Recorded at the Bavarian
        Radio, Munich, Aug. 1985.

        Wergo WER 60131 (1987).
                60131-50 (compact disc) (1987).

Two Studies for Organ

        see: Study for Organ No. 1
             Study for Organ No. 2

Violoncello Concerto

        see: Concerto for Violoncello

Volumina See: W31.

D94.   (1962) Karl-Erik Welin, organ (15:15). Recorded at the pipe organ of
        Petrikirche, Mülheim. Produced by the West German Radio,
        Cologne, May 1962. Original version.

        Electrola SHZW 904 BL.
        Heliodor 2549-003 (1970).
                3313 003 (cassette) (1970).
        MGM SE-4722 (2001: A Space Odyssey, v. 2) (3:30).
        Wergo WER 60022 (1971?).
                60095 (1984).
                60161-50 (compact disc) (1984/1988).

D95.   (1969?) Gerd Zacher, organ.

        Deutsche Grammophon DG 104 990.
                        137 003 (1969).
                        253081
                        2530 392 (1971).
                        2543 818 (1973).
        Musica Moderne MM1105.

D96.   (1970) Martha Folts playing the organ of St. Michael's Church, New York City. Recorded Dec. 1969 and April 1970.

MHS 3482 (1976).

D97.   (1971) Zsigmond Szathmáry, organ. Recorded July 6-7, 1971, at the Schuke organ, Luther-Kirche, Hamburg-Wellingsbüttel. (16:09).

Da Camera Magna SM 93237 (1972?).

D98.   (1973?) Gerd Zacher, organ. Recorded in the Kaiser-Wilhelm Gedächtniskirche, Berlin. Original version. (17:17).

Candide CE 31009 (1969). Liner notes by William B. Ober.
Columbia OW 7577 (Japan).
FSM 31009. Liner notes by William B. Ober.
Vox/Turnabout CT 4782 (cassette) (1973).

D99.   (1975) Karl-Erik Welin, organ. Recorded in the Lund Cathedral, 1975. 2nd version.

Caprice CAP 1108 (1975/76).

D100.   (197-) Werner Jacob, organ. Recorded in St. Sebald, Nuremberg.

Christophorus SCK 70 350 (Neue Klangmöglichkeiten der Orgel).

Zehn Stücke für Bläserquintett

see: Ten Pieces for Wind Quintet

Appendix I

List of Works by Category

Stage Works

Aventures et Nouvelles Aventures see: W36.
Le Grand Macabre see: W54.
Rondeau see: W53.

Solo Voices and Chorus with Orchestra

Ifjúsági kantáta "Youth cantata." see: W8.
Requiem see: W35.
Scenes and Interludes from Le Grand Macabre see: W55.

Chorus with Orchestra

Clocks and Clouds see: W50.

Unaccompanied Choral Works

Drei Phantasien nach Friedrich Hölderlin see: W61.
Éjszaka; Reggel see: W20.
Haj ifjúság see: W 12.
Idegen Földön see: W2.
Kállai kettós see: W10.
Lux aeterna see: W37.
Magány see: W3.
Magyar Etüdök see: W62.
Mátraszentimrei Dalok see: W21.
Nonsense Madrigals see: W65.
Pápainé see: W18.

Vocal Trios with Instrumental Ensemble

Aventures see: W33.
Nouvelles Aventures see: W34.

Songs

Három Weöres-dal see: W4.
Öt Arany-dal see: W13.

Orchestral Works

Apparitions see: W26.
Atmosphères see: W27.
Lontano see: W39.
Melodien see: W47.
San Francisco Polyphony see: W51.

Solo Instruments with Orchestra

Concerto for Violoncello see: W38.
Double Concerto see: W48.
Piano Concerto see: W64.

Chamber Orchestra

Ballada és tánc see: W9.
Chamber Concerto see: W46.
Fragment see: W28.
Régi magyar társas táncok see: W7.

String Orchestra

Ramifications see: W44.

Chamber Music

Ballada és tánc see: W9.
Duo for Violin and Violoncello see: W58.
Poème symphonique see: W32.
Ramifications see: W44.
Six Bagatelles for Wind Quintet see: W15.
Sonata for Violoncello see: W17.
Den Stora Sköldpadda see: W60.
String Quartet No. 1 "Métamorphoses nocturnes." see: W19.
String Quartet No. 2 see: W42.
Ten Pieces for Wind Quintet see: W43.
Trio for Violin, Horn and Piano see: W59.

Piano Music

Chromatische Phantasie see: W22.
Etudes for Piano see: W63.
Invention for Piano see: W6.
Monument-Selbstportrait-Bewegung see: W52.
Musica ricercata see: W14.
Polyphonic Etude (4-hands) see: W1.
Sonatina (4-hands) see: W11.
Three Bagatelles see: W30.

Two Capriccios for Piano see: W5.

Harpsichord Music

Continuum see: W41.
Hungarian Rock see: W56.
Passacaglia ungherese see: W57.

Organ Music

Omaggio a Frescobaldi see: W16.
Study for Organ No. 1 "Harmonies" see: W40.
Study for Organ No. 2 "Coulée" see: W45.
Volumina see: W31.

Electronic Music

Artikulation see: W25.
Glissandi see: W23.
Pièce électronique no. 3 see: W24.

Lecture

Die Zukunft der Musik see: W29.

Appendix II

A Selective List of Ligeti Concerts and Festivals

1969   Paris; "Journee Ligeti" at the Semaines Musicales.

1972   (May 14): Stanford; Ligeti Festival. *Artikulation, Poème Symphonique, Lux aeterna*, and *Ten Pieces for Wind Quintet. See*: B614.

1973   (June): Vienna; Wiener Festwochen; Concert celebrating Ligeti's 50th birthday. *Lux aeterna, Melodien, Chamber Concerto, Double Concerto*, and *Atmosphères. See*: B562.

1974   (May 7): London; Elisabeth Hall; English Bach Festival. *Ten Pieces for Wind Quintet* (Barry Tuckwell Wind Quintet); *Double Concerto* (William Bennett, flute, Michael Dobson, oboe); *Melodien*; and *Clocks and Clouds*. London Symphony Orchestra; women of the BBC singers; Elgar Howarth, conductor. Ligeti lectured prior to the concert. *See*: B390, B633, B663.

1977   (May 8): London; Elisabeth Hall; London Music Digest. Both string quartets (Arditti Quartet); both wind quintets (Stockholm Philharmonic Wind Quintet); *Monument-Selbstportrait-Bewegung* (Bruno Canino and Antonio Ballista). Ligeti introduced his new 2-piano work. *See*: W15c, W19c, W42b, W43b, B291, B351, B387, B661.

    (May 25, June 2): Paris; Insitut de Recherche et Coordination Acoustic/Musique (IRCAM). Concert series "Passage du XXème siècle." *Melodien, Chamber Concerto* (Ensemble Intercontemporain, Michel Tabachnik, conductor), *Six Bagatelles* (Barry Tuckwell Wind Quintet), *Monument-Selbstportrait-Bewegung* (Maria and Marielle Labèque). *See*: B693.

    (Sept. 15): Ghent?; Flanders Festival. *String Quartet No. 2* (Arditti Quartet), *Ten Pieces for Wind Quintet* (Belgian Wind Quintet), and *Monument-Selbstportrait-Bewegung* (Canino-Ballista). *See*: W42, W43, W52, B573.

1978   Hamburg; Concert series, "Neue Werk." *Musica ricercata* (Eckart Besch), *Monument-Selbstportrait-Bewegung* (Besch and Hans-

Jürgen Hofer), *Continuum* (Carol Tainton), *Two Etudes for Organ*, and *Volumina* (Heinz Wunderlichs). *See*: B481.

1979   (July 19-Aug. 6): Aix en Provence; Six concerts at a festival at the Centre Acanthes. Ligeti lectured on his works. Performance included *Aventures et Nouvelles Aventures* (Gertie Charlent, Marie-Thérèse Cahn, William Pearson, Ensemble InterContemporain, Peter Eötvös, conductor), the first French performance of the *Concerto for Violoncello* (Wolfgang Boettcher, cello, New Philharmonic Orchestra, Gilbert Amy, conductor), *Monument-Selbstportrait-Bewegung* and *Scenes and Interludes from Le Grand Macabre*. *See*: B292, B658.

(Nov.): Budapest; Ligeti Evening. *San Francisco Polyphony*, *Double Concerto*, and the *Requiem*. *See*: B706.

1981   Paris; Two concerts in conjunction with the Paris production of *Le Grand Macabre*. *See*: W47d.

(May 10): Munich; Ligeti Matinee. *Six Bagatelles, Continuum, String Quartet No. 2, Ten Pieces for Wind Quintet, Passacaglia ungherese, Hungarian Rock, String Quartet No. 1* (Elisabeth Chojnacka, harpsichord; Arditti Quartet; Syrinx Quintet). *See*: W15d, W19d, W42c, W43c, B585.

(Dec. 3): Vienna; Concert series "Wege in unsere Zeit." Wiener Konzerthausgesellschaft. *Melodien, String Quartet No. 2, Chamber Concerto* (die Reihe Ensemble; Friedrich Cerha, conductor; the Arditti Quartet). *See*: B393, B451, B510.

1982   (May 19): London. London Sinfonietta. *Melodien, Ten Pieces for Wind Quintet*, the *Concerto for Violoncello* (Christopher van Kampen, soloist), and *Aventures et Nouvelles Aventures* (Pamela Smith, Linda Hirst, Simon Grant, vocalists; James Holland, percussion), under the direction of Elgar Howarth. *See*: W47, W43, W38, W33, W34, B493, B666.

1983   (March 20): Budapest; Budapest Spring Festival; *Clocks and Clouds, Concerto for Violoncello* (Miklós Perényi, cello), and the *Requiem* (Júlia Pászthy, soprano; Tamara Takács, alto; Budapest Symphony; György Lehel, conductor; Hungarian Radio Choir, Ferenc Sapszon, director). *See*: B297.

(May 7): Hall (Tyrol); Galerie St. Barbara. *Melodien, Chamber Concerto*, and other works (Austrian Radio Symphony; Lothar Zagrosek, conductor).

(May 8): Salzburg; "Aspekte" Festival. Same works and performers as above.

(May 18): Stuttgart; Concert celebrating Ligeti's 60th birthday. *Horn Trio* (Saschko Gawriloff, violin, Hermann Baumann, horn, and Eckhard Besch, piano), *Ramifications* and the *Chamber Concerto* (Pierre Boulez, Stuttgart Radio Symphony), *Magyar Etüdök* (no. 1-

2), *Magány*, and *Pápainé* (Clytus Gottwald, Schola Cantorum), *Passacaglia ungherese* and *Hungarian Rock* (Elisabeth Chojnacka, harpsichord). Also included were *Die Nachtigall* by Alban Berg and Mauricio Kagel directing his own *Intermezzo*. *See:* B302, B360, B466.

(Sept. 23-25): Berlin; 33rd Berliner Festwochen. A series of concerts celebrating Ligeti's 60th birthday. 1st concert: *String Quartets Nos. 1 and 2* (Arditti Quartet), *Monument-Selbstportrait-Bewegung* (Bruno Canino and Antonio Ballista), and the *Horn Trio* (Saschko Gawriloff, violin; Hermann Baumann, horn; and Eckart Besch, piano). 2nd concert: *Hungarian Rock, Passacaglia ungherese, Continuum* (Elisabeth Chojnacka), *Six Bagatelles, Ten Pieces for Wind Quintet, Chamber Concerto*, (London Sinfonietta Elgar Howarth, conductor). 3rd concert: *Melodien, Concerto for Violoncello* (Wolfgang Boettcher, cello), *Aventures et Nouvelles Aventures* (Penelope Walmsley-Clark, Linda Hirst, and Simon Grant, soloists; London Sinfonietta; Elgar Howarth, conductor). Ligeti commented on his works. Another concert in the Kaiser-Friedrich Gedächtniskirche featured *Volumina, Two Etudes for Organ, Omaggio a Frescobaldi* (Peter Schwarz, organ), and *Lux aeterna* (Berliner Capella). *See:* B138, B642.

(Sept. 26): Bremen; Concert series "Bremer Podium." Lecture on the *Horn Trio*. *Artikulation* was played during the intermission, *String Quartets Nos. 1 and 2* (Arditti Quartet), *Horn Trio* (Saschko Gawriloff, violin; Hermann Baumann, horn; Eckart Besch, piano). The BBC film "All Clouds are Clocks" was shown. *See:* B349.

1984   (Feb. 14): Hamburg; Lecture-Concert. *Horn Trio*. *See:* B566, B618.

(May): Freiburg; Performances included *Ramifications, Monument-Selbstportrait-Bewegung, Poème Symphonique*, and selections from *Le Grand Macabre*. The conductor was Eberhard Kloke. Ligeti spoke.

(Autumn): Graz; Styrian Autumn Festival including seven concerts dedicated to Ligeti. *Scenes and Interludes from Le Grand Macabre, Clocks and Clouds* (Austrian Radio Symphony Orchestra and Chorus), both string quartets (Arditti Quartet), both wind quintets (Vienna Wind Ensemble), *Concerto for Violoncello, Melodien, Chamber Concerto* (die Reihe Ensemble), *Musica ricercata, Monument-Selbstportrait-Bewegung* (Uriarte-Mrongovius), works for organ (Zsigmond Szathmáry) and harpsichord (Elisabeth Chojnacka), *Artikulation*, and *Poème Symphonique*. A symposium on the theme, "György Ligeti: Personal style, Avant-garde, Popularity" was held simultaneously. Participants included Gottfried Michael Koenig, Monika Lichtenfeld, Martin Zenck, and Rudolf Frisius. *See:* B117, B532, B533.

1985   (May 4): Vienna. The Arditti Quartet performed both string quartets. Ligeti gave a pre-concert talk. He also stopped the performance briefly because of interfering sound from a pop concert in an adjacent hall. *See:* B507.

(Summer): Radenci, Yugoslavia; 22nd Chamber Music of the 20th Century Festival. *See*: B181.

(Aug. 28-31): Turin; Settembre Musica Festival. Performances included *Ramifications, Poème Symphonique* (Nuovo Ensemble Antidogma, Aldo Brizzi, conductor), *Musica ricercata, Monument-Selbstportrait-Bewegung* (Begoña Uriarte, Karl-Hermann Mrongovius, piano), *Omaggio a Frescobaldi, Studies for Organ, Volumina* (Zsigmond Szathmáry, organ), both string quartets (Arditti Quartet), *Atmosphères* (Orchestra Sinfonia di Torino della Rai, Zoltan Pesko, conductor), *Drei Phantasien, Magyar Etüdök, Lux aeterna, Ejszaka; Reggel* (Groupe Vocal de France, Michel Tranchant, conductor), and *Lontano* (London Symphony Orchestra, Claudio Abbado, conductor). A symposium on Ligeti's music was held concurrently, and a volume of studies on Ligeti was published. *See*: B122.

1986   (May): Frankfurt; *Six Bagatelles* (Ensemble Modern), *Aventures et Nouvelles Aventures* (Gabriele Auenmüller, soprano; Linda Hirst, mezzosoprano; Jürgen Hartfiel, baritone; Zoltán Pesko, conductor), and the *Concerto for Violoncello* (Kai Scheffler, cello; Ensemble Modern; Zoltán Pesko, conductor). *See*: B579.

(May 21): New York; Horizons '86--"Music as Theater." *Scenes and Interludes from Le Grand Macabre* (Yoko Kawahara, Olive Fredricks, Peter Haage, and Dieter Weller, soloists, Zoltán Peskó, conductor), and a new staging by Ian Strasfogel of *Aventures et Nouvelles Aventures* (Karen Beardsley, Joyce Castle, and John Brandstetter, soloists). *See*: B417, B447, B671.

1987   (June 9): London; 7th Almeida Festival. *Polyphonic Etude, Two Capriccios, Invention, Sonatina, Musica ricercata* (Louise Sibourd, piano), *Monument-Selbstportrait-Bewegung* (Keith Williams and Clive Williamson, pianos). *See*: B290.

(June 12): London; 7th Almeida Festival. *Artikulation, Ramifications, Magyar Etüdök, Concerto for Violoncello, Ejszaka, Reggel, Drei Phantasien, Fragment, Study for Organ No. 1 & 2, Melodien, Poème Symphonique* (Almeida Ensemble, Oliver Knussen, conductor; New London Chamber Choir, James Wood, conductor).

(June 22): London; 7th Almeida Festival. *String Quartet No. 2* (Arditti Quartet), *Concerto for Piano* (played twice; Anthony di Bonaventura, piano, London Sinfonietta, Mario di Bonaventura, conductor), *Ten Pieces for Wind Quintet*. *See*: B635.

(Summer): Hitzacker, Germany; Hitzacker Music Festival. This festival included performances of the three harpsichord pieces (Elisabeth Chojnacka), the six *Etudes for Piano* (Volker Banfield), and a lecture on Ligeti by Constantin Floros. *See*: W41, W56, W57, W63, B483.

1988   (Sept.): Berlin; Berliner Festwochen. Series of four concerts in two
       days devoted to Ligeti. Performances included both string
       quartets (Kronos Quartet), *Ejszaka; Reggel, Lux aeterna* (RIAS
       Chamber Choir, Marcus Creed, director), *Aventures et Nouvelles
       Aventures* (Penelope Walmsley-Clark, Linda Hirst, William Pearson,
       soloists), *Concerto for Violoncello* (Michael Kasper, soloist), *Ten
       Pieces for Wind Quintet, Chamber Concerto, Melodien* (Ensemble
       Modern, Elgar Howarth, conductor), *Etudes for Piano* (Volker
       Banfield), and *Nonsense Madrigals* (The King's Singers). *See*:
       W65a, B422.

1989   (Oct. 19-Nov. 6): London; "Ligeti by Ligeti" Festival. The festival,
       organized by the South Bank Centre included 10 concerts which
       Ligeti participated in planning. The festival featured Ligeti's music
       along with many other works. Performances included a concert
       production of *Le Grand Macabre*, British premières of the final
       version of the *Piano Concerto*, and the 7th and 8th *Etudes for
       Piano*. The first performance of *Lobster Quadrille*, the 5th
       Nonsense Madrigal took place here. The only all-Ligeti concert
       consisted of: *Hai Ifjusag!, Kallai Kettos, Ejszaka; Reggel, Six
       Bagatelles, Lux aeterna, Magyar Etüdök, Ten Pieces for Wind
       Quintet, Drei Phantasien* (BBC Singers, James Wood, conductor;
       London Winds). The composer himself introduced the series in an
       opening talk. *See*: W64d, W65b, B527, B597, B638, B686, B699,
       B724.

Index

About the Author

ROBERT W. RICHART is Head of Cataloging and Inputting Service, WLN. He has contributed to the *Double Reed* and *Library Journal Book Review.*